CHi

Revolution Day

Revolution Day

The Human Story of the Battle for Iraq

RAGEH OMAAR

VIKING
an imprint of
PENGUIN BOOKS

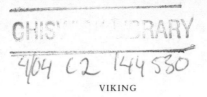
VIKING

Published by the Penguin Group
Penguin Books Ltd, 80 Strand, London WC2R ORL, England
Penguin Group (USA) Inc., 375 Hudson Street, New York, New York 10014, USA
Penguin Books Australia Ltd, 250 Camberwell Road, Camberwell, Victoria 3124, Australia
Penguin Books Canada Ltd, 10 Alcorn Avenue, Toronto, Ontario, Canada M4V 3B2
Penguin Books India (P) Ltd, 11 Community Centre, Panchsheel Park, New Delhi – 110 017, India
Penguin Books (NZ) Ltd, Cnr Rosedale and Airborne Roads, Albany, Auckland, New Zealand
Penguin Books (South Africa) (Pty) Ltd, 24 Sturdee Avenue, Rosebank 2196, South Africa

Penguin Books Ltd, Registered Offices: 80 Strand, London WC2R ORL, England

www.penguin.com

First published 2004
1

Photographic credits:
1. Duncan Stone; 2. Karen Robinson/Panos; 3. Hien Lam Duc/Panos; 4–9. Duncan Stone;
10. Rageh Omaar; 11. Hien Lam Duc/Panos; 12. Duncan Stone; 13. Rageh Omaar; 14. Duncan Stone;
15. Olivier Coret/In Visu/Corbis; 16. Duncan Stone; 17. James Hill/Getty; 18. Rageh Omaar;
19–20. Duncan Stone; 21. James Nachtwey/VII; 22. Seamus Conlan/WorldPictureNews;
23. Duncan Stone; 24. James Nachtwey/VII; 25. Kael Alford/Panos; 26. Patrick Robert/Corbis;
27. Albert Facelly/Sipa Press/Rex Features; 28. Kael Alford/Panos; 29. Gilles Bassignac/Katz Pictures;
30. Ron Haviv/VII; 31. Yannis Kontos/Eyevine; 32. Peter Nicholls/*The Times*; 33–4. Rageh Omaar;
35. Paolo Pellegrin/Magnum; 36. Rageh Omaar; endpapers: Rageh Omaar

Set in 12/14.75pt Monotype Bembo
Typeset by Rowland Phototypesetting Ltd,
Bury St Edmunds, Suffolk
Printed in Great Britain by Clays Ltd, St Ives plc

A CIP catalogue record for this book is available from the British Library

HB ISBN 0-670-91508-4
TPB ISBN 0-670-91519-X

Endpapers: The sun sets over Baghdad, and over the smoking remains of the Republican Palace
compound. The author took this photograph from the balcony of his room at the Palestine Hotel
on the day before he left Baghdad, after the city had fallen to American forces

For Nina

Contents

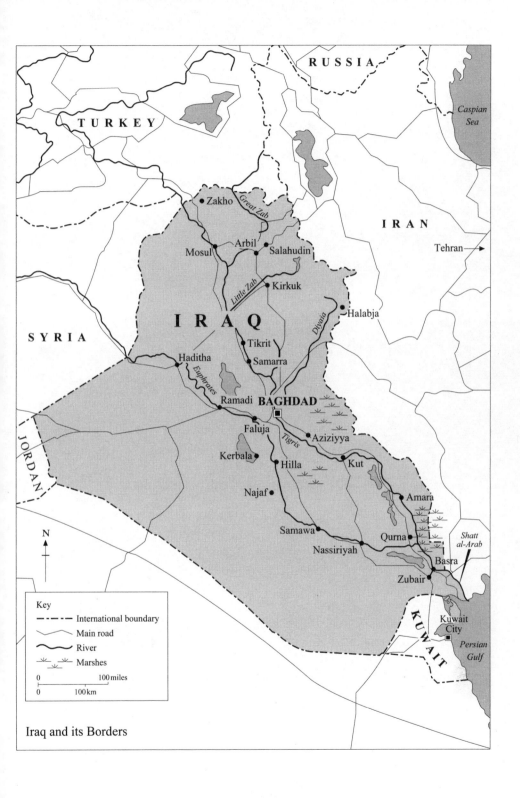

Iraq and its Borders

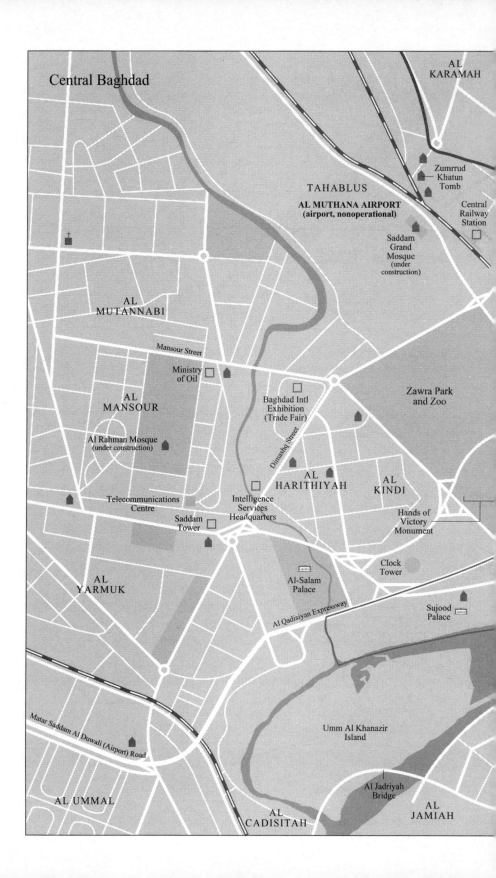

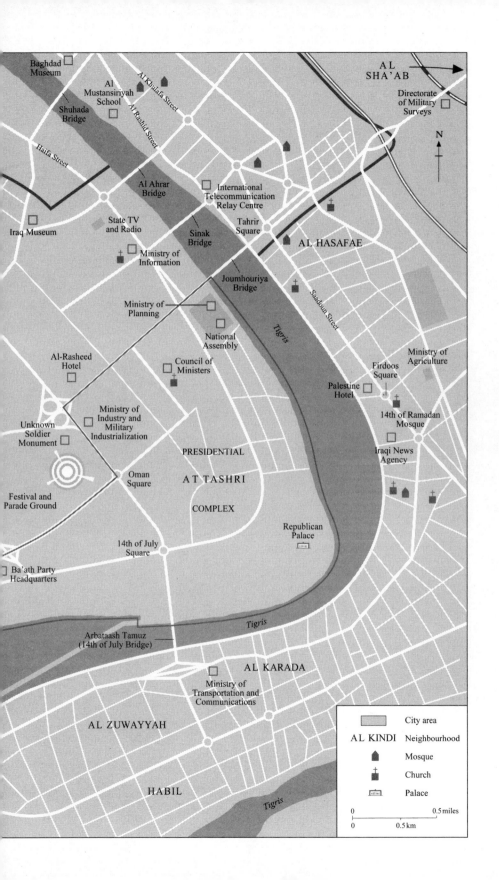

Baghdad Museum

Al Mustansiriyah School

Shuhada Bridge

Haifa Street

Al Ahrar Bridge

Iraq Museum

State TV and Radio

Ministry of Information

Al Khulafa Street

Al Rashid Street

Sinak Bridge

International Telecommunication Relay Centre

Tahrir Square

AL SHA'AB

Directorate of Military Surveys

AL HASAFAE

Joumhouriya Bridge

Ministry of Planning

National Assembly

Council of Ministers

Al-Rasheed Hotel

Ministry of Industry and Military Industrialization

Unknown Soldier Monument

Oman Square

PRESIDENTIAL

AT TASHRI

COMPLEX

Festival and Parade Ground

14th of July Square

Ba'ath Party Headquarters

Tigris

Saadoun Street

Ministry of Agriculture

Firdoos Square

Palestine Hotel

14th of Ramadan Mosque

Iraqi News Agency

Republican Palace

Arbataash Tamuz (14th of July Bridge)

Tigris

AL KARADA

Ministry of Transportation and Communications

AL ZUWAYYAH

HABIL

Tigris

N

	City area
AL KINDI	Neighbourhood
	Mosque
	Church
	Palace

0   0.5 miles

0   0.5 km

Introduction

'Have you seen the hand?' the man asked. 'Over there; look, where the group of people are standing. There's someone's hand on the steps. It was the bomb! I heard the aeroplane that dropped it. Whoosh, and then a huge bang. It just tore it off. Go! Take the cameraman with you.'

Before I could reply or get his name, he'd disappeared into the chaos. I looked over to the circle of people who stood where the stranger had been pointing, and through the crowd, there on the muddy steps, amid shards of broken glass and small pools of blood, lay a severed hand.

I'd stepped into this scene of carnage in the Al Sha'ab district of northern Baghdad a few minutes earlier, emerging from our car to the wail of ambulance sirens and crowds of people dazed and shocked among the wreckage of their neighbourhood.

The war was barely a week old, and, walking through the middle of that appalling scene, I remember asking myself how I could justify being there. My colleagues and I were certainly not driven by any love of danger. Robert Fisk, who was also in Iraq throughout the conflict, described the experience as a desire to bear witness to events that change history. In his book on the war in Lebanon, *Pity the Nation* (OUP, 2001), he writes that in such circumstances 'at best, journalists sit at the edge of history as vulcanologists might clamber to the lip of a smoking crater, trying to see over the rim, craning their necks to peer over the crumbling edge through the smoke and ash at what happens within'.

I was one of about 100 foreign journalists who remained in Baghdad through the war in Iraq in 2003. This book is a personal account of what it was like to witness the war which brought to an end nearly a quarter of a century of cruel dictatorship in Iraq, and try to describe what it felt like to be in a city under siege, in a country which had already lived through years of oppression and deprivation. This book is not only about war. I travelled through and reported from Iraq for six years before the conflict. During that time a relatively small number of western journalists, aid workers, UN officials and diplomats had the chance to observe at close quarters the brutally controlled Iraq of Saddam Hussein in the years after the first Gulf War. To have known that world and seen it at its moment of destruction was not just an opportunity to witness history. Those years gave me a better appreciation, albeit a closely monitored one, of what Iraqis have endured in the past and what the war signifies for them.

This book is not a study of battle strategy. Indeed, the account of the actual conflict presented in these pages is from the perspective of Baghdad only, where I was for the duration of the war. It is a personal and impressionistic account of the war, but it is not an exhaustive one. Neither is this book a critical examination of or commentary on the veracity of the justification for the war proffered by the British and American governments, namely Iraq's possession of weapons of mass destruction. Although I observed the work of two UN weapons inspections operations in Iraq – the UN Special Commission on Iraq (UNSCOM) and the UN Monitoring and Verification Commission (UNMOVIC) – the real truth behind the issue of weapons of mass destruction, and whether Iraq in fact possessed any in the days before the invasion, can be written only by those who were searching for them and those senior members of the former regime, the officials and scientists, many of whom are now being held by coalition forces in Iraq. So far the only thing we do know is that the evidence has not been found.

Instead I have tried, as best I could, to concentrate on the many different voices of Iraqis themselves, before the war, during it and after the overthrow of Saddam Hussein. The stories of civilians in Iraq have been little heard over the years, repressed as they were by a dictator who cared little for them, and largely unknown by western governments whose policies focused on overthrowing the Iraqi regime. For much of these past years, Iraq's 24 million people were seen only through their leader.

Before the future of Iraq can be imagined the legacy of Saddam Hussein has to be understood. Eight months before the war that would overthrow him Saddam Hussein made a speech on Revolution Day, the official day of celebration to mark the Ba'ath Party's accession to power. In his speech he addressed the enemy who were at that moment attempting to gather international support for military intervention in his country: 'You will never defeat me this time. Never! Even if you come together from all over the world, and invite all the devils as well, to stand by you.' On the evening of 13 December 2003 Saddam Hussein was found hiding in a hole measuring eight feet by six in the farm yard of his former cook, close by the village of al-Awja, near Tikrit, where he was born sixty-six years ago. At a hastily convened press conference on the day of his capture, Paul Bremer, the Americans' chief administrator in Iraq, triumphantly declared, 'We got him!' The video footage of the captive shown at the conference was unforgettable. The man who appeared on the screen was filthy, with matted dishevelled hair and a long whiskery beard, his dead, empty eyes staring out at the camera. He seemed apparently unconcerned by his humiliating circumstances, while an American doctor examined him, poking around inside his mouth with a torch and a swab. Many people in the Middle East, despite their disregard for the man himself, did express uneasiness at the images of an erstwhile Arab leader being physically examined for all the world to see by a representative of the US government.

In this most tawdry of finales, a truth was revealed about the deposed leader. During his months on the run, Saddam Hussein had issued audio recordings, which were broadcast on Iraqi television, urging Iraqis to fight 'the occupiers' to the end. His two sons and his fourteen-year-old grandson had followed these instructions to the letter, ripped to pieces as they were in a gun battle with US forces that ended their lives on 22 July. Yet when he was found, the Iraqi dictator emerged from his shabby hiding place without a shot being fired, allegedly responding to his discovery with the words: 'I am Saddam Hussein, President of Iraq. I want to negotiate,' as reported by one of the soldiers of the US 4th Infantry

Division who was present. The illusion of Saddam Hussein the warrior was finally laid to rest. However, despite the dictator's new situation, those warrior-like words in his speech in 2002 still have a kind of accidental resonance. The Ba'ath Party has been dismantled, the regime has indeed been changed. But a country that has suffered years of dictatorship, that has been isolated from the rest of the world and has been brought to its knees by years of sanctions and corruption cannot shuffle off the shadow of its leader in a matter of days.

To understand what is happening in Iraq as I write and to be able to imagine its future, we need, more than ever, to hear the voices of the people whose country is now ruled and administered by Britain and the United States. For, without doubt, the nature of the country will be determined by its people. Its future can be understood only through them, whether or not that future meets with the strategic and political interests of London and Washington.

The material for this book is based on the notes, diaries and reports I kept from the years I have been reporting from the country, and of course on my own memory and the recollections of friends and colleagues with whom I worked and travelled in the country. But this book, and indeed my whole involvement with Iraq, would have been impossible without the help and friendship of several people in particular. Their friendships and the countless risks they took on my behalf over the years enabled me not just to carry out my work, but also to see Iraq more clearly. If there are any heroes in this book they are Mohammed Darwish, Saadoun al Jannabi, Dylan Nalid and Khalil al Dulaimi; I owe them more than I can say. I also owe an enormous debt to the man named as 'Luai' in this book. He disappeared the day before Baghdad fell, and I have not seen him since, although I have been told that he is safe and well in Baghdad. I hope, one day soon, to be able to see him again to thank him in person. Many other Iraqis spoke to me, welcomed me into their homes and gave me their time. Some did not want to be named or appear in print, such was the level of danger in the old Iraq and the level of uncertainty in the new. To them all, I want to show my deepest appreciation for all their kindness and patience.

I owe an enormous debt of thanks to Paul Danahar, Andrew Kilrain, Duncan Stone, Malek Kenaan and Mustapha al Salman. As well as being close personal friends, their skill, dedication and knowledge gave me the opportunity to be able to file every single one of my reports during the war, and with their advice and encouragement they more than anyone else shaped my reports from Baghdad and provided me with an unrivalled wealth of material on which I could draw to write this book; hundreds of hours of raw, unedited footage and interviews. Paul Danahar, our Bureau Chief in Baghdad, led our team with courage, determination and passion. At many difficult times for all of us, he gave us the encouragement and focus to carry on. He also kindly read large parts of this book and offered me new insights. My colleague Paul Wood, the BBC's Middle East correspondent, was a great help to me in Baghdad and amassed a huge amount of knowledge about the complexity and subtleties of Iraqi society and politics very quickly. To him also my deepest thanks. Our bosses in London provided us with much support and understanding and allowed us the freedom to stay in Baghdad. Jonathan Baker has been an ideal Foreign Editor from the day he took up the post just before September 11 and has been a pillar of support. My assignment editors, Malcolm Downing and Mark James, were generous with their encouragement and guidance through the years that I have been travelling to Iraq and I am sincerely grateful to them and all the staff of the BBC World Newsgathering Planning Desk, who have helped me in countless ways.

Many colleagues gave me help and advice during my assignments over the past six years. From the BBC: Hedley Trigge, Carolyn Jackson and Penny Richards, who guided me when I was a television novice on my first trip to Iraq in 1997, and also Bhas Solanki, with whom I travelled across Iraq in the first years. Dominic Evans of Reuters helped me get into Iraq in the first place and I benefited over the past six years from his immense knowledge of the country and the wider Middle East. Much of my work in the last few years and during the war would not have been possible without the kindness and advice of colleagues from Reuters and Associated Press in Baghdad. Ahmed Seif and Khaled Ramahi of Reuters Television had to bear unimaginable hardship as they had to cope with the death and injury of their closest colleagues; to them my deepest thanks for everything. And also in particular to Paul Pascquale, who was injured in the attack on the Palestine Hotel. Nadim Ladki and his colleagues of Reuters News Service also gave me the benefit of their knowledge on many aspects of Iraq and I am grateful to them. Many other colleagues were helpful and supportive during the war and to them my thanks: Robert Fisk and Kim Sengupta of the *Independent*, John F. Burns of the *New York Times*, Ross Benson of the *Daily Mail* and Bob Graham of the *Mail on Sunday*, Mike Moore and Anton Antonowicz of the *Mirror*.

I owe a great debt of thanks to my brilliant literary agent, Kate Jones, of ICM Books, who encouraged me to write this book in the first place. I am very lucky to have had her and all her colleagues at ICM in London and New York to steer me as I wrote my first book. My editor at Viking Penguin, Mary Mount, has been a joy to work with and gave focus and shape to my manuscript, and looked after me by providing the space and time I needed to get the writing done. I am also indebted to Tom Weldon and Juliet Annan at Penguin for their great support and encouragement. I'm very lucky to have had the enormous experience and skills of Bela Cunha to edit my final script. To her my thanks.

My family went through far worse than I did by my long absences in Iraq, especially during the war. To my mother and father I owe everything for giving me not just the opportunities I have had in life, but for teaching me to hold on to all the precious things from Somalia. My brother and sisters – Mohammed, Rakiya and Zeinab – have always shown me love and support as we all learned our new lives and identities that straddled Somalia and the West. My two young children had to bear long periods without their father who reappeared seemingly out of nowhere as quickly as he had disappeared, so much so that each time my daughter suspects I am packing my bags for a trip she asks me if I'm going to 'ee-rok'. But my most heartfelt thanks of all are for Nina. I owe her more than I can say.

London, December 2003

1. Journeys

The end was something that I had tried not to think about. During the war, through those days and nights that seemed without end, my mind would, if only briefly, dare to envisage the last journey out of Iraq. What would the final moment look like? What would be the last thing I'd see as I left Iraq? What would mark the moment when I and the rest of the small BBC team could say it was over? Of course these were not questions that the people of Baghdad could ask themselves. For them there would be no journey out. And even now, so long after the war that changed their world has officially been declared over, there is still no 'over' for them.

During those four weeks I, and I daresay many of us who'd remained in Baghdad, had at times allowed ourselves to imagine the day we would leave Iraq. But we would rarely discuss it between ourselves. When I did think about it I envisaged an iconic, dramatic moment – something that would not just encapsulate the recent extraordinary experiences I had lived through during the war, but would also serve as a fitting resolution to the six years I had spent reporting from the country.

The end finally came on a dreary and insipid April day at the Trebil border crossing from Iraq into Jordan. Actually, it was difficult to call it a border or a crossing or anything else for that matter. It was a lifeless and eerie way-station between two worlds. It had the look and feel of a place of desolation and decay: the discarded cans of soft drinks rattling against the stony desert ground as the wind blew; the flimsy, empty plastic bottles of water glistening in the sun; and most of all, the emaciated wild dogs, who would limp from one rubbish heap to another in search of sustenance. It was usually a junction to hurry through as quickly as possible. But this day was different. As we drove through the Trebil crossing, we saw something odd amid the familiar debris of waste: flying around our vehicles were clean and crisp sheets of white paper. Hundreds of official forms, documents and immigration files were blowing aimlessly across the sand. The Iraqi border administration buildings were completely deserted; the last officials hadn't even bothered to close the doors behind them when they had made their hasty departure, and now sheaves of paper were lining the doorways to their office. It was a forsaken place where the detritus of a destroyed regime mingled with the litter and ruin. We drove slowly and stared out at the scene.

Straight ahead of us loomed the large archway that marked the border. The slow gentle curves of the arch could be seen from 500 yards away as it rose to forty feet at its highest point. From a distance it bore a faint resemblance to the golden 'M' of a McDonald's, but on closer inspection you could see it was another dismal construct of the Ba'ath Party, a monument of brown stone bricks. It had been hurriedly built. Either that or the materials the architect and builders had been given were very cheap. It was a telling example of the public monuments which the regime had erected across the country over the years: they appeared large and forbidding from a distance but up close they were flimsy structures, poorly built by workmen who were at best paid next to nothing. Just in front of the arch stood a statue of Saddam Hussein, resplendent in military uniform, mounted on an enormous horse. He held aloft a sword, urging his fellow Iraqis into battle. It was Saddam as he liked to be seen. However, on this day there was a new and unforgettable addition to the effigy. Beneath Saddam Hussein's horse stood an American military Jeep. Three young American soldiers, dressed in dark combat fatigues with splashes of jungle green and black, leaned against it. They looked different from most of the US soldiers and marines I'd seen in the last few days: men entirely kitted out in the sandy beige of desert combat clothes. These men at the border were not wearing helmets, which most of the regular soldiers did. Instead, they wore wide-rimmed sun hats. Their outfits suggested that they were from a regiment of the American Special Forces. They certainly acted the part, looking serious and purposeful with their M-16 rifles lazily slung round their necks, but with little to do except give the impression of a conquering army. They seemed mildly perplexed by our arrival.

By now, all of us had developed a certain nervousness when it came to dealing with the American military. Having lived through the war and its aftermath in Baghdad we had become paranoid about not being clearly identified as independent journalists by US forces in the field. By the end of the war, within the space of four weeks, sixteen international journalists had been killed, several of them in incidents of 'friendly fire'. Few wars in recent times have produced such a tally among the press community and when fatalities have been high – in the Vietnam War and the Bosnian war for example – it was in much longer wars. The attack on the Palestine Hotel was a very recent and graphic memory and for western journalists US soldiers on the ground were a terrifying prospect. These soldiers were young and frightened. Many of them had never set foot outside America before, and now found themselves in a strange country whose language they did not speak and where many of the local people saw them as foreign occupiers who had to be driven out. In the last days of the war, even as Baghdad fell to US forces, several American soldiers had been killed or injured by suicide bombers who had approached them in civilian vehicles. We all knew that during these very tense times, American soldiers would shoot at any oncoming vehicle they deemed suspicious. US commanders had already begun to circulate leaflets in Baghdad telling civilians: 'During all hours, please approach coalition military positions with extreme caution.' We never took our safety for granted. When the city fell and we first saw those American soldiers in Baghdad, we rolled down our windows, showed our empty hands and waved frantically. By the time we got to the border with Jordan this had become a ritual.

On this occasion the soldiers at the border barely reacted to the expressions on our faces as we passed. The figure who stood nearest to our cars just about acknowledged our presence with the slightest tilt of his head. But beneath his deliberate nonchalance, he did give away a look of surprise. We must have been the first convoy of non-military personnel to arrive at the border after the fall of

Baghdad. As we slipped through the arch on our way to Jordan, that was my last image of Iraq: Saddam Hussein side by side with his nemesis.

The border was behind me and I didn't look back. Just over a mile of no-man's land remained until we would cross the line into Jordan. The sky was dark with clouds heavy with rain approaching from the north-west, as the vast and monotonous expanse of Iraq's western desert stretched out towards the horizon. The short distance, covered within a matter of minutes, brought to an end an odyssey that had taken up six years of my life.

Our car slowed as it approached the Jordanian frontier crossing. A border guard emerged from the sentry post and ambled over to us. He was small and wiry with a receding hairline giving away his middle age and he wore the blue uniform of the Jordanian police. His light blue shirt was tucked smartly into his navy blue trousers, his beret neatly folded under one epaulette. He seemed almost excited at the prospect of finally having the chance to inspect a car coming from Baghdad. The city had fallen only four days earlier and we must have been the first civilian convoy to reach the border. There had been constant traffic across this border even through the years of sanctions but when war began the traffic became a trickle. At last, the guard could start doing his job again. He poked his head through the passenger window and immediately his expression changed from one of self-important gravity to unashamed amusement. Inside the car sat six BBC reporters who'd just driven out of Iraq; the doors and windows of our vehicle were plastered with the letters 'TV' written in heavy black masking tape. If the Jordanian official was expecting to see a group of hardened and fearless reporters he must have been seriously disappointed. We were an amusing sight, crammed next to each other, awkwardly encased like tortoises in our flak jackets, helmets tilting at odd angles on our heads. None of us had had a bath in quite a while, but if there was a rank odour inside the car he pretended not to notice.

'Welcome to Jordan and to safety,' he said, and then, as his smile broadened, he rolled his eyes skywards and added, 'thanks be to

God.' And with that he stepped back from our car and with an exaggerated flourish waved our convoy through.

It was like emerging from a sealed dark room into the light, a feeling of personal liberation after the tangible claustrophobia of the past few weeks. On the Jordanian side too, the border complex was deserted, for who would be heading to Baghdad now? And it was here at this quiet and utterly unremarkable border post in the Jordanian desert that it all ended. The daily calculations for survival and the longing to be free from a place of such upheaval and distress were behind us. But there was no euphoria. Instead there was just numbness. We stepped out of our vehicle and afforded ourselves a few light smiles and brief comments of relief. We discovered that our mobile phones worked, despite being hundreds of miles from any city. Quickly we began to call our families to tell them we were finally out of Iraq. In the midst of extraordinary times, doing what would usually seem mundane suddenly feels odd and un-familiar. This was such a moment. After so many weeks of struggling to get a connection on the satellite phone in order to speak to my wife, it was strange to be able to call Nina so easily from the middle of the Jordanian desert on her mobile phone in South Africa. She knew before she answered that it was me – my name appeared on the mobile as it rang. At that moment she was visiting the home of a close friend whose husband was also working in Iraq, embedded with US forces somewhere in Baghdad. I told her that I had just crossed the border and was safely in Jordan. Her voice was overwhelmed with the deepest relief. She was finally able to let go of all the anxiety that she had lived with for months. 'Thank God,' she said. 'Just get home as quickly as you can.'

I looked around me at the people with whom I'd worked in Baghdad. The Baghdad Bureau Chief (and my friend), Paul Danahar, paced backwards and forwards as he spoke to his wife, occasionally prodding the ground with the toes of his boots or scuffing at the pebbles, talking and gesturing as if he was in the backyard of his home in Delhi. Cameraman Duncan Stone, who, like me, had been coming to Iraq for several years, was talking to his wife and children in London. I walked past his fellow cameraman

Andrew Kilrain as he spoke to his wife Linda in Sydney. He hadn't moved from the spot where he'd first got out of the car to call home. I don't know what time it was in Australia but I could hear Linda shouting with exhilaration and relief at the news that we were all safely out of Iraq . . . Malek Kenaan, our third cameraman, leaned against a window of one of the vehicles in the convoy, quietly enjoying a cigarette. My fellow BBC correspondent Paul Wood stared out pensively into the distance, contemplating his journey home that night to see his wife and children in Cairo.

The clouds that had been ominously approaching us earlier, auguring heavy rain, instead released a soft spray that billowed and swayed in the wind as it fell. At that moment I felt the deepest sense of exhaustion: the Iraq that I knew, the country defined by the rule of Saddam Hussein, which I had travelled through and chronicled, would never return. The fact that an era had come to an end had hit me abruptly when I had first caught sight of those three young Americans standing sentry at the border post at Trebil. And the very spot where we were standing as we spoke to our families was where my voyage into Saddam Hussein's Iraq had begun. Only now as I write these words am I starting to take stock of it all. I have begun at the end because only by looking back can one appreciate how far one has travelled.

It seems hard to remember now. Harder still to recall the kind of person I was on that sweltering September day in 1997 as I queued up at the Jordanian customs post at the border alongside dozens of middle-class Iraqis fortunate enough to have been able to leave the country if only briefly. The men mostly wore dark business suits, or at the very least western jackets and ties. They carried briefcases, and those who were accompanying their wives and children wrestled with large leather pouches for important travel papers. The head of the family bore a weight of self-importance as he would plead with his wife to make sure the children didn't stray too far, or would tell his straggling group to stay together as he went to deal with the obstructive customs officials. It was a typical scene of a middle-class family on their travels. The Iraqi women tended to wear modest dresses and understated jewellery. I hardly ever saw one wearing a full Islamic veil; urban Iraqi women almost never did. Even religiously observant middle-class Muslim women would at most wear only a simple headscarf to cover their hair. It was a reminder of how strong the secular tradition had become in Iraq. Young children would often be dressed up for these important journeys, in miniature suits and glittering dresses as if they were on their way to a party.

The atmosphere among young and old was almost always one of excited nervousness, as if they were venturing into an unknown world; it was extremely difficult for Iraqi families to leave the country in the late 1990s so these people at the border gate were the lucky ones. In the years after the first Gulf War, Iraq was seen as a pariah nation by the rest of the Middle East as well as by the world beyond. Middle-class families who'd been used to regular foreign travel in the past now found their paths blocked. They were trapped between the paranoia of two worlds: the first was that of Saddam Hussein, who feared that the country's best and brightest would go into exile at the first available opportunity and so ensured that very few exit visas were granted to businessmen, scientists or administrators; and then there was the paranoia of the countries outside, who presumed that Iraqis travelling to the West were either spies for Saddam Hussein's regime, or potential refugees or asylum seekers, unwelcome in a modern world where immigration is ever more tightly controlled. The people I saw at the border were indeed the lucky few. They contrasted sharply with the large crowd of truck drivers, nearly always peasants, many of them coming from the isolated rural villages of the Mesopotamian plains, who were a permanent feature of the border crossing. Running goods into and out of a country under strict economic sanctions provided the possibility of quickly earning enough money to marry and to farm one's own land. It was a gruelling and lonely vocation and their way of life showed in their vacant, bloodshot eyes. A thick film of desert sand darkened their faces. At each destination they would have just a few hours' rest before returning with yet another cargo, unconcerned whether what they were transporting was allowed under UN restrictions. We were supposed to see only the 'permitted' items, such as vans and pick-up trucks for the various ministries in Baghdad and the consignments of cement and boxes of tea or sacks of sugar, which were carried in huge articulated lorries. However, often we did catch a glimpse of their other cargo: the household electrical appliances, fans, video recorders, televisions, sometimes even shoes and clothes. Somehow it seemed fitting that Iraq's middle classes, the very people who were benefiting from this constant flow of goods, should, if only briefly, come face to face with the men who ran the trade.

I leafed through the pages of my passport to check again that the formal journalist's visa was really there. The large green stamp with the eagle insignia of the Republic of Iraq stared out. The English inscription stated that it had been issued by the Iraqi Embassy in Amman, Jordan, and was valid for a single trip that would be cancelled if it was discovered that the bearer had been to Israel.

The BBC had been formally banned from the country, 'blacklisted' as Iraqi officials called it, for almost five years. I had been appointed as the Corporation's Middle East correspondent in the summer of 1997 and like every other BBC reporter posted to the Middle East during that time, I had applied for a visa soon after arriving in the Jordanian capital Amman, where I would be based. The conflict between Israel's Likud government led by Binyamin Netenyahu and Palestinian groups such as Hamas was at a violent peak, and I found myself making the journey from Jordan to the West Bank and the Gaza Strip often during that summer to help my colleagues in the large BBC Jerusalem Bureau report on this conflict. The crisis there meant that news from other parts of the Middle East was sidelined as so many correspondents, camera crews and resources were focused on the unravelling of the Israeli–Palestinian peace accords.

I made a conscious decision to pay as much attention as I could to the rest of the region, nowhere more so than Iraq, which was one of the central issues of the Middle East. The difficulty of getting access into the country as a BBC correspondent exacerbated the frustrating lack of reporting from Iraq, but it was a challenge for a young and newly arrived correspondent in the region. Colleagues from the BBC and other news organizations in Jerusalem encouraged me to try to get into Iraq but they also warned me, speaking as they did from experience, not to get too obsessed or sidetracked by what they feared would be a fruitless endeavour. 'Give it a go,' I remember one radio reporter saying, 'but don't end up beating your head against a brick wall. Besides, given the situation in Jerusalem there's more than enough work for everyone here.' I was determined to get into Iraq not only because it was so under-reported but also because I felt it was a story that I could pursue with a degree of independence and autonomy.

And so I applied for my visa. Usually the applications never reached the Ministry of Information in Baghdad, but lingered, abandoned, on a civil servant's desk in the embassy in Amman. This was one of the regime's most important diplomatic missions. Neighbouring Jordan was Iraq's window on the world and all westerners, whether journalists, businessmen or aid workers, had to submit their visa applications through this embassy. In an attempt to penetrate the system, I had decided to write a personal letter of introduction in Arabic to the press attaché, Saadoun Daoud.

I was called to see him one afternoon, still not holding out much hope that I would manage to overcome the ministry's solid reluctance to open the country's borders to the BBC. The enormous, bright blue embassy was situated in the centre of Amman, an indistinct jumble of buildings designed to imitate the grandeur of Iraq's ancient past. There was a large metal gate through which the Iraqi diplomatic vehicles came and went. Visitors such as myself had to use a smaller electronically operated door that led into the waiting area of the consulate. In order to get into the building you had to be able to convince the man on the other side of the door of the honesty of your intentions. This wasn't the easiest thing to do through a crackling intercom system, but I succeeded.

When I walked into Daoud's office – his desk engulfed in piles of documents and, no doubt, countless visa applications submitted by journalists – he looked surprised. He was neatly dressed in a dark blue suit and his hair was swept carefully to one side. He smoked constantly. At every subsequent meeting he would always have a cigarette wedged between his fingers. He managed to surpass the copious nicotine consumption of most of the men I'd come across in this part of the world. He spoke in very formal English but the tone of his questions and the expression on his face hinted at something close to curiosity. We talked about my reasons for wanting to see him, and he made the predictable denunciations of the BBC. These criticisms tended to focus on the Iraqi government's belief that the Corporation had a determined agenda against Iraq. 'Objectivity' was the favourite word used in these confrontations.

'Mr Rageh. We have always been willing to let the BBC visit Iraq and report from there,' Mr Daoud said, 'but why is the BBC's reporting so full of adjectives? We just want the BBC to be objective and straight and fair. Not favourable but fair. Always you twist things.' Throughout this lecture he continued to stare at me. Was he surprised by my age? Was I dressed too casually for the interview? He paused for a moment and then, suddenly switching into Arabic, he asked: 'Where are you from?' My British passport sat in the middle of his desk, the gold print of the seal of the British crown clearly visible on its cover, but I instantly knew what he was asking. I replied in Arabic, 'I am originally from Somalia although I have lived in England for most of my life.' Clearly I was not what he expected from a western reporter, but he gave nothing away. He simply responded: 'That's interesting. You are welcome, Mr Rageh. Please, I will send your application to Baghdad, and we shall see.'

At first I thought his change in tone came down to the fact that I wasn't white and that I came from a Muslim African country. With hindsight it's clear that this was not the whole story. His reaction that day revealed something of the relationship between Iraq's legions of bureaucrats and minor state officials and the westerners with whom they came into contact. His initial response to me had been defensive, a reflection of pride in his identity as an Iraqi as well as nervousness of the state he represented. The light in his eyes reflected something more: that hidden beneath his public persona as a lowly servant of a despised state, he was an individual with another identity. Most westerners met and dealt mainly with representatives of Saddam Hussein's Iraq, people like Daoud. The nature of the state they served made sure that distance was maintained, informality kept to a minimum. As a result, most official relationships between the two sides were devoid of any genuine communication. Moments of real personal contact in these state-run institutions were extremely rare, small reprieves which each person held on to when they occurred. I didn't know it then, but I suppose in some ways my relationship with Iraq began with that curious conversation in Arabic.

Two weeks later I was summoned back to Saadoun Daoud's office. I had dropped by on a colleague when I received a call on my mobile phone: 'Hello, Mr Rageh,' Daoud boomed down the line. I remember thinking he sounded oddly cheerful. I suspected that his friendliness was just a precursor to an apology and the news that my visa request had been turned down. A fortnight had elapsed since my application had been submitted and I wasn't hopeful. 'I have some good news. Please come to my office.' I barely had time to register what he'd said before the line went dead. I raced to the embassy. When I walked into the office I saw that even if the pile of papers on his desk hadn't changed, he was in an altogether different mood from at our last encounter and he was eager to share his excitement. He pressed my passport into my hands, the pages open, the crest of the Iraqi government clearly visible. He professed amazement at how lucky I was, but looking back now, I wonder how genuine his incredulity was and what role he had in promoting my application to the senior officials in Baghdad.

The journey always started before dawn, and for me, too, the road to Baghdad began in the crisp chill of the hours before daybreak. The imposition of UN sanctions after the invasion of Kuwait in 1990 meant that it was not possible to fly into Baghdad and so the only way to the city was by road and in order to complete the eleven-hour journey by nightfall it was always best to leave in the small hours of the morning. It was not a beautiful or inspiring

journey, and the landscape along the single-lane Jordanian motorway towards Trebil was not breathtaking. Far from it. It was a
procession across a flat rocky desert interspersed occasionally by
small, impoverished Bedouin villages and settlements. But this
wasn't the point. It was a tedious trip, yet it was a journey like no
other. I was travelling a distance measured in hundreds of miles,
but I was entering a country immeasurably cut off from the rest of
the world. It was a feeling that flying to Baghdad could never
reproduce.

By the end of the 1990s, as country after country began to flout
the increasingly discredited and ineffective regime of economic
sanctions, there were several flights a week from Amman to
Baghdad on board the comfortable and modern aeroplanes of
Royal Jordanian Airlines. The journey was barely an hour long –
just enough time to be served a quick drink before you emerged
into the other world that was the Iraqi capital. But the speed of the
flight jarred. It was like walking out of the foyer of a five-star hotel
and straight into a refugee camp. Journeys are about transitions,
and the journey by road to Baghdad gave the heart and mind time
to prepare and adapt for the crossing into the world of Saddam
Hussein's Iraq. Even when it was no longer necessary to travel to
Baghdad by road I continued to do so.

As I approached the border for the first time on that September
day in 1997 I was filled with the trepidation of the innocent. The
neat blue uniforms of the Jordanian soldiers gave way to the
greenish-brown dishevelled attire of Iraq's regular army troops,
their black berets inexpertly perched on their often young heads. I
had barely touched Iraq's ancient soil when I saw my first image of
the ruler in his own country. His mouth was what I noticed first.
The thick familiar moustache lined his top lip that formed an
unnerving smile. Behind the smile his teeth were clenched tight.
The frame of his skull and his jowls were heavy and square and
emanated strength. Even in a picture to welcome visitors to his
country, Saddam Hussein inspired a martial dread.

Once we were inside Iraq's borders its leader's attempts during
the 1970s to modernize his country's infrastructure became quickly

apparent. This was a time when burgeoning oil revenues had afforded him the chance to cast himself as a twentieth-century caliph. What had been a pot-holed single-lane motorway on the Jordanian side of the frontier suddenly became a smooth-as-silk expressway with three lanes in either direction. Metal barricades ran along the sides, and strong metal rails through the middle separated the traffic. There were long stretches of neon lighting along the route. No expense had been spared. The roadside rest areas were the most peculiar fixture: at regular intervals on both sides of the highway the government had thoughtfully provided clearly signed picnic areas, complete with shade from the sun and concrete seating and tables for your comfort. It was the kind of thing you would expect to find on a motoring holiday in Switzerland.

The motorway signs loomed into view: Rutba, Hilla, Ramadi, and then finally Baghdad. Emerging from the flat plains of central Iraq you pass the houses and farms on the outskirts of the capital. The road rises as you approach the main western entry point where you cross the Euphrates river. Shining in the distance is Habbaniya lake. The plainness of the rural setting is transformed by the extraordinary beauty of thousands of date trees stretching far into the horizon. Iraq was once said to be blessed with the largest number of date trees in the world and nothing so captures the spirit of this ancient land as the immortal quality of these trees.

On the wall of the sitting room in my home in South Africa used to hang a small watercolour painting by a little-known Iraqi artist from Baghdad. A typical scene from the province around the capital was depicted in gentle greens and splashes of blue and brown: a hamlet near a small tributary of the Tigris at the end of the day as the sun prepares to set. By the side of the stream a woman dressed in an *abbaya*, the long black Islamic gown worn by religiously observant Iraqi women, is walking back from her labours carrying a large bundle of date palms. Overhanging the stream are a row of date trees, their reflection caught in the waters below. One day an Iraqi friend who had not returned to his homeland for nearly fifteen years happened to notice it. He stood looking at it for several minutes. It was not the product of a skilled artist yet for him it captured the essence of the place. 'I remember going past scenes exactly like this when my parents used to take us on visits outside Baghdad,' he said. 'It makes me ache to look at it.'

Approaching the outskirts of Baghdad, the mud-daubed houses of the villages give way to small, self-built brick houses, until eventually you come to the main entrance into the city from the west. For anyone coming into the capital for the first time in the years after the first Gulf War the experience was an unusual one because the city really did have an actual entry point. The image of 'the gates of Baghdad' was a romantic western notion, suffused with the mythology of Islamic caliphates, tales of *A Thousand and One Nights* and T. E. Lawrence, but the gates of Baghdad that I saw and entered in 1997 owed little to the grand history of the city and nearly everything to the paranoia and insecurity of its current ruler. The western gate lies twenty-five miles from the centre of the capital in Abu Ghraib suburb where a military checkpoint examines every vehicle. The suburb was home to one of the most notorious prisons in Saddam Hussein's vast gulag. The prison compound was set just off the main road and its relatively modest fortifications belied the true horror of the place. Opposite it lay a huge telecommunications base, a network of antennae and radio masts rising high into the air. The receivers for military signals and security eavesdropping looked like huge fishing nets held in place by long metal cables. Prisons and military surveillance: it was a first glimpse of the instruments by which Saddam Hussein's government maintained its power.

Baghdad is a low-built city. From the fourth or fifth floor of a building you see a cityscape of small squat houses like a layer of skin hugging the flat terrain of the land. It is a quality that makes the city's streets more visible and less remote. The skyscrapers of many modern cities are sometimes like steel and concrete curtains hiding the life that goes on in the streets beneath. When you look down at Baghdad from a high point the bustle of its avenues and neighbourhoods feels more immediate. Through its heart the wide and dark Tigris river snakes its way towards the mouth of the Persian Gulf.

Baghdad had all the features of a modern city in the developing world. During the rush hour the wide western-built avenues and arterial roads carried cars of every make and description: Volkswagens made in Brazil, Japanese cars, Chevrolets and Buicks competed for advantage alongside large buses and lorries spewing out thick, black smog from their exhausts. Cars were not driven just by the wealthy in Baghdad's privileged suburbs. Many less well-off Iraqis owned cars, but in their case the vehicles were so dilapidated it was amazing that their owners managed to get them to move at all. So prohibitive were the costs of spare parts or repairing damage to the bodywork that many of these vehicles wore a coating of brown rust and often their windscreens were patchworked with cracks from repeated accidents. There wasn't the chaos of traffic that you'd expect. Commuters obeyed the traffic lights and, like motorists the world over, they also lived in dread of traffic wardens. Even in the raucous commercial and shopping districts on the eastern bank of the Tigris, the traffic flowed easily round the large roundabout of Tahrir Square. And everywhere one travelled across the city were the other basic features of a modern urban society: the bank branches, the large general and teaching hospitals, as well as clinics, schools, post offices and shops – even red double-decker buses as public transport. These weren't the original London Routemasters but I like to think that the man in charge of Baghdad's public transport system who had ordered them had done it with a sense of humour, in memory of happy days spent in London at some stage in his life.

Throughout the years that followed I made dozens of trips to Baghdad, sometimes lasting six or seven weeks. The city I crisscrossed during my reporting assignments was a place of privation, squalor and political absolutism. At least that was how a number of western reporters and publications often portrayed it: the dark murky tide of the Tigris river, the dusty and brown streets and the titanic, brutal architecture of the ministries and presidential palaces. This description was certainly true but it only represented what the city's rulers had done to it. It had little to do with the Baghdad that belonged to the 4 million people who lived there. What gave this Baghdad its life and identity was its different districts. It was not the predictable landscape of a typical 'third world' city made up of a central seat of government power, business and commercial quarters, bordered by swathes of tidy bourgeois suburbs, in turn surrounded by slums and shanty-towns. Instead Baghdad had a richer, chameleon-like identity whose look, smells and feel would change with each neighbourhood. Ironically this was a characteristic it shared with two other great cities: London and New York. Like New York's Brooklyn, Queens or the Bronx, or London's Brixton, East End or Soho, Baghdad's different areas had their own unique qualities which bred local loyalties among those who lived there.

More than any other area in the city, Rashid Street, which runs parallel to the Tigris on its eastern side, is dominated by the influence of Iraq's colonial past. Baghdad was first captured by the Ottoman Turks in 1534 and was ruled by them for almost 400 years. The beginning of the First World War saw the arrival of the British, who landed at the southern tip of Iraq to defend the oilfields against Turkish attack. They captured Basra easily and, encouraged by this lack of resistance from the Turks, moved forward to Baghdad. And so began Britain's short-lived control over the country, albeit at one remove, through a monarchy reinstated by them. King Faisal I was appointed by the British to govern the country in 1921, and the monarchy endured until the military coup of 1958, when King Faisal II and the rest of the royal family were shot dead.

However, there are no grandiose symbols of imperial power in this street, no misconceived architecture fashioned in the tastes of the colonial rulers and then transplanted on to this ancient city, and no pretentious titanic buildings glorifying foreign powers. Instead what you see in Rashid Street is the faded and gentle imprint of the Ottomans and occasional, familiar glimpses of the British who once ruled this city from a distance. The area does not bear this colonial hallmark with a sense of shame; instead it has adopted it as if it was always its own, slightly embarrassed and scruffy but ultimately embracing its past. The street's bustling pavements amble beneath tall colonnades whose peeling paint and faded stone seem only to enhance its appeal. It is a place of bookshops, barbers and tailors and traditional teashops. At times I would just stand in the middle of the pavement staring down the promenade trying to envisage British administrators wandering past the shops, or Baghdad merchants in the 1950s with their tarboushes on their heads and pocket watches tucked into their waistcoats, discussing the politics of the day.

On either side of Rashid Street there is a network of meandering alleys that double back on themselves, turning the neighbourhood into a crowded maze which only its oldest inhabitants can understand. The alleys are too narrow for cars and are squeezed on both sides by the crumbling brown brick buildings, which are home to the families you see walking past and whose children play outside their front doors. It has the atmosphere of a North African casbah. The people who live here are tradesmen, shopkeepers who work in the nearby markets and bakeries. Many of the old houses of Baghdad in their distinctive colonial style still stand among these crowded blocks. They are flat-fronted and made of narrow brick or stone, with thin galleries running along the length of the first storey. On this floor there would be just one room, empty apart from carpets and cushions scattered across the floor. The houses are framed on all sides by large glassless windows, with only wooden slats to keep out the gaze of inquisitive neighbours, but which can catch the breeze in the oppressively hot summer months.

It is the teashops most of all that give Rashid Street its distinctiveness. During my time in Baghdad, one of these teashops became for me a place of refuge and escape from the Baghdad of Saddam Hussein. Hassan Ajmi, 'Hassan the Persian', stands in the middle of Rashid Street. Its dilapidated and simple shopfront makes it seem timeless. It has no sign over the door which opens right on to the pavement. The owner always sits by a table just inside the doorway where he stores the day's takings. As soon as you step through the entrance you walk into a large open salon with rows of benches and wicker seats. They are broken and old and the bindings of the wicker have grown loose and frayed from years of use. Its large floor-to-ceiling windows allow the men inside – and there are only ever men inside – to watch the world go by. On your left as you enter is a series of old brass and copper urns and pots constantly bubbling and steaming with fresh tea. Hassan Ajmi has its own unique sound. Morning, afternoon and night there is a constant tinkling as spoons are stirred in the glass thimbles full of sweet black tea with cardamom, and the rattle of domino pieces as men huddle around the tables to play. It was a meeting place particularly for writers, journalists from various state-controlled newspapers, aspiring poets and translators, and it was also the watering-hole for local shop owners and businessmen. Throughout the days and evenings the energetic young waiters would rush around the low tables, handing out endless glasses of tea and water-pipes.

Hassan Ajmi was not just somewhere I went to take in the charms of an old Arab teashop; it became a place where as a foreign journalist I could socialize with and talk to ordinary Iraqis. Far too often the only way western reporters met Iraqi civilians was in the course of their daily assignments. The nature of a controlled society like Iraq, where foreign journalists are monitored and accompanied by 'minders', makes it hard to meet ordinary people in any setting other than a formal interview, where both sides are usually focusing on a recent political event. Being able to speak Arabic meant it was much easier to talk to the people I met and to learn more about how this society worked. My being from Somalia meant that it wasn't immediately obvious to the customers in the shop that I was a reporter. Only on the occasions when I visited Hassan Ajmi as part of a television news crew to interview people in the teashop were they aware that I was a western journalist. For most people in a society such as Saddam Hussein's Iraq, the television camera represented a tool through which they could be monitored. Those who agreed to be interviewed were at best cautious about what they said about the regime. But in the absence of cameras and notebooks, in Arabic conversations, people were prepared to shed at least some of their inhibitions. They would never reveal their real thoughts or emotions, but through their willingness at least to broach certain subjects and sometimes end their sentences with a telling look or a wink, I began to get a better sense of the concerns of Baghdad's inhabitants.

It was in places like Hassan Ajmi that I got to know people. There and in the BBC's cramped and windowless office in the Ministry of Information I was introduced to the city by a number of Iraqis with whom I formed deep bonds over the years.

It was in 1997 that I met the two people who would become fundamental to my understanding of the country and its inhabitants and to whom I would turn time and again as war approached in 2003.

In November 1997 the world's media descended on the Iraqi capital to report on another crisis between Saddam Hussein and Britain and the United States. It was the beginning of what would become a defining theme in the war that would eventually destroy the Iraqi leadership six years later. UN weapons inspectors had been prevented from carrying out their operations because Baghdad – rightly as it eventually transpired – accused them of passing intelligence to London and Washington. It had all the feel of a staged drama. Aircraft carriers and troops were dispatched to the Gulf, while the Ba'ath Party leadership maintained its customary defiance. It was against this backdrop that I met Mohammed Darwish, a man who would come to have a formative impact on me. The BBC had been absent from Iraq for a long time because of its blacklisted status and was only then beginning to re-establish an office in Baghdad. I was its only correspondent there at the time, and it was up to me to find a translator. Mohammed had been recommended by an Iraqi friend who was working as a journalist for a western news agency in Baghdad.

When Mohammed walked into the small, uncomfortable BBC room at the Ministry of Information he was wearing what would become his trademark wool tweed jacket with black-rimmed reading glasses peeping out of the breast pocket. He was courteous and greeted me warmly. One of the first things I noticed about him was that, unlike the vast majority of Iraqi men who, in imitation of Saddam Hussein, grew thick moustaches, he was clean shaven. Growing a moustache, which in the West had come to be seen as passé, even mildly ridiculous, was an important symbol of political identity here. It was an act of imitation intended to show devotion

and loyalty to Saddam Hussein. It was *de rigueur* to wear a moustache
if you were a senior official – a general in the army or a cabinet
minister for example – but quite a few of the older, educated
Iraqis were clean-shaven. They had no desire to demonstrate their
machismo and to be clean-shaven was a quiet act of independence
from the state. However, many Iraqi men also sported moustaches
simply to project an image of strength and virility. They continued
to do so even after Saddam had been deposed, unlike the men in
Afghanistan, who ceremoniously shaved off the beards they had
been forced to grow during the Taliban's reign as soon as the
Taliban were overthrown.

Mohammed had spent several years during the 1980s studying in
Britain at universities in Edinburgh and York. His interests lay in
the world of literature and the arts. He had effectively opted out
of the political system and was happier at the idea of editing a
literary magazine than a national newspaper. He had also never
joined the Ba'ath Party – a requirement which was routine, indeed
necessary, if you had any ambition to work in public institutions in
Iraq – but that had not, so far, got him into hot water.

Mohammed's Iraqi co-worker in the BBC would be Saadoun
al Jannabi, who had begun working as the office manager the week
before. Saadoun had been the head of the Press Centre during the
first Gulf War and had formed many friendships with western
correspondents over the years. He too had studied in Edinburgh in
the 1980s, where he had got to know Mohammed. Saadoun and
Mohammed differed from each other in a number of ways: where
Mohammed's interests were largely artistic and academic, Saadoun
was an experienced figure in the media and a great 'fixer'. Having
worked in the Ministry of Information in the years of isolation and
upheaval that followed the first Gulf War, Saadoun knew the official
mind of the Iraqi bureaucracy better than many. He understood the
fear, paranoia and stifling restrictions that were the hallmarks of the
system and had worked out ways of manipulating it. Saadoun was
most at home in the company of western journalists and friends he
had made during his time as a civil servant. He frequently met the
latter group in the Alwiyah Club, an old private club favoured by

Baghdad's anglophile middle-class families, who would go there to play bingo and reminisce about the past.

Mohammed and Saadoun more than anyone else taught me to see beyond the Baghdad of Saddam Hussein. I realized quickly that it would be an education based on trust, and that trust had to be earned. Lifting the lid on the realities of a tyrannized society to a foreigner, and a journalist to boot, was not something to be taken on lightly. Friendship and camaraderie were not enough to make it worth the risk, even if your job and livelihood depended on western news organizations. It took a long, long time before these Iraqi friends came to trust me with their inner thoughts about their country's agony. This was about far more than simply confiding in a friend and colleague, and far more dangerous. Years later, Mohammed would say to me: 'In dictatorships, the last place left that is free is the inside of your head.' Trusting somebody was about letting them into that last hiding place. It began with small, sometimes comical, acts of mutual trust between the three of us. During the first Gulf War when foreign press dispatches from Baghdad were censored by Iraqi officials, some BBC journalists dreamed up their own code so that they could talk about Saddam Hussein without any Iraqi official being aware of whom they were discussing. Saddam Hussein went under the codename of 'Eric'. I decided to revive the idea with the agreement and participation of Mohammed and Saadoun. Many conversations took place about Eric's whereabouts, his habits, his tactics and of course the history of all he had done. The codename served a practical purpose, and we mischievously delighted in its absurdity. However, for people like Mohammed and Saadoun to take part in this faintly ridiculous charade was a brave and risky process.

Under UN sanctions many basic and crucial things became increasingly hard to get hold of, particularly medicines. Before each assignment back to Baghdad I would always telephone Mohammed and Saadoun to ask if there was anything they needed. I got to know the exact types and dosages of various blood pressure and kidney infection tablets members of their families required but were not able to obtain in Iraq. I also knew that Mohammed wanted books, and occasionally Saadoun would ask me to bring him some too. Initially I brought novels, poetry and volumes on literary criticism, as well as magazines and periodicals. However, as our trust grew, I began to smuggle in books on Iraq and Saddam Hussein for both of them. Our belongings were often given a brief inspection at the border, but if they were found I could claim them as my own and the worst that would happen to me as a westerner would be to have them confiscated. The consequences for an Iraqi found in possession of such works were far more grave.

Over time I began to bring works on the modern history of Iraq, books such as *Cruelty and Silence* by Kenaan Makiya, a haunting and anguished examination of the suffering of Iraqis imprisoned, tortured and exiled by the Ba'ath Party, and *Out of the Ashes* by Patrick and Andrew Cockburn, probably the best account of how Saddam Hussein regained total control over Iraq and saw off British and American attempts to overthrow and undermine him after the catastrophe of the first Gulf War. An Iraqi caught in possession of such books would be seen by the authorities as an opponent of the Ba'ath Party and the Iraqi leader himself. Only someone with strong political connections would stand a chance of extricating himself from the grip of the security and intelligence agencies if he were caught with such provocative literature in his possession. Even then, your card and that of your relatives and friends would be marked for life and you would be permanently watched for any signs of dissent. You would never be given permission to leave the country, your career ambitions would be stopped in their tracks, your children would almost certainly never gain entry into the main universities or colleges. This is what you could expect, if you were fortunate.

I would bring the books to the BBC office concealed among my equipment and would take them out in the editing room at the back where officials rarely went. I would have covered them in different book jackets, often just making them up from old newspapers. On one occasion I used an old cover from a second-hand work on development economics. In order not to attract attention, I avoided using images from the Middle East or from recent conflicts. I would close the door to the editing room before handing the books over to Mohammed or Saadoun and they would immediately tuck them under newspapers and hide them in their carrier bags or briefcases before leaving the room.

The trust that came to underpin our friendships was cemented by more than these acts. When I spoke to them about their families, their recollections of life in Iraq before and during the rule of Saddam Hussein and their fears about the future, I did so in Arabic. I reciprocated with recollections of my childhood in Somalia, of how my family came to leave the country and settle in Britain and what had happened to relatives and close family friends during the long years of military dictatorship and civil war in Somalia. In these exchanges and intimacies a sense of cultural connection developed. It made them believe that I understood – or at the very least could imagine – the nature of their lives. What is more, they believed that, having grown up in a family which understood the cruelty of dictatorship, I realized the importance and value of keeping secrets and that you had to know when, with whom and where you could talk.

Many of our conversations took place outside the Press Centre in the Ministry of Information, either on the street or in the ministry's car park. We would instantly change the subject when someone we did not know passed by. At other times, in exactly the same circumstances, we would simply carry on talking because we felt it safe to do so. It became a shared sixth sense often based on nothing more than the way the stranger looked or how they were dressed. Invariably, 'secret' policemen would be kitted out in their own distinctive 'uniform', in broad-shouldered black leather jackets or very smart suits. Their clothes immediately identified them as government employees – no one else had the funds for or access to such expensive, foreign clothes. They would wear their uniforms with the swagger that only someone with complete confidence in the safety of their position can flaunt. Many of course were not so obvious, remaining more unobtrusive and sinister, but there were certainly a large number who had clearly watched *The Godfather* too many times.

Mohammed and Saadoun's friendship guided me as I learned to operate as a reporter in Saddam Hussein's Iraq, and gave me a glimpse into the lives of the people of Baghdad, trapped in a tragedy they were powerless to change. They gave an authentic voice and identity to a city that had for so long been seen only through the image of its ruler.

In our long discussions over the years I learned much about the conditions of life for Mohammed, Saadoun and their friends. It was they who brought home to me what life had been like since the Gulf War and the reality of the phrase 'the march to war' which was so overused in the months leading up to the conflict in March 2003. The truth is that the people of Iraq had already been traumatized by a decade-long war. Its weapons were not smart bombs or laser-guided munitions, but the harsh and silent reality of economic privation, known euphemistically as sanctions. Even now I am stunned at the lack of public examination in Britain and the United States of the long-term economic and psychological damage that policy caused the Iraqi people in the 1990s. The direct impact of sanctions on their lives came to define how millions of Iraqis viewed western policy. It is the damage that sanctions have caused Iraq that has so undermined the ability of the coalition to make Iraqis feel that the war to overthrow Saddam Hussein has changed their lives for the better. More than anything else it is the effects of a decade of sanctions that are leading Iraq to such a blighted and chaotic future. It is only by examining how sanctions ruined the lives of middle-class Iraqis, and how the system was manipulated by Saddam Hussein's government, that one can begin to appreciate just how badly prepared Britain and the US were for governing Iraq after Saddam Hussein.

2. Illusions

The world changed utterly for Saddam Hussein after his invasion of Kuwait on 2 August 1990. When the first Gulf War ended in March 1991 the US and Britain were adamant that he should never again be in the position to make such forays. The sanctions imposed by the UN Security Council on 6 August 1990 to persuade Iraq to leave Kuwait remained in place when the war ended and would do so, with tragic consequences, until war broke out again in 2003.

In December 1997 I arrived at the Saddam Children's Hospital for the first time to check for myself the reality of the reports by journalists, aid agencies and the UN on the worsening humanitarian crisis that faced the Iraqi population as a result of international economic sanctions.

Above the entrance to one of the wards at the end of a corridor was a portrait of Saddam Hussein who'd given his name to what was now this place of unspeakable suffering. The doctor's eyes darted back and forth between me and the three children lying on beds in the ward. He said, 'The children are not suffering just because of a lack of food. This is of course one issue, but the problem is lack of clean water and the chronic sanitation in many parts of Baghdad and of course other cities in Iraq. This is what lies behind the many cases of diarrhoea, intestinal infections and other diseases.' He paused for a moment and then, looking down at his feet, he said, 'This is the reason for so many deaths amongst children in Iraq.' He showed me the thick bundles of paper which constituted the clinical accounts, and the broken medical equipment that could not be repaired because of insufficient funds and which lay uselessly gathering dust. You could hear the crying of children along the corridors. The smell of the cheap old disinfectant being sloshed on to the floor from battered tin buckets was overwhelming. The bags of blood to be used in transfusions for some of the young children were stacked on metal trays, alongside cotton wool balls stained brown with bromine.

I headed out of the hospital and had to stop myself from breaking into a run and betraying my desperation to escape the scenes I had just witnessed. I took great gulps of air once I got outside while Karim, the minder appointed to me for the day by the Ministry of Information, clambered into the front passenger seat of our car. We headed back to the BBC office in the ministry and none of us spoke. I wanted to say something, some expression of sorrow for the patients inside, such as a young girl called Salma, who was suffering from leukaemia and whom I'd just seen in a terrifying condition in a bare room of the hospital. Karim sat stony-faced as he gripped the handle above the window. He was slight, with a hooked nose above a thick moustache, and he always wore the same light-blue wool blazer, dark tattered tie and shiny polyester shirts. He'd excelled as a language student in Baghdad during the early 1980s, specializing in Spanish, and so had had the opportunity to travel and study abroad, and his looks had attracted some rather unusual attention during a trip he had taken to Mexico in the mid 1980s: 'Many Mexicans I met could not believe that I was an Arab. They said I looked exactly like General Zapata, the revolutionary Mexican leader. Many times people shouted out to me, "Zapata! Zapata!"' He did look exactly like the legendary Mexican bandit and he would tell this story often, roaring with laughter as he did so. On the day of our hospital visit, however, there was no sign of Karim's usual humour. He didn't even raise his head to look outside the window as we drove but fixed his gaze on the dashboard. I said something about being unprepared for what I had seen in the hospital and how upsetting it was. Karim looked up. 'Mmm? Sorry, I did not hear you.' I repeated my comments. 'Oh yes, the hospital. Yes, very bad. It is always like that.'

Karim never took his job as a minder very seriously and never eavesdropped on any of my interviews. He often chose to wait outside and have a smoke rather than stay in the room while I worked. When we arrived back at the Press Centre after the hospital visit, I shook his hand and he headed for the room behind the director's office where the minders would listlessly wait to be assigned to journalists. Then suddenly he turned back and said that he wanted a private word. He slipped his arm under mine and pulled me aside. 'Mr Rageh, I want to ask you something, but please don't be angry and please, don't tell it to anyone. I consider you as an Arab brother so please keep this between us . . . Mr Rageh . . . I am wondering . . . it's a small thing . . .' He was tentative and embarrassed. 'Mr Rageh. I have some difficulties in my family and as you know the situation in the country is very bad. Please, I need some money, to help my family you understand, not for me. Can you help me, please?' I did not want to say anything that would add to his palpable embarrassment. What was a small sum for me was for him a month's supply of food. I briskly patted him on the back, said I would see what I could do and quickly walked away, to avoid his having to thank me. I did not want to prolong the process of supplication.

Deciding how much to give was a delicate and difficult thing. Was £50 enough? Should I just say no? What would be the consequences? Would other minders find out and report him? Would I be starting something that I would later come to regret? The official salary for a civil servant in the ministry, or for that matter any Iraqi ministry or state organization, company or commission, was 5,000 Iraqi dinars a month, which in the late 1990s was the equivalent of about £1.70 a month. Many officials, translators and technicians in the Ministry of Information desperately wanted to be hired by western news agencies in Baghdad because translators for a TV network could earn up to £200 a month – a hundredfold pay rise. But this was no easy transition. There was no job security, no way of telling how long the journalists or their organizations would maintain an office in Baghdad. Of course, working alongside westerners also meant that you were effectively keeping company with people over whom the intelligence services were casting a watchful eye. That gaze would sooner or later fall upon you too. Karim did not want to take such risks. He wanted a quiet life and to avoid any sort of trouble, so he never sought out this kind of work.

The next day, before I left my hotel room, I folded £100 in my pocket. I saw Karim smoking a cigarette at the gate of the ministry car park. I went over to him, pretending that I just wanted to cadge a cigarette. We started chatting: what was he doing that day? Had there been any new arrivals among the press corps? I stubbed the cigarette out on the ground, said goodbye and held out my hand to shake his. In my palm were the crumpled up banknotes, which I slipped into his hand. He caught my eye for an instant before saying goodbye, withdrawing his hand into his pocket. That was the last either of us said on the matter.

After the end of the first Gulf War the United Nations sent a special mission to Iraq, headed by Under Secretary-General Martti Ahtissari, to report on the economic and social conditions facing people in the wake of the conflict. In his report the Finnish diplomat wrote:

I and the members of my mission were fully conversant with media reports regarding the situation in Iraq and, of course, with the recent WHO/UNICEF report on water, sanitary and health conditions in Greater Baghdad. It should be said at once, however, that nothing that we had seen or read had quite prepared us for the particular form of devastation which has now befallen the country. The recent conflict has wrought near-apocalyptic results upon the economic infrastructure of what had been, until January 1991, a rather highly urbanized and mechanized society. Now most means of modern life support have been destroyed or rendered tenuous. Iraq has, for some time to come, been relegated to a pre-industrial age, but with all the disabilities of post-industrial dependency on an intensive use of energy and technology.

In the next decade, those prescient words came to define a truth that lay beneath public perceptions of economic sanctions in Iraq. They demonstrated the futility of a policy aimed at punishing a dictator but which instead ended up making the members of the ruling elite rich and ripping to shreds the social fabric of a people we would later wage a war to liberate. They underlined the corrosive influence that this policy was having on the reputation of the United Nations within the country and outside. All this from an organization whose founding charter speaks of its determination 'to promote social progress and better standards of life'.

The effect of sanctions against Iraq has remained a treacherous issue for international commentators. To doubt the efficacy of sanctions was problematic given that commentators on both sides wanted to see Saddam Hussein's power curtailed and given that the sanctions themselves were used by him as propaganda against the West and to cover up the shortcomings of his regime. The point, however, is that sanctions are always a complex issue and this complexity needed to be grappled with if the Iraqi people were not to suffer. For it is impossible to deny – indeed the UN itself has confirmed it – that innocent people became the victims of a policy that had supposedly not been aimed at them. The sanctions imposed in 1990 failed to force Saddam Hussein to withdraw from Kuwait and thus failed to avoid military conflict, and they failed in that conflict's immediate aftermath to dislodge him from power. But they were nevertheless maintained, with disastrous results. The UN was the only international institution that could be an alternative to the US provisional authority in the post-war occupation of Iraq, but for many Iraqis it would always be tainted by having been the body that oversaw and administered the decade-long sanctions regime. 'Nothing that we had seen or read had quite prepared us for the particular form of devastation which has now befallen the country.' Those words described exactly how I had felt standing in the corridor of the Saddam Children's Hospital.

Nowhere were sanctions more corrosive and debilitating than among the middle classes of Iraq. Until the first Gulf War Iraq had imported virtually everything necessary to the day-to-day functioning of an urbanized and mechanized society: cars and spare parts, electrical equipment, machine tools for factories, even household products. Sanctions, however, made all economic trade with Iraq illegal unless approved by the UN. At a stroke the country's economy collapsed and with it went the livelihoods of the large merchant class whose family-run businesses facilitated much of this trade. Those who did remain in business were basically criminalized, having to resort to black marketeering and smuggling.

The new system gave rise to a new class of *nouveaux riches*, relatives of senior officials who had the clout and political connections to circumvent the rules and restrictions of sanctions and remain protected. For the older established trading families it meant only ruin.

In 1997 I first witnessed the tangible effects of this economic ruin for a large section of urban Iraq. Driving along the eastern bank of the Tigris towards the commercial district of Karada on an afternoon just before Christmas, I spotted an arrangement of chairs and tables lined up along the pavement. The furniture was not advertising the wares of any shop as all along the street there were only shuttered offices and food stalls. The chairs and tables were of particularly good quality: the wood was a deeper and richer brown than the light tan of the more usual cheaper softer wood and the carving on the legs was of a much higher standard than the mass-produced furniture more often found in the city's shops. Mohammed explained: 'This is an auction market. Families come to sell their expensive furniture and luxuries to raise money.' He sighed. 'This bloody embargo.'

These auctions were rarely advertised and took place almost in secret. That evening I decided to go and see one for myself. I wanted to go there alone without a minder hovering in the background. The system of minders in Iraq was never as ruthlessly efficient as many in the outside world might have been led to believe. The minders were supposed to accompany us only if we were going out to work, either filming or interviewing. They never accompanied us if we wanted to drive around the city, go out to dinner or visit the homes of friends, and most of our equipment was too big to be taken out surreptitiously. So that evening, I went to the Al Rasheed Hotel in central Baghdad to pick up a taxi, pretending I was just off to dinner. The hotel had been built on a lavish scale by Saddam Hussein to host a summit of Arab leaders during the Iran–Iraq war. No expense had been spared to keep those visiting dignitaries safe from incoming missiles. The inch-thick glass in the windows stood behind concrete blast deflectors and the hotel had its own reinforced underground bunker, as well as the more usual trappings of a five-star hotel. It also had an extraordinary mosaic in the foyer. Depicted in hundreds of tiny, brightly coloured tiles was the face of President George Bush Senior, beneath which the inscription read: 'Bush is Criminal'. It was impossible to walk across the foyer without treading on the former president's face – a deliberate intention, no doubt, on the part of the artist. The hotel's exorbitantly expensive restaurant had become the haunt of the new moneyed elite during the sanctions years, a place where they could display their recent wealth. The short taxi ride from the Al Rasheed to the auction houses marked the boundary between those who'd been dispossessed by sanctions and those who'd profited from them.

The collection of BMWs and Mercedes outside the blank-faced building where the auction was being held indicated the background of the customers. There were also a number of large white Japanese four-wheel-drive vehicles with 'UN' painted on their sides. In the crowded passageway the auctioneers yelled instructions to their assistants. There were about sixty people milling about the small hall. The atmosphere was part traditional auction and part indoor market. Whole lives were on display. The owners of the BMWs and the UN vehicles, who were able to pay for the bargains on show with hard currency, seemed to be there for the few antiques: Bokhara and Tabriz carpets, family silverware and china bowls, figurines of lapis lazuli and topaz. But among these refined pieces there was an eccentric array of household goods: old refrigerators, a Telefunken colour television from Germany, video recorders and their remote controls, a juice blender, and dilapidated pieces of furniture. I had expected to see the Persian carpets and the china. Despite the obvious pain involved in parting with these heirlooms, families realized that they were luxuries that they could ill afford, even if they fetched only a few hundred pounds. What I had not expected to see were the old fridges, kitchen equipment and sad pieces of furniture.

These goods had belonged to families who couldn't afford mantelpiece decorations inlaid with semi-precious stones, who had not inherited wool and silk handmade carpets to spread on the floors of their homes. These were the belongings of people who had

painfully clung to a middle-class existence, whose few possessions
would have meant everything to their fragile sense of status. Their
owners would have been badly paid civil servants like Karim, or
junior managers in state factories, or shop assistants and restaurant
managers. They would probably be described as 'the aspiring
working classes' by sociologists. Most of these people lived in the
small houses or flats in the old neighbourhoods which run off
Rashid Street or in the outer edges of the Mansour district in the
west. The fridge or television would have had pride of place in
their homes, perhaps alongside other hard-won purchases such as a
stove or radio. Perhaps those too would soon be auctioned off.

I went over to talk to a middle-aged man who'd come here for
a second time to sell off more of his possessions. He probably
assumed that I was a UN official on the hunt for some bargains,
but my notebook and questions in Arabic soon identified me as a
journalist. He was forty-one years old, stocky and wearing spectacles. He told me that many people from his neighbourhood came
here to raise some ready cash and had been doing so since the early
1990s. He was an engineer by training and used to work at the Oil
Ministry which he had left two years before because the £5 or so
he earned each month was hopelessly inadequate. At first, like
thousands of other middle-ranking officials and bureaucrats, he
moonlighted. However, he said rather euphemistically, the arrangement had not been sustainable and so he had left his government
job to work full time for a friend who owned a large car workshop.
He now earned about £40 a month.

The collapse of Iraq's economy under sanctions, entailing massive
devaluation of the Iraqi dinar and huge hyperinflation, had made
state salaries almost worthless. In the 1980s 1 Iraqi dinar was worth
about £2. In the mid 1990s, when the effects of sanctions were
becoming truly debilitating, you needed 3,000 Iraqi dinars to buy
£2. Savings were obliterated and take-home pay, even for engineers
in the Oil Ministry, was almost meaningless. As a result many
in the educated and technocratic classes were forced to abandon
their official careers. Over the last few years in Iraq I have met
and interviewed many university graduates working as shop assis-

tants, primary school teachers selling cigarettes in markets, one mechanical engineer driving a taxi.

One of the most catastrophic effects of this state brain drain was on the education system. Already facing chronic shortages in teaching equipment and materials, the state school system imploded as teachers were forced to find work elsewhere. Many of them resorted to giving private tuition to children of wealthier families whose parents were keen to get their sons and daughters into the best universities. In this sense sanctions effectively facilitated the mass privatization of education. Many parents with more moderate incomes saw no point in their children continuing to attend schools that had hardly any equipment and whose teachers rarely turned up because they were getting paid for private lessons. It was more useful to take the children out of school to earn money for the family by working as runners for shops or simply by begging. According to figures from the United Nations Children's Fund (UNICEF) after the first Gulf War ended 70 per cent of all schools in Iraq needed repairs, and 60 per cent of girls and 50 per cent of boys stopped attending secondary schools. What went largely unreported was the soaring levels of crime, prostitution and street begging in a country which until the early 1990s had had little experience of such things.

Growing concern within the UN at the dire humanitarian consequences of sanctions, and frustration in Washington and London at their failure to dislodge Saddam Hussein, led to the 'Food for Oil' deal in 1996. The aim was to alleviate the effects of sanctions on poor Iraqis. It allowed the regime to sell around £1.4 billion worth of crude oil every six months under the tight supervision of the UN. The funds were placed in a bank account in New York controlled by the UN, against which Baghdad could buy food and medicines. The sanctions committee of the UN could still veto any orders or contracts which it felt could also have a military purpose, so-called 'dual use' items. Two-thirds of the money went on buying food and medicines, the other third went on paying for the operations of the UN weapons inspectors, and paying compensation to Kuwait for the 1990 invasion. The UN

Office of the Humanitarian Co-ordinator for Iraq, which oversaw
the food importation, shared its offices in Baghdad with the
weapons inspectors. It was an uneasy coupling.

The first thing I saw when I entered the reception hall of the
UN building was a large display cabinet. Inside it was a strange
collection of basic foodstuffs: a pile of grain, a jar of cooking oil, a
bag of sugar, a small mound of tea. Beneath the cabinet was stated
that this was the monthly food ration for an Iraqi family. At first
this seemed to be a distasteful and offensive exhibit given the
deprivation that existed in the city in which the offices stood.
But I later realized that this was a mildly subversive act by UN
humanitarian staff, many of whom felt strongly about the inad-
equacies of their own operations. The display was actually an
admission of guilt and an expression of discontent. Once Iraq had
paid for the operations of the weapons inspectors and paid around
£130 million in compensation to Kuwait every six months out of
its oil revenue under the scheme, it left the UN humanitarian
operations with around £127 to spend on the needs of each Iraqi
in the country for the whole year. That works out at 30 pence a
day to cover the food and medical needs of one Iraqi. On top of
this, under the terms of the UN resolutions, no money could be
spent inside Iraq on the repair of civilian infrastructure. As everything in the country was controlled by the state, there was no way
of repairing sewerage pipes, for example, without paying the Iraqi
regime to do so. The UN could not take some of the money from
the 'Food for Oil' programme and give it to the regime even if it
truly did intend to use it to build teacher training colleges or repair
power stations.

The most damaging and self-defeating aspect of the sanctions
regime lay in how it transformed the nature of the relationship
between the dictatorship and its captive people. The Ba'ath regime
was built on cruelty and violence. It was, in essence, a dictatorship
of fear. However, because of the way sanctions were implemented,
it was transformed into a dictatorship of need. The regime paid for
the importation of food and medical supplies, and the UN oversaw
its administration, but the monthly food rations were actually

distributed by the Iraqi Ministry of Trade. At various points in neighbourhoods all over the country, from local shops, administrative offices, shopping centres, Iraqi families took their monthly coupons to their local private grocery shop which was authorized to act as an agent by the Ministry of Trade. Each family was registered with its local shop, which kept a detailed record of the families in the area, the number of people in each family and their ages, so as to determine the rations for each household. Families would collect their goods in exchange for their monthly coupons. Unable to trade goods freely between themselves or with the outside world the Iraqi population actually *needed* Saddam Hussein's state to sustain them. A policy whose aim had been to undermine Saddam Hussein was entrenching him more deeply. The dictator's presence was now a necessary and unavoidable part of everyday survival. The system also gave Saddam Hussein the chance to promote a new personality cult in the style of his true historical mentor: just as Stalin had insidiously presented himself to the Russian people as 'Uncle Josef', so Saddam now portrayed himself to Iraqi families as the great provider. For many UN staff working in Baghdad this was an agonizing truth to confront.

I saw the display cabinet at UN headquarters in the autumn of 1997 when I went there to interview the UN Humanitarian Co-ordinator. Denis Halliday had only just taken up the post and he welcomed me courteously into his comfortable but understated office. A tall, thin man with a neatly trimmed beard, he was an Irish Quaker and had served in numerous UN development postings around the world in a career with the international body that spanned over three decades. By the late 1990s he was an Assistant Secretary-General of the UN. He was profoundly serious about the job in hand and had a firm grasp of his brief. During our first few interviews he was factual and circumspect in his assessment of the work of the UN in Iraq. He expressed concern about the humanitarian crisis which had already been made public in the reports from various independent aid organizations, but he also believed that he and his colleagues were making a difference. All journalists liked him and found him humorous and approachable.

But in the year that followed, we watched him gradually lose faith
in the sanctions system that he had been charged to administer.
He began to talk openly in interviews of how sanctions were
creating 'a lost generation'. He repeated the unofficial estimates
that he had received from his colleagues at the UN World Health
Organization that between four and five thousand children were
dying every month directly as a result of sanctions. He explained,
just as the doctor at the Saddam Children's Hospital had done, that
although the 'Food for Oil' programme meant desperately needed
food supplies were being imported, the lack of clean water, appalling sanitation, broken-down treatment facilities, sewerage in the
streets and dilapidated health facilities left infections and disease
unchecked.

By the autumn of 1998 it was becoming clear that Denis Halliday
could not carry on for much longer. We met, for the last time as it
turned out, in September at the UN office in Baghdad. By this
time we knew each other very well. He told me that he was looking
forward to a holiday with his family back in Ireland, 'the land of
saints and poets' as he would jokingly refer to it. In that meeting
he reiterated to me what he had been saying for some time. He
described sanctions as 'a form of warfare', and said that the UN
humanitarian operations were 'having the same effect as band-aids
on gaping wounds'. He railed at being in the position of 'overseeing
the de-development and de-industrialization of a modern country'.
He resigned a few weeks later with a withering attack on the system.
He called sanctions 'a totally bankrupt concept [that] probably
strengthens the leadership and further weakens the people of the
country . . . Sanctions are starving to death 6,000 Iraqi infants every
month, ignoring the human rights of ordinary Iraqis, and turning a
whole generation against the West. I no longer want to be a part
of that.' He also pointed an accusing finger at his political masters
at UN headquarters in New York. 'I find myself being second-
guessed by a headquarters that does not understand the Iraq that I
understand, living and working here.' Indeed in a 1996 television
interview, when Madeleine Albright, the then US ambassador to
the United Nations, was asked about the cost of sanctions in terms

of the half a million Iraqi children who had lost their lives, she responded: 'We think the price is worth it.' A statement which was not forgotten in Iraq or in the wider Middle East.

In May 1996, a team of economists from the London School of Economics travelled to Iraq to do a detailed survey on the effects of UN sanctions on the civilian population of the country for the Centre for Economic and Social Rights (CESR). One month earlier, the CESR had conducted surveys on child mortality and nutritional status, as well as public health and sanitation infrastructure. It is the kind of report you might expect from academic economists: sober, rigorous. It is hardly the work of commentators with a political agenda, and it is for this reason that the findings of the report are so shocking. Issued in November 1997, it found that

Iraq had relied heavily on oil revenues in the past, and its economy had developed around the surpluses generated by oil exports. As such Iraq was particularly vulnerable to an oil embargo . . . The impact on earnings and livelihoods has been disastrous. Real earnings fell by around 90 per cent in the first year of the sanctions, and then fell by around 40 per cent more between 1991 and 1996 . . . The human and economic cost of the sanctions has, indeed, been enormous, and it has largely been borne by the civilian population of Iraq. There can be no question of seeking justification for policy-induced human suffering of this magnitude.

The report also discussed sanctions in the context of its initial aim – that of disarming Saddam Hussein's regime. The report acknowledged that there had been a degree of success in this regard during the 1990s but that, even if sanctions had contributed to this success, the economic privations were still misguided and self-defeating. It went on:

The sanctions may have succeeded in forcing the Iraqi government to submit a substantial proportion of the stock of long-range rockets and nuclear and chemical materials and facilities for their manufacture. The continuation of sanctions may help to unearth and destroy what has until now been concealed; but it would not change the Iraqi leadership or change the character of the regime. It would prolong the suffering of the Iraqi population and contain Iraq through a stranglehold on its economy. These conditions are likely to hinder rather than help the cause of meeting 'the ongoing challenge of building long-term peace and stability in the region'.

Denis Halliday went beyond just a personal expression of disappointment and used his resignation to give a warning which in retrospect was as unwelcome as it was insightful. In November 1998, a month after leaving his post, he delivered a speech at Harvard University in the United States in which he detailed the various and complex long-term effects that the experience of sanctions would have on Iraqi society. His comments back then have extraordinary and frightening resonance in present-day Iraq:

The sanctions have also served to isolate the intelligentsia, the professionals, and others in Iraq from the world at large. One of the offshoots of this isolation is alienation. That is the growth of a younger generation of men and women who have not travelled overseas, cannot study overseas and cannot communicate overseas . . . With a younger generation of Iraqis finding a situation that they deem to be impossible and discriminatory, one can only visualize the formation of a radical movement to reverse the conditions imposed by sanctions which utilizes the despair and discontent existing among the younger generation as a basis of support. One can only fear therefore what history's most comprehensive and debilitating sanctions regime may have on the future of Iraq, the region and the world. As a result of isolation, the danger of breeding fanaticism, deep-seated resentment and the chances that such characteristics will come to influence the future decision-making process in this country are very real.

Had Denis Halliday been the only senior UN official to resign his post in protest, one could dismiss his resignation as an individual response with no wider relevance to the work of the UN in Iraq or its sanctions policy. However, Denis Halliday was replaced in 1998 by the respected German UN career diplomat Hans Von

Sponeck. Given the nature of Mr Halliday's departure, UN head-quarters in New York were hardly likely to appoint a highly strung maverick to replace him. Yet he too travelled the same road to disillusionment. He too began his posting in Baghdad by immersing himself in detail, arguing forcefully and cogently about the different ways he and his colleagues within the UN humanitarian agencies were trying to alleviate a chronic situation. But then he too began to speak of the creation of 'a lost generation' under sanctions, he too began to question bitterly what the UN was doing in Iraq. The reports of child mortality, rates of malnutrition among children under five and the number of households without clean water continued to appear. After less than two years in the job, Hans Von Sponeck also resigned as UN Humanitarian Co-ordinator in Iraq, bringing to an end a thirty-six-year career at the UN. Like his predecessor, he used his departure to protest against the present situation. 'As a UN official, I should not be expected to be silent to that which I recognize as a true human tragedy that needs to be ended,' he said, adding, 'The humanitarian programme has failed to meet the needs of Iraq's 22 million people . . . As a UN official I should not be expected to be silent. How long must the civilian population be exposed to such punishment for something that they have never done?' Two days after Hans Von Sponeck's resignation, the head of the UN World Food Programme in Iraq, Ms Jutta Burghardt, another German diplomat, offered her resignation as well in protest at economic sanctions. In just over two years, three of the most senior UN humanitarian officials in Iraq had resigned. All of them were career UN diplomats and could hardly be described as naturally inclined towards rebellion.

Several months after he resigned, on 6 May 2000, Mr Von Sponeck gave a speech at a conference in London. Like his predecessor, Denis Halliday, he tried to highlight some of the lesser-known effects of the economic restrictions imposed on Iraq:

Cyberspace? [he asked rhetorically] Cyberspace in Iraqi skies does not exist. All computers requested for education have been put on hold as being 'dual use' for the Military. Prostitution of young girls, unheard of in a Muslim country; a girl from an educated family is a part-time prostitute to make some money in order to prepare, to get what she needs, for the school year. This is not a story, this is a reality . . . The US Postal Services Regulations forbids even the import into Iraq of sheets of music. The song that the Bruderhof Children's Choir has just sung to us, their sheets of music would not be allowed to reach Iraq according to US standards. So it is killing not only the physical needs but also it is killing the whole ethos, the mindset of a society that should live under normal conditions.

Mohammed slumped into one of the benches in Hassan Ajmi and ordered me what I always had whenever we went there, a glass of Hamuth, a type of tea peculiar to Iraq. It is made from dried whole limes cut into quarters, seeded and then soaked in boiling water, and produces a fine, light golden liquid with a sharp, clean taste. It's reputed to be an aid to good digestion, which I never saw as a reason for drinking it. It was April 1998 and I had been in Iraq almost continuously since December. The teashop was pretty quiet on that mild spring afternoon, and as we settled in for a welcome break from the day's work Mohammed began to explain how he had arrived at his present position. He had studied translation at Heriot-Watt University in Edinburgh for just over a year in 1982, followed by another course in York. On his return to Iraq he had landed a job with the *Baghdad Observer*, Iraq's only English-language newspaper, where he met his future wife, Samira, who was working in the proof-reading section after graduating from Baghdad College. They married in 1986 and a year and a half later had their first child, a daughter called Teeba. The Iran–Iraq war was in its seventh year, and it was a time when the two enemies were bombarding their capital cities with long-range missiles. 'After getting married I rented a small house whose monthly rent was the whole of my monthly salary, so I had to find other means to support my family and this is how I began to translate literary works for publication.' This was when the Iraqi dinar was worth £2.

Mohammed chose to translate a book of literary criticism by Colin Wilson, *The Art of the Novel*. He submitted it to the official body that oversaw the translation of foreign works and it was accepted. He was paid a decent fee and felt the satisfaction of getting a work into print. The translation was very well received among the academic fraternity in Baghdad and he was soon embarking on translating another work of literary criticism, *A Double Exile* by Gareth Griffiths, which talks about the identity struggle among African and Caribbean writers educated and domiciled in Britain. His love of literature and his growing success in translation persuaded Mohammed to help establish an English language literary magazine called *Gilgamesh*. It took its name from the oldest epic poem of Iraq, written in the Sumerian language, which tells the story of a king vainly looking for immortality. While he was pursuing his literary interests, Iran's missile attacks on Baghdad, the so-called 'war of the cities', were becoming increasingly ferocious. Mohammed and his young family lived in a rented house in the Jamila district of eastern Baghdad, which was hit several times. 'I was worried as a father that my family was at risk. But suddenly in August 1988 a peace deal was agreed with Iran. There were so many celebrations in Baghdad at that time. I thought that at last it was all over, but I didn't realize that Saddam was preparing a new war.'

The following year, Mohammed and Samira had a son, Marwan. Like many Iraqis, after the unimaginable long nightmare of the war with Iran, they looked forward to a new beginning. This feeling was to last only a year. 'Like every other Iraqi citizen, I heard the news of the invasion of Kuwait at around midday on 2 August 1990. When I heard the news I was stunned. How, after eight years of war with Iran, could this now happen? But of course everyone believed that Saddam had gone to Kuwait to stay, because we thought that he had been given a green light for the invasion by the USA.'*

* Saddam Hussein did not believe that the US would worry about the Iraqi army entering Kuwait. Perhaps, if he had limited himself to the disputed Rumailah oil fields and only a partial invasion, he might have been right. However, by attempting to take the whole country he invoked the wrath of the US and Britain, who decided he had to be stopped.

The looming reality of a Gulf War left Mohammed fearful, like everyone else in the country. 'I now had a son to worry about,' he said, 'so my worries were doubled.' But it was the enclosed world that Iraqis like him were forced to inhabit in the years after the Gulf War that Mohammed said had had a more profound and long-term effect, on himself and his family, more perhaps than even the allied bombing. 'Iraqis had got used to travelling abroad a lot. The dinar was worth a lot in those days, so even lower-middle-class Iraqis could visit Egypt and Syria and the middle classes would travel to Europe. Sanctions meant all of this stopped, and culturally sanctions buried Iraqis in a sort of grave. We had no new books or contact with other peoples.' Mohammed listed the many pernicious effects of sanctions: prostitution, declining literacy and educational stan-dards, and of course the arrival of the auction houses, which he said had 'emerged like a cancer in the city'.

In the years that followed Mohammed wrote articles on Samuel Beckett's poetry, and translated, among others, *Immortality* by Milan Kundera, Kingsley Amis's *Lucky Jim* and *The Memoirs of a Survivor* by Doris Lessing. By the time I got to know him he had been working for some time on a Ph.D. thesis on the 'semiotic approach to translation' and was writing about the challenges of translating James Joyce's *Ulysses*. In 1999 an Irish colleague from the BBC who had by then taken up my former post in Jordan had written in the *Irish Times* about Mohammed's monumental effort to translate Joyce. It prompted Stephen Joyce, the author's grandson, to invite Mohammed to that year's Joyce Festival in Dublin. It took several months to arrange the permissions for him to travel by land to neigh-bouring Jordan, and then to Ireland via London. It was the first time since the late 1980s that Mohammed had travelled out of Iraq. When he arrived at the immigration queue at Heathrow he girded himself for the inevitable interrogation by immigration officers. 'The official looked at my Iraqi passport, and asked me why I was travelling to the UK. I said I had been invited to attend a literary symposium in Ireland because of the work I'd done on translating *Ulysses* into Arabic. The official looked at me and, without even a smile, he said I should first translate it into English because he'd tried to read it several times and found it impossible to understand!'

On that occasion Mohammed was lucky and able to overcome the rigid controls that existed between the two countries. He described another occasion when he was not so lucky and which reveals the extent, and absurdity, of many of the controls which sanctions imposed. In the course of research for his Ph.D. Mohammed wrote to the British Library asking for particular extracts from *Ulysses* to help him in his work. The British Library responded, accurately, but with just the slightest note of incredulity in their reply: 'I regret to inform you that we cannot process these requests because of trade sanctions that have been imposed on your country by our Government.'

It is not easy to convey the overwhelming sense of intellectual isolation which was felt most strongly by the educated class of Iraqis of which Mohammed was a part, a group which, as Andrew and Patrick Cockburn point out in *Out of the Ashes*, 'had helped propel Iraq out of the third world and constituted a resource hardly less valuable than the oil fields'. Mutannabi Street on the eastern bank of the Tigris river and round the corner from the Hassan Ajmi teashop is a place that brings home this isolation like nowhere else in the city. Compared to the maze of narrow alleys around it, the street is wide and open. But every Friday only a lane of the uneven and pot-holed tarmac is visible. Looking down from the top of Mutannabi Street all you can see is a carpet of paper: books, journals, magazines and newsletters. The sellers and hawkers set up their little stalls on the pavements and the magazines and papers are laid across the ground with their covers on display. The titles spill out on to the road, leaving just a narrow path for the browsing walkers. Many of those who came to Mutannabi Street were young university students who would also come to buy notebooks, rulers and pens from the stationery shops on Rashid Street. Others were just middle-class Iraqis, fluent in English or French, who wanted copies of classic novels, or back issues of *Time*, *National Geographic* or *Paris Match*. I went to Mutannabi Street many times. It held a particular fascination, not just for what it said about the reading tastes of Iraq's intelligentsia, but because it was a living record of recent times. In the spring of 1998 I remember coming across an issue of *Time* magazine from late 1979 which talked about President Carter's agony over the Iran hostage crisis. I found a British football magazine from 1988 describing Wimbledon's surprise victory over Liverpool in that year's FA Cup Final.

Just before the war, in January 2003, I went back to Mutannabi Street and saw another English football magazine with a pull-out calendar of the best-known stars from the English Premiership – pictures of David Beckham in England colours and David Seaman stretching to stop a goal. All the highlights of British football were on show in that crowded street. On that day three young men were looking over each other's shoulders at the football magazines on the pavement. I asked them if they didn't think it was a bit strange to want to read about British footballers when bombs from Britain were about to land on their city. They laughed at my question and one of them replied in English, 'We like the English teams and players. Manchester United, Liverpool, Arsenal, Chelsea. All young Iraqis like them. Football is very popular here. We like it too much, so we follow all the best teams in the world, and the English league is one of the best. So we try to find out more about it.' His friends nodded keenly in agreement.

Most of the publications on sale were from the 1980s and were hopelessly out of date. Pink-jacketed romances lay next to ancient encyclopaedias and worn copies of British classics such as *Great Expectations* and *The Hound of the Baskervilles*, their spines cracked with use. There were also rows of paperbacks by African and Arab writers of the 1960s. I found an old copy of Frantz Fanon's *The Wretched of the Earth*. It was the kind of book that a young educated Iraqi might have read at the time of Nasser, Suez and the growth of the non-aligned movement, the international alliance of newly liberated former colonies in the Third World led by figures such as Nehru, Kwame Nkrumah and Tito that served as a focus for the economic and political aspirations of the educated middle classes in countries throughout the Arab, African and Asian world. I imagined its owner coming to Mutannabi Street, older now, perhaps in his seventies, selling it in order to raise a quick bit of money.

The beginning

1. Baghdad before the war, looking north–west

2. A father and son sell their possessions on the street at the height of sanctions

3. A mother sits with her seriously ill child in the Kerbala paediatric hospital

4. The market on Mutannabi Street

Baghdad communities
5. Making a live recording from Rashid Street in December 2002

6. Making the tea in Hassan Ajmi teashop

7. A meeting in Hassan Ajmi teashop

8. Mohammed and I talk to a customer in Hassan Ajmi teashop

War approaches

9. Photographing UN inspections in a Presidential compound in Baghdad

10. A chocolate stall in Shorja market before the war began to impinge on people's lives

11. Customers crowd a stall selling duct tape in Shorja market the day before the war began

12. A parade of young soldiers in Baghdad in March

13. A military parade of women in Tikrit in February

14. Boys parade in Baghdad outside the Ministry of Information, some slightly more seriously than others, in March

War

15. The 'Shock and Awe' campaign begins, as seen from the Palestine Hotel

16. Oil fires surround the city

17. Members of the 1st Marine Division endure a sandstorm near Nassiriyah

18. The tents and satellite dishes of news organizations on the roof of the Ministry of Information

19. The team having lunch: Paul Danahar, Killa and Dylan Nalid are first, third and fifth from left

20. Preparing for a broadcast on the roof of the Palestine Hotel three days before it was bombed. The 14th of Ramadan Mosque is behind me

People would take hours over which of the ancient issues of magazines and periodicals to buy. They would gingerly leaf through a copy of *Time* magazine from 1987, or some lifestyle journal from the late 1970s, slowly and reverently turning each page – such was the hunger for images and writing from the outside world. But it would be wrong to think that they came here to buy these now useless publications because they hankered after the lives of people in America or Europe. They came to buy these old magazines because these journals stood as a record of the lives they themselves had once led, lives that included new literature, art and design, political comment, sporting prowess, cities and countries around the world where they had once studied. The pages piled high in this one Iraqi street were mirrors into lives once lived. It was as if the despotic regime and the system of sanctions had converged to cut the very lifeblood of this city, not only literally but also in terms of the inner intellectual lives of its educated people.

3. Twilight

'I was here in the BBC office, in this very chair, when I saw it,' Mohammed said, as he tapped his finger hard on the desk. 'There were no BBC journalists in Baghdad as it was a quiet period, and I had come in just to check if there were any messages. As I was walking into the Press Centre I overheard someone saying there had been some kind of attack in America. When I got to the office I switched on the television immediately – as you know, the Press Centre was the only place we had access to international channels. Everyone gathered round to watch. They just kept playing the images of the planes hitting the towers again and again. My God! We all just sat there staring.' I asked him what he had thought would happen next, after he saw the towers collapse. He gave a nervous smile. 'At that moment I was convinced that they will bomb Iraq. Even within the following few days some commentators on American networks were asking whether Iraq was involved. I thought it was just a matter of time.'

Mohammed and I were having this conversation as we sat in the BBC offices in Baghdad in March 2002, exactly a year, as it turned out, before the war on Iraq would begin. I had returned to Iraq after a few months' absence. Since the events of September 11, I had spent nearly all my time in Afghanistan, where I had covered the siege of Kabul and witnessed the collapse of the Taliban. Even though I was based in South Africa as the BBC Africa correspondent, I, like many other journalists all over the world, now found that the attention of all of us was focused on the 'War on Terror' irrespective of where we were based.

Whatever politicians have said since and however tenuous the link between September 11 and Iraq is, that date has to be seen as the starting point for the war that followed eighteen months later. Mohammed's ominous response to the events of September 11 was by no means unusual in Iraq at that time. Many Iraqis were frightened that the appalling attacks on New York and Washington would have profound repercussions for them. It must have been one of the few occasions when the Iraqi people and those who ruled them were thinking the same thoughts.

In the week following September 11 the biggest international news organizations, such as Reuters, Associated Press, BBC, CNN, ITN, ABC America, Fox News and many more, tried to send their correspondents and crews to Baghdad in the belief that Iraq was high on the USA's retaliation list. I was among them. On 17 September 2001 I sat in one of the central five-star hotels in Amman, in neighbouring Jordan, surrounded by hordes of western reporters and television crews. The foreign news media is not an appealing sight when it swarms towards places of impending tragedy with its ludicrous mountains of satellite and editing equipment, generators, rations and protective clothing. This was by no means the first wave of journalists that had attempted to cross the border into Iraq in the last four years. News crews had arrived in Amman when the crisis over weapons inspections was reaching its climax, and during the ongoing air strikes in the so-called 'no-fly zones' in northern and southern Iraq. By that time, unlike in the past when it had isolated itself from the vagaries of the western media, the regime understood perfectly the value of allowing journalists to report these crises from Baghdad's perspective and it was used to granting visas and permits to reporters who were then carefully monitored once they reached Iraqi soil. But after September 11 the atmosphere changed utterly and the international political crisis looked profoundly dangerous for the Iraqi regime. Not one western journalist was allowed in, irrespective of their organization, or whether they had a permanent office in Baghdad or not, and no matter how often they had reported from the country before or however many impressive official contacts they had. The government of Iraq was terrified.

Saadoun would spend hours every day trying to process the applications from our BBC team, waiting outside the offices of senior officials, carefully and as diplomatically as possible explaining exactly why we wanted to come to Baghdad at that time. But it was clear that the policy of refusing all applications had been dictated from the highest levels of the regime. Saadoun phoned me several times a day to give me updates. 'I think there is no chance, to be honest,' he said finally after nearly three days. 'The government wants to keep everything cool and they do not want *any* link whatsoever to be made to events in America, so I believe that no visas will be given at all.' This blanket policy was the clearest sign that the regime harboured the same fears that Mohammed would express to me when we met the following March. Even after the war in Afghanistan had ceased to appear on the front pages of our newspapers and it began to look as though Washington was not going to make a link between the twin towers and Iraq, the citizens of Baghdad still remained extremely nervous. I spoke to Mohammed and Saadoun regularly and they told me that people in the city overwhelmingly believed that Iraq would become the next target in the 'War on Terror'.

Early on the morning of 30 January 2002, when I was on my way to a radio studio in Cape Town, I received a call from Saadoun in Baghdad. It was the week after President Bush's State of the Union address. 'This is it,' he said anxiously, 'the war will start very soon.' I laughed and dismissed his comment. Saadoun was highly sensitive and could sometimes be melodramatic. But it was important to remember that he and his family had lived through the first Gulf War and the memory of what they had experienced then was still fresh. The fear they felt at the prospect of another war was clear in his voice. 'But did you hear what he said?' he asked, referring to Bush's speech. 'He said, in black and white, Iraq is part of an axis of evil and that it is a threat to America. It is clear what he means, and he has decided to finish the work of his father. No question.' I asked Saadoun if other people he knew were reacting to Bush's speech in the same way. He responded emphatically, his voice rising in pitch: 'Of course! Everybody is.'

When I got back home I read again the words of the speech that President Bush had made in Washington on the night of 29 January, and the despair in Saadoun's voice seemed justified:

Iraq continues to flaunt its hostility toward America and to support terror. The Iraqi regime has plotted to develop anthrax, and nerve gas, and nuclear weapons for over a decade . . . This is a regime that has something to hide from the civilized world . . . States like these, and their terrorist allies, constitute an axis of evil, arming to threaten the peace of the world . . . The United States of America will not permit the world's most dangerous regimes to threaten us with the world's most destructive weapons.

If the days and weeks after September 11 had led the Iraqi regime to fear the future, Bush's 'Axis of Evil' speech in January 2002 made them realize there was no way back to the uneasy stand-off that had marked their relations with Washington before that terrible event. And so, tentatively and in the hope of gaining some PR advantage, the regime began to readmit western journalists. Paul Danahar, Andrew Kilrain, or 'Killa' as he was known, and myself were the first British television team to get into Iraq in March. The three of us had worked together in Africa and Afghanistan as part of the BBC Africa Bureau in Johannesburg and had become close friends. Killa, a quiet, softly spoken man with a tinder-dry sense of humour, had been to Iraq several times before in the mid 1990s. He loved working in the Middle East, a place whose sensibilities he knew well. It was Paul's first trip to Iraq. He was undoubtedly our team leader, a man of prodigious mental and physical stamina and an extraordinarily resilient sense of humour. We would spend the next year working together, and continued as a team until after the war was over in 2003.

We drove out of Amman before dawn on 27 March. Iraq was beginning to look like a very different place from the country I had first visited. By the end of the 1990s the Iraqi regime was striving to break down the animosity and suspicion that had previously marked its relations with the rest of the Arab world. It was also widening its reach, to Europe and to countries in Africa and Asia. London and Washington had failed to topple him, and now, with Muslim and Arab popular opinion no longer willing to tolerate the effects of sanctions on Iraqi civilians, Saddam Hussein saw an opportunity to undermine the unity of the international effort to ostracize his country. As sanctions began to crumble, his government courted anyone who was prepared to listen. Senior officials were sent around the world to attend international conferences and sign treaties on 'mutual co-operation and friendliness', to use the jargon of the Iraqi state newspapers. Increasing numbers of anti-sanctions protest groups – such as 'Voices in the Wilderness', a US-based group of activists who consciously broke some of the more ludicrous sanctions restrictions to bring medical supplies to Iraq – began to travel to Baghdad. Actors and politicians also began to protest against sanctions: former US Attorney General and anti-sanctions campaigner Ramsey Clark and the Hollywood actor Val Kilmer both visited the capital. By the end of the decade, the economic embargo was being ignored more than it was being observed, without any official changes in international legislation having taken place. After a ten-year absence direct flights from Amman to Baghdad were resumed. All kinds of goods and consumer products were being imported into the country. Things which had been hard to find when sanctions had been at their worst were now within the reach of many Iraqis. There were air-conditioning units, spare parts for cars, computers, even brick-like old mobile phones that dated from the late 1980s and which worked only within a twenty-mile radius from the centre of Baghdad. Where old and rusted vehicles used to line the main roads to the capital, new Land Rovers or BMWs were now queuing to get into the city. The economic elite which had grown rich under sanctions were further and more explicitly aided by the slow collapse of the economic embargo.

Shorja market lies in the centre of Baghdad. Open to the wide skies of the city, on the eastern banks of the Tigris, hundreds of stalls jostle for space, selling everything from almonds glazed in honey to lightbulbs to tall bottles of pink shampoo. The market straddles one of the main thoroughfares of the city and an iron pedestrian bridge carries you over the streams of traffic from one side of the sprawling mass of corner shops and food stalls to the other, the narrow pathways shaded beneath swathes of tarpaulin.

We were there one late afternoon in March just as the city's rush hour was hitting its stride, and dark, heavy fumes from the long line of exhausts shrouded the stalls in a grey haze. Every lane of Shorja market was alive with urgent shoppers. The long skirts of black *abbayas* flapped in the afternoon breeze as mothers pulled their children through the heaving throng. The market's porters, in their loose shirts and trousers covered in the dust of the market floor, pushed me aside and trod on my feet as they ran through the market, shouting and carrying huge sacks of tea or boxes of soap above their heads.

While the atmosphere had not changed, the stalls themselves had changed utterly from the early 1990s. Mars bars, Snickers and large family tins of Quality Street were piled up on tables, along with crates filled with cans of Fanta, Pepsi and even Diet Coke. The stalls for cosmetics which had previously carried rather grim and limited collections of lethal-looking bottles now displayed jars of hair gel and 'Leave-in Conditioner with extra Jojoba Oil'. I assumed that the black market had exploded and that everything would be exorbitantly priced. '*Besh hatha?*' I enquired from one store owner. Ten pence for an imported can of Coca-Cola. It was no longer the black market.

One corner of the market specialized in pasta, rice, pulses and cooking oils. Hands flashed in the sunlight as flour flew from great sacks on to the scales and then into the waiting paper bags of the expectant customers. As they weighed and poured, measured and counted their change, portly, beaming stallholders shouted out their bargains: 'Indian rice, Indian rice!' 'Olives! Olives! Good prices!'

Moyid Mohammed Mustafa ran a small stall selling imported pasta and dried beans. He stood behind his wares, elevated on a wooden crate, beadily surveying his supplies. 'From what TV channel are you?' he asked as we approached. 'Ah! British,' he said mischievously. 'Welcome, welcome!' I asked him if, as a seller of more traditional fare, he was dismayed to see this new range of luxuries that surrounded him. 'It's good!' he shot back. 'We are trading more with other nations now who see the injustice of sanctions.' He said that although sanctions were still in place and the rationing system remained a lifeline for many poor families, the breakdown in the sanctions regime had made little luxuries such as chocolate affordable again to most middle-class Iraqis. They were no longer the exclusive domain of the corrupt elite. Everyone came to shop at Shorja market, the poorer middle-class women who were more often dressed in traditional Islamic dress and whose husbands worked as clerks or low-level civil servants, as well as the richer women, usually in western clothes, who belonged in Mohammed and Saadoun's world.

The new cars in evidence on the road to Baghdad could be seen as the direct results of Saddam Hussein's drive to forge new relations with the outside world. Now, shoppers in Shorja market could perhaps feel less isolated, the fruits of international trade clearly on display. And perhaps Iraqis were meant to feel further reassured by the increasing numbers of stage-managed international conferences shown on their televisions each evening. On the day I visited Shorja market, the leaders of the Arab world were meeting in Beirut. In the centre of the city in a luxurious hotel rigid with security staff, the heads of state sat at a horseshoe-shaped table, microphones placed discreetly in front of them and a bank of advisers and deputies seated discreetly behind them like a row of butlers. Saddam Hussein had not left Iraq for two decades, unless you count the visit to his troops in Kuwait shortly after they invaded the country in 1990, and he had rather got out of the habit of foreign travel. So he sent his official number two, Izzat Ibrahim al Douri.

The majority of the Arab leaders and their entourages had taken their seats when the most theatrical moment of the conference took place. A carefully choreographed moment it may have been, but it was no less dramatic for it. Saddam Hussein's emissary walked into the middle of the chamber with Crown Prince Abdallah of Saudi Arabia, and the two men embraced. The other Arab dignitaries rose to their feet and gave them a standing ovation. The scene was beamed live around the Middle East, and if the Iraqi leader was watching on television in one of his palaces, it must have brought a self-satisfied smile to his face. He liked theatrical gestures that

reinforced his sense of Iraqi tribal tradition. Not for him the trans-
parent processes of negotiated agreements drafted by civil servants.
He loved the idea that agreements between 'Arab brothers' could
be sealed with an embrace, conveniently forgetting the fact that as
a secular leader he was in a minority in the region and that there
was little love lost between him and his neighbours. At this conference, the men who had, eleven years earlier, enthusiastically opened
their countries to western forces and enabled them to invade Iraq
and destroy Saddam Hussein's grip on Kuwait and the region,
were publicly welcoming him back. There was a message here for
President Bush: how can you dislodge me now when those who
helped your father are, these days, openly expressing their solidarity
with me?

The performance in Beirut was also meant to reassure the people
of Iraq, but most Iraqis were sceptical about this claim of solidarity
and, even if it were sincere, they wondered what difference it
would make. Their fear of invasion remained pretty much unas-
suaged. This public nervousness was reflected in Iraq's economy.
It is not only the stock exchanges of democracies that reflect public
mood; even in dictatorships, the money men provide an accurate
gauge of the feelings of the populace. By this time in Iraq the black
market in hard foreign currency had effectively become the *de facto*
official market. Although one was supposed to change foreign
currency at state banks, who held to absurd valuations of the Iraqi
dinar, even government officers ignored the system. This was hardly
surprising given that the black market was controlled by Saddam
Hussein's family and closest allies, and most notably by his eldest
son, Uday.

The US dollar was virtually the only foreign currency that the
money changers would be willing to countenance. Even then, they
were very particular about the sort of dollar bills they would accept.
They were suspicious of any $100 banknotes minted before 1998,
saying they were easier to forge than later ones. The shops openly
advertised their trade in the commercial districts of Baghdad, with
large signs over their doorway saying 'exchange', beneath which
pictures of Iraqi dinar notes bearing Saddam Hussein's portrait were

pasted alongside the Queen's face staring out from English £10 notes. Behind desks piled high with bundles of dinars tightly wrapped in elastic bands would sit the money changers, their faces serious and inscrutable, their pens moving frenetically across the pages of their notebooks.

The day after the Arab Summit in Beirut I visited a money shop in the Al Wahdah district of Baghdad. Here there was little evidence that people had been reassured by events in Beirut. The rate of the Iraqi dinar against the US dollar had hardly risen, stuck stubbornly at around 1,890 dinars to the dollar.

The appalling state of the economy went some way to explain the reluctance of Iraqi ministers to be interviewed. They were all extremely nervous of exposing themselves or their government at this time of political strain. I had written several letters to the office of Foreign Minister Naji Sabri, whom I had known for five years. Suave and likeable and a great anglophile, he had been a senior official in the Ministry of Information during the first Gulf War and enjoyed the company of foreign journalists. At times this seemed incompatible with his ambition for high office in the Iraqi government. Tellingly, he was one of very few officials who, like Mohammed, had not grown a moustache. He was also one of very few officials with whom it was possible to conduct a rational and relatively open conversation. The only thing he refused to discuss was the execution of his brother by Saddam Hussein for suspected involvement in an attempted coup. As a consequence of his brother's supposed actions Sabri had been barred from any official function for a number of years, but by the late 1990s had been slowly rehabilitated. After that the regime recognized the usefulness of his innate intelligence and diplomatic charm and he was rapidly promoted to Foreign Minister. His long friendship with Deputy Prime Minister Tariq Aziz, with whom he shared an urbane manner, also helped him. And now that Sabri had joined the cabinet, a moustache had begun to grow on his top lip.

After a week of persistent calling on my part, Sabri's private secretary responded, saying that unfortunately the Foreign Minister was unwilling to give an interview until he had heard what Prime

Minister Blair and President Bush had to say at their summit in Texas. Every other minister I tried gave a similar answer. This was a tacit acknowledgement that, despite Saddam Hussein's hopes, the display of brotherly love witnessed in Beirut had done little to dilute the threat from Washington. It had been six months since those dreadful events of September 11, but few in Baghdad believed that the Bush administration had abandoned its desire to overthrow the regime.

The Al Rasheed Hotel was a forlorn place to return to each evening. It was the hotel where all foreign journalists and businessmen stayed and it was where the heads of the teams of UN weapons inspectors were accommodated. But it had a gloomy atmosphere made worse by the knowledge that many of the suites were bugged. I hardly ever went to the hotel's restaurant – eating there only intensified my feelings of claustrophobia as it was filled with the sort of rich elite so familiar in countries of corrupt dictatorships. I chose instead to go to the small, cheap Arabic restaurants where most of the families in the downtown districts of Baghdad ate. The Al Rasheed was prohibitively expensive for most local people and the little cafés and restaurants, like the teashops in Rashid Street, were usually much livelier places to sit and chat – and the food was better too.

The window in Paul's room at the Al Rasheed looked out across the west of the capital and the warm orange glow at sunset flooded the sitting room as darkness encroached. The haunting reds of the final minutes of the day lit up the gargantuan construct that dominated the low cityscape of western Baghdad. Three cranes rising hundreds of feet in the air stood like modern dinosaurs, looming above a circle of enormous dark-grey concrete pillars, looking like giant's fingers grasping at the clouds in the sky above. The construction had taken several years to reach this still rudimentary stage and it would take still more before it would be finished. It was to be the largest mosque in the world, larger even than the holiest Islamic shrine of all, the Grand Mosque in Mecca.

As sanctions had taken their toll on the civilian community of Baghdad in the years after the first Gulf War, attendance at mosques had risen astronomically. Saddam Hussein noticed the new religious fervour in the country and responded by referring to his leadership as 'Islamic' increasingly often. He introduced punitive laws under a nebulous religious umbrella, and it soon became clear that this 'Islamification' of his rule was just another way for him to control and persecute his people. In 1994 he further reinforced the 'Islamic' image by embarking on the construction of this enormous mosque. We would often stare out at the awesome sight and wonder whether its founder would get the chance to finish this latest homage to self-aggrandizement.

That evening we were in Paul's room trying to access the press conference for Bush and Blair's summit in Texas. Paul disentangled the wires and cables for his satellite radio and tilted the small receiver dish at the right angle by the window, pointing it in the direction of the nearest satellite. Within a few seconds, the crisp tones of international broadcasting stations boomed out of the radio, along with their optimistic theme music. Even though the Al Rasheed was the main hotel in Baghdad for foreigners, like the rest of the country it never showed international news channels. I switched on the television in our room to see how state television would mark the moment when Iraq's new destiny was set in motion; a moment which few Iraqis could actually witness for themselves given the lack of access to independent foreign media coverage in the country. As our satellite radio tuned into live reports of a press conference, Iraqi television was showing a soap opera set in the court of a mythological ancient Arab ruler. While the Iraqi people were being regaled with the plot twists of a television soap, thousands of miles away two men were meeting at a ranch in a small corner of Texas to decide their fate.

This encounter between Tony Blair and George W. Bush on 6 April 2002 at the President's residence in Crawford was a defining moment in the march to war. It was the first clear instance in which the British Prime Minister committed himself and his government to the same overall aim which had been expressed by President Bush in his State of the Union address, namely the overthrow of the Iraqi regime, or 'regime change' as it would soon come to be known. Exactly a month earlier, on 6 March 2002, Tony Blair had told the British Parliament: 'We have not agreed any action in respect of Iraq at the moment, so it is important that before anyone takes a position condemning it or supporting it, we see what the government propose we should do.' A month later in Texas he gave a clear indication that he had now crossed the Rubicon. At that meeting in April the Prime Minister disclosed for the first time – and perhaps in the clearest and most undiluted way – his true intentions towards Iraq and his support for President Bush's baldly stated aim of deposing the Iraqi leadership by force if necessary. In that press conference you could hear Tony Blair reaching for the words, the conviction which his ally had arrived at weeks, if not months, before. It was the moment when he made the decisive political, psychological and irrevocable leap towards removing Saddam Hussein by force. We listened, incredulous, to every word.

It is easy to lose sight of how the path to war was laid, muddied as our memories are now by the fog of war, the chaos of its aftermath and the British government's subsequent need to respond to the urgent doubts of public opinion. At the press conference in Crawford, Bush and Blair began by making general remarks on the need to continue to fight terrorism, but once the reporters' questions started, the subject of Iraq dominated.

PRESIDENT BUSH: The Prime Minister and I of course talked about Iraq. We both recognize the dangers of a man who is willing to kill his own people and harbouring and developing weapons of mass destruction. This guy, Saddam Hussein, is a leader who gasses his own people, goes after people in his own neighbourhood with chemical weapons, he is a man who obviously has something to hide . . . I explained to the Prime Minister that the policy of my government is the removal of Saddam and that all options are on the table.

The simplicity of it, the matter-of-fact way in which President Bush expressed this last thought, 'the removal of Saddam', and its sheer wilfulness were astounding. Although he had professed the same intention before, President Bush had never stated so unequivocally that he and his government had already decided that Saddam Hussein must be overthrown by any means.

When Bush came to the end of his devastating statement, it was Tony Blair's turn. There wasn't even a follow-up question, everyone's gaze just fell automatically on the British Prime Minister, wondering how he would follow this extraordinary proposition. His words were delicately chosen.

PRIME MINISTER BLAIR: I can say that any sensible person looking at the position of Saddam Hussein and asking the question: would the region, the world and not least the ordinary Iraqi people, be better off without the regime of Saddam Hussein, the only answer anyone could give to that question would be yes. Now, how we approach this, this is a matter for discussion, this is a matter for considering all the options.

One of the journalists immediately cut to the chase and asked the question that Tony Blair seemed keen to avoid:

JOURNALIST: Prime Minister, we have heard the President say what his policy is directly about Saddam Hussein, which is to remove him, that is the policy of the American administration. Could I ask you whether that is now the policy of the British government?

PRIME MINISTER BLAIR: You know it has always been our policy that Iraq would be a better place without Saddam Hussein, I don't think anyone should be in any doubt about that for all the reasons I gave earlier. And you know reasons to do with weapons of mass destruction also do with the appalling brutality and repression of his own people.★ But how we now proceed in this situation, how we make sure that this threat that is posed by weapons of mass destruction is dealt with, that is a matter that is open . . . you cannot have a situation in which he carries on being in breach of the UN resolutions and refusing to allow us the capability of assessing how that weapons of mass destruction capability is being advanced, even though the international com-

★ Tony Blair's mangled speech was probably evidence of the pressure he was under.

munity has made it absolutely clear that he should do so. Now as I say how we then proceed from there, that is a matter that is open for us.

As we sat silently in that hotel room in Baghdad listening to the words coming through on the radio, I imagined how the Prime Minister might have looked. I pictured a man who had been asked to show his loyalty by taking part in some sort of initiation rite. Having paused briefly to think about what he was embarking on, he had decided to sip from the holy grail of 'regime change', and from this point on there was to be no return. Here was a British Prime Minister who was morally convinced of the necessity of ridding the world of Saddam Hussein and determined that Britain should remain a resolute ally of the United States but who was also aware that his own party and country were divided on the issue and that the UN had not yet given any mandate for a policy legitimizing the use of force. No wonder his voice was hesitant when he was asked if it was also his government's policy to remove Saddam Hussein from power.

President Bush immediately saw the painful dilemma that Tony Blair faced in front of the questioning journalists. As soon as the Prime Minister had finished his reply, George Bush piped up and attempted to lighten the tone. In his inimitably 'folksy' style he tried to draw a line under the questioning. But it didn't quite work.

PRESIDENT BUSH: Maybe I should be a little less direct and be a little more nuanced and say we support regime change.
JOURNALIST: Is that a change in policy?
PRESIDENT BUSH: No, it is really not, regime change was the policy of my predecessor as well.
JOURNALIST: And your father?
PRESIDENT BUSH: You know I can't remember that far back, but it is certainly the policy of my administration. I think regime change sounds a lot more civil, doesn't it?

It seemed that a countdown to a direct confrontation had effectively been set. Both President Bush and Prime Minister Blair were asked to explain the link, if indeed there was one, between the 'War on Terror' and the Iraqi regime, since, as one reporter put it, 'Europeans . . . can see the linkage between Al Qaeda and Afghanistan, [but] they can't see a direct linkage with Saddam Hussein.' The two leaders did not want to be caught on this un-steady ground, and instead put at centre stage the issue of weapons of mass destruction and UN resolutions calling on Saddam Hussein to disarm. They laid out what would quickly be the next step in the overall aim of 'regime change' which was to press the UN for a new resolution demanding the return of weapons inspectors to Iraq. The inevitable failure of this mission would lead inexorably to the use of 'all necessary means', a euphemistic term for military invasion.

As soon as the press conference ended Paul got up quickly from his chair to turn the radio off. 'It's begun,' he said, 'it may be months and months away, but having just heard that, I find it hard to believe that this won't end in war, and that all of this,' he gestured towards the Baghdad skyline, 'will be reduced to rubble.'

Saadoun was even more frustrated than we were and we were about ready to give up trying to make contact with any member of the Iraqi government. Levels of anxiety within the leadership had clearly risen to fever pitch. A regime which in recent years, in an attempt to break out of international isolation, had so assiduously courted the outside world and which had, in the last six months, allowed western journalists to come to Iraq to meet defiant-sounding senior officials, was now extremely cautious of allowing interviews in response to the ominous pronouncements by Presi-dent Bush and Prime Minister Blair. Getting an interview with an Iraqi minister had never been easy and it could take up to a week to arrange, but I could usually be confident that the meeting would happen in the end. If there were many journalists in Baghdad, figures such as the Deputy Prime Minister, Tariq Aziz, or the Chief Scientific Adviser to the government, General Amer al Sa'adi, who was at the centre of negotiations with the UN weapons inspectors, would even hold press conferences. This recent unwillingness of

Iraqi officials to grant interviews to foreign journalists exposed the grim truth that they did not have much confidence in their standing with the Middle East and the rest of the world and they realized that protection from a British–American attack was extremely unlikely.

'Another letter asking for an interview isn't going to help, the Foreign Ministry must be sick of seeing BBC embossed letterheads,' Saadoun said. We decided to make one last attempt to speak to the Foreign Minister's assistant. The Foreign Ministry building was less than five minutes' walk straight up the road from the Press Centre, but the telephone line hissed and whined as if we were phoning from a different continent. I introduced myself to the Foreign Minister's assistant and, after a brief exchange of pleasantries, asked him when we'd be able to meet the minister. 'He is very busy at this time, he has to prepare for a meeting with the UN Secretary-General in New York next week as you know. I think it will not be possible. I'm sorry, Mr Rageh.' I persisted, but nothing seemed to work. I then tried a different tack, asking if my colleagues and I could just pop in to see him for an off-the-record chat. 'Just to say hello and to catch up as I haven't seen the Foreign Minister for a few years,' I said. There was a pause, and the official said he would be in touch the next day.

We sat around in our hotel until after lunch, unable to go out into the city for fear of missing a possible appointment with the Foreign Minister. The last time I had seen Sabri he was working as the senior adviser to the Minister of Information. He would occasionally come down to the offices of the various western news organizations in the Press Centre to greet people. More often, we would go up to his office on the eighth floor where there would always be a long queue of reporters or producers waiting outside his door seeking help and advice with getting interviews or cajoling him to speed up permits to bring in additional equipment. He would often work at his desk until ten or eleven o'clock at night, wearing a shirt but no tie. Mischievously he would sometimes invite several news organizations into his office at the same time to discuss their points or grievances, agencies which would more often

than not be in direct competition with each other. 'So CNN [or
BBC or ITN or CBS etc . . .], you say in your letter here that you
want to submit a request for an exclusive interview with Mr Tariq
Aziz,' he'd say, and wait for the reaction of the competition to this
minor revelation. It was an effective way of undermining the ruthless
ambitions of many of the journalists who invaded his office.

On this occasion we decided to take all our television equipment
with us just in case our 'off-the-record' chat did develop into an
interview. Saadoun shepherded us through the ministry's layers
of security and protocol, until eventually we were sitting in the
reception room outside Sabri's office. It was furnished in a way that
would have seemed impressive for a senior Iraqi official twenty
years ago, but which now looked kitsch and slightly dilapidated.
Three dreary carpets were scattered across the floor, underneath
heavy, dark wood tables. On one of them stood a small glass vase
filled with dusty artificial flowers. In one corner a large Iraqi flag
was surrounded by pots of glossy indoor plants. Lined up along
the walls were a series of rather dark, gloomy paintings depicting
traditional village life and idealized labourers hard at work in the
fields. And, of course, there was the familiar portrait of Saddam
Hussein. There were huge sofas with overstuffed cushions and
chairs so deep they forced you to lounge like a student in a common
room. I perched on the edge of one of them.

Finally the door opened and in walked a slightly thinner man
than I remembered, dressed in olive green military uniform, surrounded by four officials in dark suits whose sole purpose seemed
to be to clear the way for their boss. Sabri's soft silvery hair was
combed neatly to one side, the moustache was darker than it
had appeared in recent television pictures. His easy, light-hearted
manner had vanished and he had adopted, instead, a deep, almost
lordly tone of voice. '*Ahlan, Ahlan, Ahlan,*' he said in Arabic.
Immediately I realized that he did not want any displays of familiarity, and so I replied courteously and formally. I introduced Paul
and Killa and we proceeded to talk generally about how he was.
He barely touched on the comments by Tony Blair and George
W. Bush, referring to them only once when he accused the two

leaders of bringing 'the law of the jungle' into international affairs. I noticed he was wearing a large and shiny new Rolex on his wrist. I asked him if he wouldn't mind speaking to us on camera, 'which we usefully have in the next-door room,' I said rather hopefully. 'You are hoping to ambush me, huh?' he said. It was the briefest of flashes of the old Sabri, and it lasted just a few seconds. 'No, I made it clear that this was to be an informal chat, to say hello to you and your colleagues here in Baghdad, but I am not ready for any interview now.' We talked for a few minutes more until he concluded our meeting and briefly said goodbye. The defences were definitely up in the offices of government.

Saadoun Street runs parallel to the Tigris on its eastern bank and was the route to a good local restaurant where we often ate. Less than half a mile before the turning to Al Ghota restaurant, the road passes the Palestine Hotel and enters a wide and busy roundabout known as Firdoos Square. In the middle, surrounded by the traffic, is a large paved circle with a lawn at the centre. There are a few stone seats where on quiet afternoons I would sometimes see old men deep in discussion or mothers walking with their children.

In April 2002 Firdoos Square was a building site, carpenters and builders milling about urgently, carrying ladders and pointing up at the scaffolding which screened the new monument in the centre of the square. A semicircle of columns was in position at the edges of the little park. The pillars formed a curtain of stone, rising gradually in height until they reached the middle. In front of the highest one was a plinth, about twenty feet in height. A figure, whose shape could only vaguely be distinguished beneath its white shroud, stood grandly on the plinth. Beneath the sheet you could just make out the head of the statue and an outstretched arm that seemed to be reaching out in a gesture of imperious possessiveness over the city below. It was due to be unveiled on Saddam Hussein's birthday, 28 April. Little did he or the craftsmen working at his feet know that this statue would last less than a year, and that its destruction at the end of the war would come to be the defining image of the collapse of his rule.

Paul and I had ventured down to the square one morning, as heavy dark clouds gathered over the capital, to interview the workers and engineers erecting this new effigy of the Iraqi leader, just at the moment when Britain and the United States had committed themselves to his removal. As the likelihood of war increased, so too did the number of statues going up in squares all over the city and the number of portraits being hung in every available public space. The chief engineer and the official from the city municipality came over to talk to us. They said we could not interview them unless we had written permission from the municipality. I explained it was for a simple radio report, but they refused. As the workers continued to chip away at the concrete slabs they were preparing to lay, Paul, who was standing a few feet apart and was pretending to put his microphone away, instead switched on his recorder. I carried on talking to the official. 'Do you think it will be ready in time?' I asked. 'God willing. Everything is going smoothly.' 'Even though the Americans are threatening war?' I asked. 'We don't care about such things,' he said, 'we follow our leader, Saddam Hussein, may God preserve him. This statue is in honour of what he has achieved for Iraq. Our leader and everything he has built will be here for many years to come. He will survive because he is loved by his people.'

4. The Last Hours of a World

It was supposed to be a picture of a meeting of the Iraqi cabinet, but the large photograph on the front page of the *Iraq Daily* looked more like a group of men planning a bank heist. The mastermind, in a beige jacket and with a tie peeping out from beneath a dark V-neck sweater, leaned back in his chair at the head of the table. His eyes had that blank look so familiar from the thousands of portraits that hung from the walls of teashops, banks and institutions across the country. His lieutenants, lined up on either side of the table, sat eagerly on the edge of their chairs, leaning forward to hear their leader's words. They had come dressed in preparation for what they knew he was about to say, neatly suited as they were in green military uniforms, starched berets aslant on their heads. Only the leader's younger son and heir, who sat among the other *capos*, wore a civilian suit like his father. Notebooks were lined up in front of each officer and each man held a pen at the ready, poised to write down the words of wisdom and instruction that the man in charge was about to deliver.

It was two days after the Texas summit between Prime Minister Blair and President Bush, and the piece in the newspaper which accompanied the photograph reported what Saddam Hussein was apparently telling his deputies, among them not just his son Qusay, who was in charge of the Special Republican Guard as well as other key security organizations, but also the Minister of Defence and the commander of Iraq's air defences. Saddam Hussein was warning his senior advisers that Iraqi officials were getting soft – and he wanted to see an end to it. The report quoted him as saying: 'Your enemy is weak and you are strong. Even if half your air defences were to be destroyed, you would fight with the other half. And even if the enemy destroys that half, you would fight with daggers.' These were the words of a man who had accepted that war was certain and was now summoning all the guile and willpower he possessed in response. It was clear that even then, only two days after that meeting in Crawford, Texas, he fully realized the urgency of the new situation.

At noon, only a few hours after that edition of the paper had appeared and at a usually quiet part of the day – in fact there were few western journalists in Baghdad then as no one had anticipated a major event or speech to follow so soon after the Texas summit – the office of the Press Centre's director became a frenzy of activity. One of the senior minders hurried into our room and said a few words to Saadoun, and then was gone as quickly as he had come. 'There is to be a presidential announcement in about an hour's time,' Saadoun said in a state of agitation, 'it will be televised.'

Saddam Hussein made national television broadcasts on only a few occasions each year, and almost always to mark particular anniversaries such as Army Day, which was a commemoration of the founding of the Iraqi national army; or the anniversary of the end of the Iran–Iraq war; and, of course, Revolution Day on 17 July to mark the moment when the Ba'ath Party came to power. Large numbers of middle-class Iraqis across the towns and cities owned televisions and would have witnessed the nationwide speeches of their leader. Less wealthy Iraqis saw them too, in public places such as teashops, restaurants and shops, where there was often a television propped up on a chair or hanging above the diners' heads. If the television was switched on you wouldn't have been able to watch anything else as Saddam's speeches were shown on all state channels simultaneously. And, even if they hadn't been, it would have been too risky to try to change channels in public anyway.

It was very rare for Saddam Hussein to make an unannounced national speech, and so everyone assumed that something dramatic was about to happen. Performance and drama greatly appealed to the Iraqi leader; he loved the idea that the world moved when he spoke. Mohammed reacted to the news wearily. 'What does he have in mind now?' he said quietly.

Two hours later the impeccably made-up news presenter on

state television announced the 'national address by His Excellency President Saddam Hussein, the warrior leader, may God preserve him'. The screen cut to the Iraqi national flag and the thumping, martial tones of the national anthem. The leader appeared, behind a podium overflowing with flowers. He spoke in his distinctive, ponderous voice, which gave full expression to the florid classical Arabic which distinguished his set-piece speeches. This style, never used in colloquial conversations in Arabic even in highly educated and academic circles in the Middle East, was intended to portray Saddam Hussein as an intellectual. It was the kind of language used in ancient Arabic literature and poetry, and he used it to convince his audience that he was well versed in classical Arabic history and traditions and thus enhance the image of him as an Arab nationalist that the Ba'ath regime tried to foster. His language was grammatically flawless if highly contrived and would be almost impossible to understand to anyone not familiar with classical Arabic verse.

Saddam Hussein is reputed to have been a voracious reader, and he even wrote two novels himself. In December 2001, a novel entitled *Zabibah and the King* suddenly appeared in almost every library and bookshop in the country. The author was in theory anonymous, but the fact that the book had been printed and distributed all over the country and was accompanied by fulsome reviews in every national newspaper and magazine meant that it could only have been the work of Saddam Hussein. Amazingly he found time to write a second novel, *The Impregnable Fortress* (an ironic title for a book by Saddam Hussein if ever there was one), in the year before the war, and this time it was publicly acknowledged that he was the author.

He began his speech in the manner that had become so familiar to his viewers: 'Great Iraqi people. Heroic people of glory, faith, jihad, sacrifices and bravery . . . Peace be upon you.' His first subject was the ferocious and bloody conflict between Israel and the Palestinians in the Occupied Territories. 'The killing, destruction and humiliation that is ongoing in Palestine, are being carried out against the Arab and Islamic nation, not just the heroic and glorious

Palestinians,' he bellowed, 'who are facing the Zionist enemy and its aggressive forces with stones and simple weapons, using their chests which are full of faith, for ammunition.' But where was he going with this? This sudden, attention-grabbing address had to be offering more than the usual predictable musings on the Israeli–Palestinian conflict. And if I was reacting like that, I thought, what would most Iraqis be thinking? I looked over at Mohammed and Saadoun, who were staring, unmoved, at the television screen.

'Dear Brothers,' Saddam went on, 'the Zionist aggression . . . is perpetrated by a common arrangement between the Zionist entity★ and the American administration.' The Iraqi leader's bluster and outrage now began to reveal his true purpose – how he planned to make use of the region's turmoil in his confrontation with Washington: 'The Revolutionary Command Council†, the Iraqi leadership of the Ba'ath Arab Socialist Party, and the cabinet in their meeting on 8 April 2002,' (he made it sound as if his imminent announcement was the result of an open debate between the mass ranks of officials which made up these bodies, rather than what it was, the decision of a corrupt and ageing autocrat), 'declare in the name of the faithful, honest, mujahid, noble Iraqi people; stopping oil exports starting from this afternoon . . . for a period of thirty days after which we will reconsider, or until the Zionist entity's armed forces have unconditionally withdrawn from the Palestinian territories they have occupied.'

He had thrown his cards on the table with all the bravado of a poker player who has a hopeless hand but boundless self-belief. Saddam Hussein had not set foot outside Iraq for over twenty years, and imagined the Middle East to be still as it had been in the 1970s, when the West was heavily dependent on the region's oil supplies and the Arab world could use the threat of suspension of oil exports as a political and economic weapon. It was Saddam's misguided

★ The government of Iraq never mentioned Israel by name – it was always referred to as 'the Zionist entity'.
† The Revolutionary Command Council was the highest decision-making body in the government below Saddam Hussein.

belief that by announcing the suspension of Iraqi oil production, he would throw western economies into turmoil. But the world had changed and Iraq no longer had the power to shake the economies of the US or Europe.

The speech said much about the isolated, deluded world which Saddam Hussein inhabited. It was a place filled with terrified courtiers and advisers who said only what they thought their leader wanted to hear. In the years after the first Gulf War, stories about Saddam Hussein and his political inner circle did the rounds in Baghdad. One story tells of a cabinet meeting as the regime set about the vast reconstruction of key civilian infrastructure, focusing particularly on Baghdad. Many of the bridges across the Tigris river had been destroyed during the bombardment of the city that had lasted nearly forty days. According to the story, Saddam Hussein walks into the cabinet meeting, obviously pleased by the news that one of the bridges in the city has been rebuilt. Surprised by the speed of the repair, he turns to the minister responsible and asks him how much it cost to hire the engineers and workers to carry out the work so quickly. The minister is said to have answered: 'Two tons of paper and a small amount of concentrated ink, Your Excellency.' In other words, the minister had simply printed as many banknotes as was necessary to pay for the rebuilding of the bridge. Then there were the more chilling stories of the purging of party members soon after Saddam Hussein came to power in the 1970s. These stories were easily verified as he insisted that the scenes were filmed as a warning to other party members who might have been thinking of conspiring against him. In one of the videotapes the Iraqi leader is sitting on a stage in an auditorium, surrounded by several hundred officials and party members. Those in the audience that he accuses of treason are ordered to leave. There is no doubt as to what their fate will be.

As soon as Saddam Hussein's televised speech was over, the state channel began playing archive footage of the violence that had taken place across the West Bank and Gaza Strip that year. The disturbing image that so shocked the world, of a father desperately trying to protect and cradle his young son as they were caught in the middle of a gun battle in which both of them ended up being killed, was shown repeatedly.

This day of theatre ended with rallies and marches across Baghdad which had been timed to coincide with the end of the televised address. Senior officials in the Press Centre fanned out to the various media offices to inform us of these 'demonstrations', trying to insinuate that they were spontaneous and unexpected outpourings of public sentiment. It was an absurd fiction. Each of the capital's neighbourhoods had been prepared and drilled by the local Ba'ath Party office for the rallies. We drove to the Al Sho'la district in north-east Baghdad, where the main road had been cordoned off for one of these supposedly unprompted shows of allegiance to Saddam Hussein's declaration. We saw a group of men, ranging in age from early twenties to late fifties. Almost all of them looked as if they had been summoned from their workplace to attend the rally. The young men wore neatly pressed trousers and crisp short-sleeve shirts, and they probably worked in the shops and small offices that lined the street where they stood. Others were clearly mechanics from the car repair yards round the corner, their shirts splashed with grease and oil. One old man, flashing a toothless grin as he waved an AK-47 in the air, wore an old padded winter jacket. He was probably a night-watchman on his way to work, wrapped up to keep out the night-time chill ahead. Whenever the television cameras pointed in their direction they brandished with great gusto the AK-47s they'd been given for the occasion and cried out rather half-heartedly: 'With our souls and with our blood, we will sacrifice for you, Saddam.' Until, that is, the local bigwigs drew up in a pick-up truck – at which point their shouts grew more animated.

It felt more like a street party than a frightening display of political aggression. Young children and teenagers ran excitedly about, chasing each other in and out of the crowds, the women taking part in the chanting became giggly and coy whenever the cameras came near them. Some laughed shyly and tried to cover their faces, more because they didn't want to be photographed without their make-up on than because they didn't want to be photographed by westerners. In fact I don't think anyone there was taking it seriously. The so-called 'demonstrators' certainly weren't, nor were the journalists, the onlookers, even the local party officials, who looked rather bored and somewhat embarrassed.

This scene seemed to me a glaring example of just how far apart the Iraqi leadership was from its people as the days and weeks slowly progressed towards war. The dramatic televised images staged by Saddam Hussein of defiant, chanting Iraqis, waving guns in the air, seemed entirely divorced from the unseen daily lives of people I met in Baghdad. Throughout the summer there were, of course, tense and often sensational twists. There were the sombre gatherings at UN headquarters in New York where Britain and the United States pressed for a stringent new resolution demanding the return of weapons inspectors. Then there were the vast military exercises that Britain was holding in the Omani desert, as George W. Bush went on telling visiting heads of state of his determination to overthrow the Iraqi dictator. But the reality of life for the capital's civilians was much less dramatic.

It felt as if the whole city was sleepwalking towards war. In April 2002, less than a year before the war would start, there was no hysteria, no hoarding of goods, no rise in the prices of basic foodstuffs, not even a change in the value of the Iraqi dinar against the dollar. Just a strange, dignified and sad sense of normality. I say sad because this 'normality', these scenes of people going about their daily business as their country plunged into political chaos, was an eloquent reflection of the trap in which most Iraqis found themselves. The truth was that they were entirely powerless in the decision-making that would affect them and their families for years to come. They were caught between a dictatorship which, by its very nature, was at best ignorant and at worst distrustful of the views of its subjects, and two western nations which had no access to them; two western nations whose understanding of the Iraqi people was severely limited by the fact that they had had no diplomats in Iraq for twelve years, since the invasion of Kuwait, and whose primary focus – some might say, obsession – was to overthrow Saddam Hussein. The number and seriousness of the warnings and threats against Saddam emanating from Washington and London increased and from the government in Baghdad came only arrogant, ill-founded defiance. In between stood the faceless, unheard Iraqi people.

It became difficult to convey the real story of this country on the verge of conflict. Pictures of people going shopping or driving home from work are hardly newsworthy and yet they were, given that this was a country which would be at war within eleven months. I remember in particular doing live interviews from the roof of the Ministry of Information, attempting to convey something of the mood in the Iraqi capital. The ministry stood on the western bank of the Tigris, next to a large avenue which took you across the Sinak Bridge to the other side of the river. The road was always thick with traffic, something new presenters interviewing me from the studio in London remarked on: 'Rageh, we can see the traffic of a normal day in Baghdad behind you, is there any sense of panic among ordinary people? Are they worried by what the Prime Minister said in Parliament yesterday?' No, was usually the answer, which must have left viewers perplexed.

As the crisis deepened, increasing numbers of journalists were allowed into Iraq that spring, and it now seemed as if every TV station on earth was represented beside me on the roof of the ministry. Standing at one end of the long gangway at the side of the building you could see a row of about twenty tents with camera positions, microphone stands and endless miles of straggling black cables leading to the round faces of the satellite dishes behind us. The names of TV channels were emblazoned in spray paint on the ragged tarpaulin tents: BBC, ABC America, NBC, Reuters, ITN, CBS, Fox News, etc . . . It had become very crowded: there was no more than about two or three feet between each of us.

People around the world were reading and watching the frequent and increasingly dire reports of the escalating crisis from Baghdad. There were the leaks from Washington about various war plans, which Pentagon officials always tried to play down even though the various battle plans had been leaked by someone in the Pentagon in the first place; there were scenes of frenetic haggling in the

Security Council for a tough new resolution on Iraq, and British ministers rushing around the world trying to gain support from non-permanent members; there were reports of more troops and warships setting off for the Persian Gulf. Then I would come along and describe a city where people's only concern was to get on with their daily lives as best they could. This was not the reaction of a people who did not know or realize the momentous upheavals that their society was heading towards, it was the response of an economically exhausted and brutally repressed people who yearned for change but were powerless.

Mohammed was both bemused and irritated by the notion that he and other Iraqis should be running around in a wild state of panic. 'What the hell are we supposed to do?' he once asked us at lunch. 'We have been through this kind of thing already. Even now there are continued airstrikes in the south and the north of the country where British and American planes are attacking under the disguise of patrolling the no-fly zones. The Gulf War was only ten years ago. We all know what that hell is like.' Paul acknowledged this, but explained that it would still be difficult for people back in Britain, with their secure, peaceful lives, to imagine themselves reacting with anything other than blind panic had they been facing the same future. Mohammed gave a sad smile of resignation. 'This is our life,' he said.

It was late afternoon, and we had just arrived in the centre of the city, at the BBC offices. It was August, the worst time of year to be in Baghdad. The breeze is what hits you first. You look to it for respite, but in Iraq during the summer the atmosphere has been cooked to such a pitch that the breeze becomes blasts of agonizing, hot air. In the office we found Mohammed, and Paul gave him the books and the boxes of chocolates for his children and Saadoun's family which we had hidden in our bags. Mohammed told us that we had been assigned a new minder who would now work with us exclusively, as opposed to our being given a minder by the Press Centre on an *ad hoc* basis.

The minders who accompanied all foreign journalists were

controlled by the Press Centre in the Ministry of Information. It was a system that was intended to limit the access of international reporters to Iraqi society; to make sure that anything the regime deemed to be damaging was not filmed – presidential palaces, intelligence buildings, military bases and prisons. It was also meant to ensure that no Iraqi spoke subversively when interviewed, but such was the atmosphere of fear that no Iraqi would dream of doing so anyway. Sometimes the minders came in handy. In some working-class or rural areas, unused to the sight of foreign pressmen, minders had to explain to people who were nervous of the foreigners in their midst that we were allowed to film; their alarm at the sight of us showed just how isolated many people were from the outside world. However, the monitoring of the media was actually pretty haphazard and censorship relied largely on the con-stant sense of fear that the regime evoked among its people. With or without the presence of minders most Iraqis were just too terrified to speak candidly to foreigners about the government.

Luai was sitting in the hallway outside our office. He was short and round and immaculately turned out. He didn't wear the instantly recognizable foreign-made clothes that senior intelligence officials and secret policemen wore, such as leather jackets and dark, modern suits. Instead he wore a neatly tucked shirt and sweater, more out of self-respect than in an attempt to show his position. He had a gentle, almost baby face that broke into a broad beam when we were introduced. His English was slightly broken, but more than enough for him to be able to communicate reasonably well and at times, when he was grasping for a particular word or phrase in English, I would respond in Arabic. We all shook hands, and I told him that we had no work planned for that day but would meet him again the following morning. He was courteous and said goodbye. I hadn't seen Luai in the Press Centre before and he couldn't have been seconded from one of the official translation sections from other ministries because his English wasn't good enough. 'He is from that office,' Mohammed said, gesturing sky-wards. 'But he is a good man. He is not nosy and interfering. He stays outside the office when we don't need him and he does not try to block your work. I think he is fine, really.' It was not the first time that someone from one of the intelligence agencies had been assigned to us. However, it spoke volumes about the increasing paranoia of the government.

We arrived the next morning to find Luai already sitting outside the office. And so began what would become a ritual over the coming months. I would ask him if he'd like to come in for a cup of tea. He would decline, bringing his hand up to his chest in the traditional Arab gesture of polite refusal and say, 'Thank you, thank you.' He would sit back down and return to his newspaper. This was hardly the behaviour of a determined secret policeman eager to monitor our every word and thought. When he accompanied us on our assignments around Baghdad he took the same approach. He would always stand a little apart as he waited for us to finish filming.

There were a few occasions when we wanted to film near places that were classified as 'sensitive' by the Iraqi authorities and on these occasions he was more a help than a hindrance.

One morning we set off to film one of the most important and well-known monuments in Baghdad, the Hands of Victory. An enormous arch straddles a long military parade ground in the centre of the city, overshadowing a wide open field laid out to celebrate Iraq's rather hollow victory at the end of the Iran–Iraq war.* Two crossed scimitars form the arch and where the two blades meet the Iraqi flag flutters on a pole. The scale of the arch is overwhelming but the most bizarre and unnerving part of the monument is the massive, black, iron forearms that emerge from the earth to grasp the handles of the scimitars in thick, muscular fists. The metal for the swords apparently came from the melted-down guns of dead Iraqi soldiers. It is said that the hands were modelled on Saddam Hussein's own. Too big for the foundries of Iraq, the arms were

---

* Iraq's war with Iran lasted eight years and ended with Iran's Ayatollah Khomeini's acceptance of a ceasefire in 1988, when he realized that the US had joined the Iraqis. Iraq, with a population then of only 17 million, suffered 200,000 fatalities with 400,000 wounded.

apparently cast in Basingstoke. It is a monument where the venera-
tion of war, death and sacrifice is clear. Huge iron nets surround
the bases of the arch. They are filled with the helmets of thousands
of dead soldiers. The helmets, many of them dented by shrapnel or
punctured with bullet holes, were from Iranian soldiers who lay on
the battlefields at the mouth of the Persian Gulf. They now lie here
to decorate Saddam's empty victory.

We drove to the far end of the parade ground and began setting
up our camera. One solitary Iraqi soldier guarding the monument
ambled towards us and spoke to Luai. 'He says that you cannot
film in this direction, because in the background are important
government buildings, like the Ba'ath Party headquarters,' Luai
said. He continued talking to the soldier, carefully explaining that
his charges were simply recording the BBC correspondent and
not the backdrop of government buildings. The soldier looked
unconvinced and worried that he was about to land himself in
trouble. We let Luai do the talking. When the conversation seemed
to be taking a turn for the worse, Luai whisked out his official
security ID from his back pocket, showing it to the guard for just
long enough for him to realize that he was dealing with someone
from the terrifying intelligence department. 'It's okay,' Luai said
triumphantly, but quietly added, 'but please, do not show the
official buildings too much.' Paul told him not to worry, the
background would be blurred, and then patted him on the back
and thanked him. Luai smiled, looked at all of us, and said, 'I am
one of your team.' It might seem an innocuous comment, but for
a man employed by the intelligence services it was a significant
statement.

We all liked Luai. He was the perfect minder: broadly observing
the letter of the laws governing his job, but never wishing to fulfil
their spirit. When we weren't out filming, he would not seek to
come into our office. If we told him we were going to spend the
day there, he would ask if it was okay for him to go home early.
But this wasn't the main reason we all warmed to him; it was
because he began to trust us. During discussions over lunch he
would volunteer stories about his family that would illustrate how

difficult life was under a dictatorship. It cannot have been an easy thing for him to do. Unlike with Mohammed and Saadoun, my relationship with Luai had not been fostered and cemented over years. My colleagues and I were only now getting to know him, an intelligence official, during one of the most sensitive periods of his country's recent history. As our confidence grew, we began to say things in his presence that his bosses would certainly have deemed subversive. We'd talk about Saddam Hussein's propensity to miscalculate the political landscape and we would openly doubt how stable the edifice of his regime would prove to be once the military onslaught began. He listened to all this, sometimes giving us his broad beam of a smile, at other times just quizzically raising his eyebrows.

Even though he was an Iraqi security officer, it was Luai's other identity that guided his actions. He was a middle-class Iraqi, living in Baghdad with his young family, who, like everyone else, feared the future. He was an exception to the often accurate caricatures of Iraqi intelligence and security officials as the loyal henchmen of a brutal dictatorship. The images from western newspapers and television reports of the ominous 'Iraqi intelligence officer', the henchman or 'bogeyman' who seemed closer to a figure from a Hollywood film than to real life, were just too much of a generalization when it came to a person like Luai. As Britain and the United States continued to augment what was looking increasingly like an invasion force, few Iraqis in Baghdad doubted who would be the victor in any war. And Luai, despite his position, was certainly no different.

On 6 August a series of military parades was to take place across the city. Such parades had been unheard of in previous years, and the formation of a civilian militia was a direct response to President Bush's recent threats. In part, the parade was a 'smoke and mirrors' exercise on the part of Saddam Hussein, an attempt to exaggerate the military prowess of his regime, to hold out the spectre of a long and bloody war, in the hope that the American aversion to high military casualties might discourage an invasion.

We headed out to a district in north-east Baghdad. It was late afternoon and hundreds of people had gathered to see what the Iraqi leader had described as his 'Army of Eight Million'. The march past had already begun by the time we arrived and the columns of troops seemed to stretch for miles. This was the civilian militia the Iraqi government said would be at the heart of an urban guerrilla campaign in the event of war. The show was reminiscent of scenes from Cold War Russia – vast lines of marching figures disappearing into the city's horizon. However, when we looked more closely, what we saw was more an example of just how weak Iraq's military regime had become. One of the columns was made up of middle-aged women carrying machine guns. They tried to keep time, struggling in their thick rubber-soled sandals, their painted toenails peeping out beneath their long black skirts. Another section of the march seemed slightly more menacing. Young men stomped by, wearing spotless white paramilitary-style boiler suits and gloves, only their eyes visible above the swathes of white scarves wrapped around their heads. Sticks of dynamite were strapped to their waists. They looked like rows of marching Action Men in snow suits, and there was something deeply unconvincing about them. I suddenly realized what it was – the 'sticks of dynamite' around their waists were actually cardboard tubes that had pre-viously held nothing more dangerous than rolls of kitchen towel. The wires were stuck in haphazardly, as if *Blue Peter* had suddenly gone in for making sticks of dynamite. Luai looked on without saying a word.

Two days later, members of the dreaded Republican Guard set up their artillery guns on the banks of the Tigris river, to fire a military salute in honour of their fancifully titled 'Great Victory Day' to mark the end of the Iran–Iraq war. Saddam Hussein used the occasion for another television broadcast in which he declared that a British–American attack would be 'doomed to failure', that the two countries were motivated by 'arrogance and greed' and that their efforts would 'fall to hell'. We watched as the men to whom he would entrust his survival set about celebrating his pronouncement. As they loaded the ancient guns beneath a fero-cious sun, their uniforms began to darken with sweat. Wearily they stepped back a few paces before pulling the firing cord. The guns were so old that most of the tan camouflage paint had peeled off, and large patches of rust crawled their way along the barrels. This display was evidence of the catastrophic effect that defeat in the first Gulf War had had on the military forces on which Saddam Hussein had previously expended so much of the country's wealth. It also showed that sanctions and international isolation had succeeded at least in crippling his efforts to reconstitute his armed forces and thus have a whip-hand over the region. His regime could now hope to rely only on a shabbily equipped, demoralized and largely conscript army to keep it in power. What match was that against the armies and modern machinery being assembled in the Gulf, which could deliver destruction to within a few feet of its target from hundreds of miles away?

In November, as the summer heat gave way to the first cooler days of autumn, the UN weapons inspectors arrived in Baghdad. Unsurprisingly, having baulked at the notion of readmitting what he saw as an intelligence-gathering operation under the guise of the United Nations, Saddam Hussein eventually relented in the face of a unanimous UN resolution that threatened 'serious consequences' if he refused. It was to be, as British and American officials often repeated, 'Saddam's last chance'. The technical and scientific experts who made up the revamped UN disarmament and monitoring teams came to Baghdad against a backdrop of a continuing process of military fortification by Britain and the United States. Tens of thousands of troops, warships and fighter aircraft were already positioned in the Gulf, largely in Kuwait. In the same month as the UN inspectors returned to Iraqi soil, the US Central Command announced that it would be holding a military exercise at a multi-billion-dollar new command and air base in the Gulf state of Qatar that had been under construction throughout the summer. Four hundred British officers joined about 2,000 US soldiers already at the Al Udeid air base, where they played the computerized war games that were aimed at testing command and control operations. The base was directed by General Tommy Franks. It is little wonder that the Iraqi people barely looked up when the weapons inspectors arrived. The value of the dinar to the dollar hardly budged.

The actual start of the first genuine inspection was a closely guarded secret. Or at least it was meant to be. There were hundreds of foreign journalists in Baghdad and every day they would gather in a vast crowd outside the Canal Hotel, the headquarters of the UN in the capital. The inspectors usually began their operations at nine o'clock in the morning. By 8.30 there would already be a large gathering of journalists waiting outside their offices, their car engines running and their drivers waiting anxiously for the order that could have come straight out of an Ealing comedy: 'Follow that car!' Any UN vehicle that drove away from the UN parking lot was immediately followed by at least twenty cars full of reporters. At times witnessing history can be as surreal as it can be banal. I am still amazed that no one was killed when journalists gave chase to the white Jeeps of the weapons inspectors as they set off on their daily searches.

It could be quite cold in Baghdad during December, and the inspections could last all day at sites far from the city limits. So journalists arrived not just laden down with their cameras and microphones, but also armed with thermoses of tea and coffee and boxes of sandwiches. They looked like a very odd assortment of day-trippers.

It was important to be able to distinguish between the biological and nuclear teams. In their reports, weapons inspectors – and the UK and US governments – laid particular emphasis on suspected biological weapons programmes, so you could be sure that the UN visits to those sites would always be attended by a long line of press vehicles. Once we got to know the nationalities of the different inspectors it was easier to tell which teams were headed by American inspectors – they always attracted the longest queue of followers. Before heading to the facility they wanted to search, the inspectors had to meet their Iraqi liaison officers who were meant to ensure there were no obstructions or delays at the suspected sites. So the UN inspectors would first drive round the corner to meet the Iraqi liaison officers in an unused piece of open land. Once they had met, the chase began in earnest. This was the most unnerving bit of the day. The inspectors, under the false impression that they could shake off the pursuing reporters, would drive at breakneck speed through the city. The Iraqi officials, in turn, would swerve through the pack of newsmen to get between them and the inspectors. The journalists would do whatever it took to get the best pictures. Normal traffic screeched to a halt when confronted with this cavalcade of thirty four-wheel-drive vehicles racing through the streets at more than eighty miles an hour.

I remember my first experience of the chase. Our driver, Dylan, who quite rightly boasted of his driving prowess, even if it left us a little shaken, had manoeuvred our car so we were driving right next to the lead car of the UN inspectors. Our windows could not have been more than six feet apart. As I clung rigidly to the headrest in front of me, I looked over at the UN vehicle and caught the eye of one of the inspectors sitting in the back. We stared at each other as our cars hurtled along the road side by side. The inspector was in his fifties and resembled an academic with his trimmed grey beard and spectacles, but with a rather incongruous perky blue UN cap on his head. Under furrowed eyebrows, his jaw hanging open, he displayed an expression of both fear and outrage. He pointed at the side of his temple and made a series of wide circles with his finger. It was indeed a strange and shameful madness.

Thereafter I tried to do whatever I could to avoid going on these inspections. I wasn't alone. Few other BBC colleagues relished the prospect of these frightening and ultimately fruitless journeys. When the UN vehicles arrived at the site for inspection, leading a trail of vehicles behind them, a few bemused guards would amble up to the front gate. The UN inspectors would be allowed in, while journalists were denied access, and cameramen and photographers had to jostle for pictures outside. A long line of photographers would end up lying on the dusty ground outside the building, trying to peek through the thin crack between the bottom of the gate and the floor.

The pursuit of the weapons inspectors served only to deepen the strange atmosphere in Baghdad. The detailed legal and scientific work of the UN disarmament teams became the focus of the crisis for the outside world. Questions about the phrasing of the regular reports from the chief inspectors to the Security Council came to dominate the debate. Would there be a mention of 'material breach of UN resolutions'? Did the fact that an Iraqi official turned up late to allow weapons inspectors into the facility constitute obstruction, and if so was Iraq deliberately blocking the work of the UN teams? Did Iraq try to buy raw uranium from Africa, as the British government continues to assert, even though the head of the International Atomic Energy Agency described this claim at the time as 'baseless'? The obscurantist way in which the crisis was being presented made it increasingly difficult to see what was actually happening.

It was extraordinary to realize that, in the last weeks, days and hours before this nation was submerged beneath full-scale bombardment and its existence changed utterly, there seemed to be no connection between its citizens and how they were viewed by the world outside. Living in Baghdad, reporting every twist of the weapons inspections saga, while watching an ancient city go through the last days of a dictatorship it had known for twenty-five years, was like living a double life. Western journalists, UN inspectors and Iraqi officials acting as spokesmen for the government inhabited a hermetic bubble concerned with the minutiae of dossiers, of leaked reports and carefully managed press conferences. It was the view of the crisis that we transmitted around the world. Inside this bubble, it felt as though the entire world were hanging on the words of the weapons inspectors and the Ba'ath Party officials. But outside, in the streets and homes of the inhabitants of the city, the inspections seemed not to exist. Just as the people of this country did not appear to matter either to the Iraqi government or to the press conferences of the coalition, the inspections meant little to a people who knew that war was coming and that they could do nothing to stop it.

It was a bitterly cold December day, just before Christmas. The wind from the northern Kurdish mountains had brought with it an unfamiliar chill which swathed the Iraqi capital. It was, I suppose, the only thing that connected Baghdad with the Christmas season in Europe and North America. In the far east of the city, in an area called Hay Muhandisiya, is the Church of Our Lady. It is a parish of the Chaldean Church, a Catholic denomination of the Eastern Christian Church to which the vast majority of Iraq's estimated 700,000 Christians belongs.

Saddam Hussein liked to portray himself as the leader for all Iraqis. However, in both religious and ethnic terms Iraq is one of the most diverse countries in the Middle East. The regime, dominated as it was by Sunni Muslims, was only too aware of its position as a minority in a country where Shia Muslims were the majority. Saddam Hussein attempted to overcome this vulnerability by some very clumsy propaganda: appearing in posters around the country in a variety of costumes according to local faiths or ethnic and class backgrounds. For the Kurds he was depicted in traditional Kurdish clothes; for middle-class urban Iraqis he was a metropolitan businessman in a western-style suit; and for the rural farmers and peasants in the central Sunni heartland, he wore Bedouin robes. However, the Christian community in Iraq was so small that Saddam did not view them as politically threatening and therefore did not feel the need either to court them or, more importantly, to persecute them in the way he did the Shia Muslims.★ In fact, the regime looked to the Vatican and the Christian churches outside the country as valuable diplomatic allies.

I'd spent two previous Christmases in Baghdad, and on both occasions I'd gone to see Ishlemon Warduni, an auxiliary bishop and leader of the estimated 400,000 Chaldean Christians in Baghdad. The church building is a modern construction which shares a compound with the church offices and store rooms. It was about an hour before the evening service. Just inside the door of the church there was a small metal stand which held a dozen thin white memorial candles that had been lit by parishioners who'd arrived early and

---

★ Tariq Aziz was the only prominent figure in the regime who was a Christian, and he had no political constituency outside the Ba'ath Party.

had taken up their usual places on the narrow wooden pews. Three women sat together near the front, huddling in long black overcoats, their heads covered in black lace headscarves. I made my way through to the bishop's offices, where a young man showed me to a drawing room to wait. Framed photographs of Pope John Paul II, including one of the Holy Father greeting Bishop Warduni, were proudly hanging on the whitewashed walls.

'Hello, hello, nice to see you again,' Bishop Warduni beamed as he walked into the room. 'How is the BBC? Busy, eh!!' He was short, with a plump face and an infectious grin. He had a playful sense of humour, but was also intolerant of what he deemed intolerable. He eased himself on to the sofa while I prepared my microphone. I reminded him of the last time I had come to visit him, on the eve of Christmas in 1998, just after Britain and the United States had bombed Baghdad in Operation Desert Fox, in reprisal for the expulsion of UN weapons inspectors. 'Yes, I remember clearly,' he said, 'and it seems that nothing has changed.' I explained that I wanted to record a radio programme for the BBC, a sort of 'letter from Baghdad', in which contributors would describe what Christmas means to people around the world. 'The programme is called "Joy to the World",' I remember telling him, 'and it tries to explore what the spirit of Christmas represents to them.' 'Mmm . . . well I will try to provide some joy, but I am not hopeful,' he said with a rueful smile.

The bishop went back to Christmas 1998. 'I think the lights were off,' he said. 'There was a power cut, we had bombing. The night of the peace, but yet we had missiles. We are hoping that it doesn't happen again, anyway you are welcome.' I asked him what he would be telling his congregation this Christmas, when an even greater military onslaught appeared to be almost certain. He gave a deep sigh. 'I will tell them the message of Christ, of heaven, of God that loves all men.' I asked him if he felt connected to the Christians in Britain and America at this time. 'All Christians are one in Christ. For that I feel this connection with them, because we have the same baptism, the same sacraments. And for that, I ask them to pray for all the people, for all nations, but especially for Iraq.' He stressed this last point. 'I ask them to pray for their brothers in Christ and for their friends in religion, so we must pray for one another to have peace. As a real Christian I must love everybody, even my enemies, and I tell them to love us as God and Christ tell us.' I thanked the bishop for his time, and then, with a charming and sincere smile, and without my prompting, he leaned into the microphone and said, 'And a very merry Christmas to everybody, but they must pray for their brothers in Iraq.'

I switched off the recorder and asked Bishop Warduni if he was at all optimistic about the coming weeks and months. He raised his arms towards heaven and shrugged his shoulders. 'I trust only to God,' he said. I responded: 'What about your parishioners, how would you describe the mood among the families who attend your church?' He paused for a moment, then leaned forward, 'They are living their lives even in these difficult times because it is all we can do. We can't do anything about the present situation. But war will have terrible effects. It is the fear of chaos that terrifies everyone. That will be very dangerous for Iraq and the region, and nobody can tell what will be done in such a scenario.'

I then asked him about an upcoming report to the Security Council by the chief weapons inspector on the progress of their work in Iraq, and whether he thought the report would prove to be negative enough to bolster the British and American case for military action. The bishop looked at me quizzically, as if I had just branched off into an unfamiliar language. I stopped mid-sentence. 'Nobody cares for these things,' he said more coldly. 'If there will be war, it will be because the British and American governments have decided it. Not because of what the inspectors say. Look! Blix and the inspectors are saying they need more time, does anyone in London and Washington listen to them? I don't believe that President Bush or Tony Blair are going to have their minds made up by Mr Blix and Mr al Baradei★. Go and see how the Iraqis are getting on with their lives. You will see that people feel that they have been condemned to war.'

★ The head of the International Atomic Energy Agency.

His words were both sobering and true. News means drama. All of us who were in Baghdad reporting the steady steps towards conflict necessarily had to focus on the significant milestones that would eventually and inexorably lead to the invasion of Iraq. The reports of the inspectors, the reactions of British and American government officials, the defiant declarations of Saddam Hussein and his ministers were the material for our live broadcasts. None of this bore witness to how Baghdad and its people lived through those last days of peace. This side of the city seemed entirely separate from the events deciding its fate. At times it was as though these unnamed, unreported people were clinging on to a life that stood still as the world outside rushed towards violence.

The family's story

It was January 2003. We were off to visit a family who was about to move house. We had been put in touch with them by our driver, Khalil, a great bear of a man who now looked after us. In the 1980s Khalil had driven supply trucks to Republican Guard bases and positions around Tikrit and also in the western desert. He came from a prominent Sunni clan from the area around Tikrit, and so, even though he was poor, he was able to use his background to get work with the Republican Guard rather than with other conscript regiments who were not as well paid or well equipped. Despite his connection to the Republican Guard, however, he was utterly loyal to the BBC and was indispensable to us throughout the war.

We turned off the expressway down a narrow side street lined with small stone and concrete houses. Halfway along the empty lane we saw a removals lorry. Two little boys had climbed up the mountain of boxes and sat on a couple of armchairs, screeching with laughter, perched on top of the pile of possessions. Three men were walking through the metal front gate weighed down with enormous wooden crates. They shouted at the young boys to get down from the truck and out of the way. The men were obviously exhausted and eager to finish packing their family's belongings.

The British and American military build-up in the Gulf was almost complete and war seemed certain. It was obviously a good time to get your family out of Baghdad.

But the Abdel Ghani family was not moving out of the city. Ahmed Abdel Ghani emerged from the house and greeted us with a loud shout of welcome. He was short and solidly built, with a harelip and a flat, boxer's nose. He did not look like the rich owner of a garments factory which is what he was. He told us we'd arrived too late if we wanted to see him packing up his things, as there were only a few large items left. It was a small, modest and simple brick house just like the others alongside it down the street. There was nothing ostentatious about it, the self-standing air-conditioning units in the rooms being the only indicators of wealth. The furniture that remained in the empty sitting room was comfortable, the legs of the sofa decorated with imitation rococo carvings – tasteful but also well-used. This was a comfortable Baghdad family with a future ahead of them. They were moving into a large new house in the south-east of the city. Ahmed's youngest daughter ran about us excitedly, keeping a firm hold of her doll all the while, anxious that it shouldn't be forgotten. Ahmed's wife looked pleased and proud. She invited us in to film the last bits of furniture being removed from the kitchen, hoping that when we saw her new kitchen we'd compare it to the one they'd left behind and thus appreciate how far the family had come. It was a strangely touching moment. Her delight in the new life ahead and her keenness that we should witness it seemed so normal that for a moment it blotted out any thoughts of what was about to happen in this city.

Once the belongings had all been packed tightly in the back of the truck, Ahmed slammed the front gate closed and padlocked it. He did not give his old family home a backward glance. We followed him as he drove behind the van in his Toyota, keeping a keen eye on the back of the van in case any of the precariously perched furniture fell out. It was a surprisingly short drive to their new home and we arrived fifteen minutes later. It was directly underneath a major flyover, and, more worryingly, across the road from an electricity sub-station, but looking up at the tall, newly built two-storey mansion, I could see why the Abdel Ghani family had moved here. There was a broad paved courtyard, with space for two cars by the side. The front door was heavy with dense, richly varnished wood. Encircling the first floor was a veranda lined with thick marble columns. An airy, light hallway gave way to a vast kitchen and living room behind, while a wide staircase led to the four bedrooms upstairs. This was a world away from their previous home. The children helped to unload the van, laughing and running into the house with several pots and pans under their arms, and whatever else they could carry in their hands. It was a bewildering sight. Ahmed, seeing the surprised look on my face, read my thoughts. 'We've been through many wars,' he said. 'The Iran–Iraq war and the Gulf War – then we lived in a central area of Baghdad which was heavily bombed. This might be safer. Who knows? Anyway, we will need this house in the future, whatever happens.'

The well-digger's story

A hammer tapping against a metal drum makes a strange hollow, clinking sound, a sound that rang out across the residential districts of the city in the months before the war began. 'Clink! Clink! Clink!' It was followed immediately by shouts of 'Water wells, water wells!' This mantra continued either until the well-digger was stopped by a potential customer, or until his horse-drawn cart laden down with tools and pipes trotted out of earshot. The echoing call of the well-diggers plying their trade to the families preparing for war is a sound that brings back those last days of peace. Wars have an insidious way of creating economic opportunities. As Baghdad moved into a strange half-world between peace and war and people finally started to turn their attention to the worrying future, they slowly began to stock up on supplies to last them through the siege. They needed somewhere to store their water during the conflict and well-digging became one of the few boom-ing businesses in the city. The well-diggers trawled the middle-class districts, not just because the people there had money, but also because they had gardens where a hole could be sunk.

Jamal Salman Marmous was ambivalent about his new-found prosperity. He had trained as an agricultural engineer, and for many years he and his workmen had made a living digging wells for farmers in the rural provinces around Baghdad. He described it as a hard existence, but one which was also rewarding, both psychologically and financially. Not as financially rewarding, however, as digging water-wells for fearful urban families. 'I do about seven to ten wells on a good day,' he said, 'but I wish I didn't have to. War has led me to this.'

On a crisp February morning, as the sun shone through the clear cold sky I stood in the front garden of his home in the Al Dora district of Baghdad, as the men he usually employed to drill holes for other people began work for a well in his own tiny front garden. An uneven concrete patio was surrounded by carefully nurtured shrubs and plants: soft pink winter roses, a thick, rambling bougainvillea and low evergreen hedges. The workmen took a long metal spike to the centre of the patio and began hammering. Once they'd made a deep enough puncture, they placed the nose of a large manual drill into the hole. A metal bar like a giant corkscrew was threaded through a hole in the middle of the drill. Slowly it began to burrow through the concrete and the soft earth beneath it. As the bar across the drill got lower, it would be threaded through a higher hole on the drill, and the process would begin again. Jamal looked on, occasionally issuing instructions to his men. He had a noble face, with clearly defined features and sharp, high cheekbones. He was tall and strongly built, but his voice was weak and soft, the result, he told us, of 'heart problems'. He couldn't have been more than forty-five years old.

I had expected to meet a man who was satisfied with his new-found wealth but instead I had found a melancholy figure. His voice was distant and empty of emotion when he described his new livelihood. 'There is a big demand to dig wells,' he said in a matter-of-fact way. 'People are worried that if there is war, the power will go, and that they will therefore lose their water supplies.

And what life can there be without water in a city?' Whatever reassurances Britain and the United States had been giving about preserving the city's infrastructure and resources in the event of any conflict had clearly fallen on deaf ears. As people finally forced themselves to face the future, their attitudes became immediately clear. After the years of war and sanctions, ordinary Iraqis had learned to trust their own instincts.

5. 'Unsheathe Your Sword'

Our team had assembled in the suite of the Mansour Hotel, on the western bank of the Tigris river, just across the road from the Ministry of Information. Such was the suffocating nature of the Al Rasheed Hotel – and our certainty that it would be a military target during a war because it was fortified with underground bunkers – that we had made the decision to move out of it by early February. The BBC team in Baghdad now consisted of myself, Paul and Killa, and two other correspondents, Paul Wood and Andrew Gilligan. Malek Kenaan, a vastly experienced Lebanese cameraman who had worked for the BBC all over the Middle East, had also joined us, along with Duncan Stone, another cameraman and senior picture editor, who had been reporting from Iraq since 1998, and Mustapha al Salman, a young American-educated Iraqi engineer, who had joined our team to take responsibility for our lifeline to the outside world, our satellite broadcasting dish.

Paul had called us in to say that each of us had a decision to make. Of course every one of us had been quietly thinking about this decision throughout the previous week but this was the first occasion we discussed it openly together. The sleepwalking was over and it felt as though the city had been jolted awake to face the war that was now only a matter of hours away. 'I've had a conference call with all the bosses in London who are very, very concerned about whether we stay or whether they pull us out,' said Paul. 'They've said that given how long we've been preparing for the story and the infrastructure we've built up they have the confidence to trust our judgement. They said that they'd come very close to pulling us out. Jonathan* said that the whole news management board were seriously taken aback not so much by the decision of

* Jonathan Baker, the BBC's much-liked Foreign Editor.

most of the remaining American networks to pull out, but by the decision of Associated Press Television. For a major international news agency to remove its foreign staff gave our bosses a major jolt, and, rightly, they're wondering if they're being naïve by agreeing to let *us* decide if we want to stay. But the main thing I want everyone to think about is what they want to do. If anyone wants to leave, I guarantee that that person will have complete and total support. Put it this way, if we're here when the war starts, our bosses will leave it entirely up to us when we send reports, and they've said from the very top, that if we want to keep our heads down for several days and not make a single report, that's absolutely fine with them. But look, everyone needs to talk to their families and think hard about whether they want to stay.'

I thought I had spent exactly a year preparing for this moment, but that morning I realized I had only ever thought about it in the abstract. 'When the war starts', 'During a siege of Baghdad', etc . . . Those words had been so easy to say over the past year but it proved much harder to confront what was really about to happen. We had all been gathered together on the day which President George W. Bush had described the previous evening as the 'moment of truth', and for the first time his words accurately captured the mood of Baghdad. He'd made his speech at a hastily arranged summit with Tony Blair and the Spanish Prime Minister José María Aznar at a military base in the Azores in the mid-Atlantic. Having failed to muster enough support in the UN Security Council for a new vote authorizing the use of force, the British and American leaders chose this surprising setting to issue an ultimatum to the world body. You might have expected them to give such a speech in Washington or London, and perhaps it was in order to avoid anti-war protests that they chose to do it in the middle of the Atlantic. The two men gave the UN a twenty-four-hour deadline to enforce the terms of existing resolutions after which the Anglo-American coalition would go to war.

'Tomorrow is a moment of truth for the world,' President Bush had said. 'Tomorrow is the day that we can determine whether or not diplomacy will work.' Tony Blair spoke with a bluntness that he had not been able to muster in Crawford, Texas, the previous April. Tense and grim-faced, he said: 'We are in the final stages, because after twelve years of failing to disarm him now is the time when we have to decide.' The two leaders had effectively abandoned all hope of getting majority agreement within the UN Security Council. The ultimatum, which they must have known stood little chance of being heeded by other Security Council members, would free them to pursue the path on which President Bush and Prime Minister Blair were now firmly set: a war to disarm Iraq of weapons of mass destruction with or without the backing of the United Nations.

Saddam Hussein had not waited for this missive from the mid-Atlantic to show publicly that he realized war was certain and imminent. A national decree was issued just as the summit was being convened in the Azores. The Iraqi leader announced that in preparation for the attack the country had been divided into four defensive commands: the North, under the control of Izzat Ibrahim al Douri, deputy head of the Revolutionary Command Council; Baghdad and Tikrit, which would be in the hands of Saddam Hussein's younger son, Qusay; the South – where the invading armies would enter – entrusted to the command of another family member, Ali Hassan al Majid, better known in the West as 'Chemical Ali'; while Saddam himself was taking overall control of the air defences. The decision, the communiqué said, was based on the need to take 'the necessary steps to repulse and destroy any foreign aggression'. Even if Saddam Hussein appeared to be taking things in his stride, this 'moment of truth' shook Baghdad to its core. In an instant, a city that had for so long existed in a state of almost anaesthetized denial became gripped by panic and anxiety. And it showed.

I could hear people and shouting as we approached Shorja market, yet from where we stood, the place looked half empty. The narrow walkways between the stalls selling mountains of pulses and rice were not thick with shoppers. There was no sign of where the noise was coming from. But then we walked further into the covered market, to the part which was usually much calmer and emptier, and there we saw the crowds of shoppers bustling between the long trestle tables where rows of batteries, kerosene lamps, matches and packets of candles were neatly laid out. The fingers of the stallholders busily counted off the bundles of dinar notes as each box of matches or roll of tape was handed over, then the men quickly turned their attention to the next customer. One man was asking for masking tape. 'Wide tape,' he insisted, 'I need thick, wide tape which is strong.' He bought two or three rolls and put them in the flimsy plastic bag already bulging with packets of batteries. No doubt that night he would unroll the sticky tape and stretch it across the glass windows of his house, perhaps starting with the window in the children's bedroom. It was disturbing to watch these people, whom I usually saw haggling over the price of bread or cooking oil, striding through the market with such efficient determination, knowing exactly what they and their families needed at this time of crisis. It is a difficult thing, to say the very least, to realize that you have only a few hours in which to collect together the necessary supplies to protect you and your loved ones during an aerial bombardment by the most powerful armed force the world has ever known.

Think about it for a moment. You have a bit of money, and a few hours. You are in an open market along with hundreds of others. What do you go for? Rations of food first? Maybe some blast-proofing? When there is no masking tape, when the last roll has been sold to the woman in front of you in the queue, what do you look for as a substitute? The power is bound to go very quickly. What about light? Candles and matches? Or kerosene lamps? Most people knew that it was better to buy things that were fuelled with kerosene rather than diesel because in times of conflict most supplies of diesel would be requisitioned by the army for use in their vehicles. It is a desperately sad measure of what Iraqis have been through this past quarter of a century, that they knew exactly what they needed and, indeed, the market sellers knew what they had to provide. Ordinary life, which Baghdad's citizens had so insistently continued to live until that moment, had suddenly stopped, but there was a clockwork efficiency in what should have been a scene of panic and mayhem.

Adnan Mustapha Hamid had not gone to work that day at the restaurant where he was a manager. 'All the staff have gone to be with their families,' he told me. 'The owner told us to go and he gave us our money and some food to take with us to our relatives.' I asked him what he made of President Bush and Prime Minister Blair's strong undertaking to do everything possible to avoid hurting Iraqi civilians. 'I know the British and Americans say they will spare civilian targets,' he said, as other shoppers gathered to listen to what he had to say to the camera, 'but few of us believe them. I think they're going to bomb everything, and most of us are just going to stay at home.' Others nodded in agreement. It was finally happening. There was no more doubt, no more having to speak in the conditional tense about the 'prospect of war'. If war is a state of mind, an emotional condition as well as an actual event, then war was already in Baghdad, even before the first bomb hit its target.

Journalists reacted similarly. The Press Centre at the Ministry of Information went through its own version of the scenes we witnessed at the Shorja market. The office of the Centre's director was in chaos. It was the last opportunity to get exit visas before the borders closed. Beneath the dense haze of cigarette smoke that hung above the main hall where correspondents gathered, angry voices rose in strained conversations. One colleague from a British news organization was struggling to hold back her tears. Having worked in Iraq for several years, reporting from the country when many others were not, she was now being asked by her bosses to leave for her own safety. Her frustration was palpable. It took me more than an hour to walk from the director's office to the BBC's office, which was less than 100 yards away, as I said goodbye to journalists, cameramen, photographers and satellite engineers from America, Britain, France, Kenya, Russia, Australia and South Africa who were on their way out of the country either willingly, or more often reluctantly, under orders from their programme chiefs.

It was hard to watch experienced and dedicated colleagues leave Baghdad, and more than anything else it left me severely doubting my decision to stay. I had reported on other conflicts where I had seen many of the same people who were now leaving, trying desperately to either get into besieged cities or do their best to remain there once they had arrived. I never imagined that I would see so many news organizations deciding to withdraw their foreign correspondents and crews from a major news event. In those last three days of peace I oscillated constantly between deciding to leave and feeling committed to stay. It was the hardest decision I have ever had to make. I had pledged to my family that I would not stay in Baghdad if I had any serious misgivings about whether foreign journalists there would be targeted by the regime. I was the one who knew the country and had witnessed the preparations for war and so it was I, not my family, who ultimately had to make that decision for us all. Our families were not in the position to weigh up the risks and help us to decide. Nina said that she would trust me to make the right decision as long as I had not a grain of doubt about my safety. The decision-making process was made only more torturous by the paranoid conversations that were occurring among the dwindling group of correspondents.

I had many agonizing discussions with colleagues and friends from all over the world about the painful decision of whether to stay or go. Having reported from the country for six years under sanctions and repeated military strikes, I was keen to stay to witness a defining moment in its history. More than that, as often happens in such situations, I had formed strong personal bonds with people in the city. Leaving now felt as if I was abandoning them, even if they would never have wanted or expected me to feel that way.

Paul, our Bureau Chief, had to consider every eventuality, every risk. I saw him talking to Suzanne Goldenberg of the *Guardian*, who was a friend from his days working in South Asia. 'Suzy, the *Guardian*'s staying, right?' Suzanne shrugged her shoulders and said she thought so. 'Come on, Suzy, I'm asking you as a fucking mate, not just another hack, are you going to stay or not, because there's no more time to think about it and I need to know how many other British journalists are going to be here in Baghdad.' He didn't mean to sound aggressive, and Suzanne was not trying to be evasive, it was just that those last few hours were extraordinarily tense. 'Yes, Sean★ and I are going to stay.'

Up on the roof, television engineers worked quickly to dismantle the tons of satellite equipment, cables and makeshift editing suites and box them up before getting the necessary permission to take them out of the country that evening. It seemed that as each journalist left the city, the level of neurosis rose correspondingly. There was a widely held belief that those who stayed would be used by the Iraqi authorities as human shields. And this was just one of the increasingly bizarre scenarios that were being envisaged by many of us who remained behind. One story had it that on the first night of the bombing, journalists would be tied to the bridges across the Tigris river. Another rumour suggested we would be taken as 'guests' to one of the presidential compounds, 'for our own safety'. Somehow these scenarios did not square with the picture I had of the low-ranking Iraqi bureaucrats who would have been charged to carry out such orders. I just couldn't picture the poorly paid, silently resigned minders I had met tying me to a bridge and waiting for the bombs to fall. But even if these visions did seem paranoid and far-fetched, as the days passed there was plenty of ammunition to fuel them. The supplies of nerve agent antidotes and the unwieldy chemical and biological warfare suits began to arrive in boxes at our hotel, and with them the fears about weapons of mass destruction seemed to gain credibility.

Northern Baghdad contains one of the main Shia enclaves of the city. Its heart is the Khadimiya Mosque, one of the most important Shia shrines in Iraq. Shia Muslims are the majority in Iraq and live mostly in Baghdad and the plains of the south. The domes and minarets of the mosque compound tower above the horizon, their roofs inlaid with gold leaf shimmering in the sunlight. The mosque

★ Sean Smith, *Guardian* photographer.

is believed to have been built nearly 500 years ago, and a large Shia community has grown around it over the years. Running along the wide boulevard that stretches from the main square by the shrine's front gate is one of the city's biggest gold markets. The street is lined with narrow jewellery shops owned by generations of old Baghdad families. Close by are the dozens of small pilgrims' guest houses for the thousands of Shia visitors who travel to the mosque from all over Iraq and from neighbouring Iran. The huge, heavy wooden doors of the shrine's main gate lead on to a vast courtyard laid out in blue and white tiles, which wraps itself around the golden mosque standing regally in the middle. We went to film at Khadimiya Mosque just hours before President Bush's deadline.

It was early evening and young Shia conscripts from the Iraqi army were among the crowd of worshippers in their elegant lace caps, making their way into the shrine for evening prayers. The sight of these young men in their uniforms going into the mosque to pray on the eve of war was both touching and unnerving. As Killa filmed by the front gate, I took Luai aside and explained that I wanted to speak to him as a friend, even as a brother. He nodded his head earnestly. 'You've heard all the fears among many of the journalists, Luai, of what the government might do to them once the war starts. I am asking you, with that in mind, do you think we should stay or return to our families?' He didn't pause to think about it for a minute. 'Rageh, nothing like this is going to happen to you. I guarantee it. Even from our briefings from my office' – the intelligence agency he worked for liaising with the Ministry of Information on the foreign journalists working in the country – 'there are absolutely no plans or thoughts like this. Believe me. They need the international media to be here.' Then he said something extraordinary. 'This war will not last more than four days. Everyone, they will just go home. No one fight. If you and Paul and Mr Duncan and the others, if you like, I will give you the keys to my home to stay there for your safety.' Then a brief smile crossed his lips, 'And I will stay with you at my home!'

Both Mohammed and Saadoun had told me almost exactly the

same thing a few days earlier. They assured all of us that no one, least of all the authorities, was going to harm western journalists who remained in Baghdad during the war. Both of them were absolutely certain of this but, interestingly, they too believed that the war would be over within a week, so rapid would be the collapse in the face of bombardment and invasion.

It was after these conversations that I decided to stay. I simply did not recognize the Iraq presented in the images and fantasies of the wholesale murder and execution of foreign journalists, even by a brutal dictatorship like the one of Saddam Hussein. Luai was right, the regime wanted the western and Arab media to report the war from Baghdad. When the war finally did end, no foreign journalist had been killed or wounded by Iraqi forces; even when, in the middle of the war, about nine western reporters who were covering the conflict as 'unilaterals'* were found in southern Iraq, by Iraqi forces. They had no Iraqi visas or permits, they were Australian, French, Italian and one was an American, and they were carrying sophisticated broadcasting equipment that could easily have been used for espionage. Several I spoke to after the war said they had feared the worst, and thought they would be executed as spies. In the end, they were brought to Baghdad by the authorities and had their equipment confiscated, but they were free to stay at the same hotel as the rest of the western journalists who were covering the war from Baghdad. When the city fell, they managed to get their cameras and computers back by breaking into the room where their confiscated equipment had been taken and were able to report on the defining moment of the war. One of the Australian journalists joked that if he had known that he would get to report on the fall of Baghdad by being arrested by the Iraqis at the start of the war, he wouldn't have wasted so much time at the beginning of the war trying to avoid Iraqi soldiers.

By 18 March there were about 140 foreign journalists, cameramen, engineers and photographers left in Baghdad. There were fewer farewells as it became more difficult to get out of Iraq. By

* In other words, completely independent from both sides.

now all the remaining reporters were based in the Palestine Hotel, on the eastern bank of the Tigris, opposite the main Republican Palace compound. Most of the rooms in the Palestine Hotel had been block-booked by journalists as early as the end of January, which shows just how convinced many of the world's news organizations were that the crisis would end in war. It is as revealing as the fact that our colleagues who were to be 'embedded' with British and American army units had been asked to make their way to register with them in February. There they were met not only by media officers from the army, but also media spokesmen seconded from Whitehall.

We had a series of rooms with balconies connected together to form a large suite, on the thirteenth floor. The Meridien Hotel was built by the Meridien international hotel group, in the 1970s judging by the style of the architecture and decor. It was nationalized and, as its name suggests, Arabized, to become the Palestine. It stood across the road from the former Sheraton, which after nationalization became the Ishtar Hotel. In the past, few journalists or businessmen stayed at these two admittedly rather grotty hotels, but several factors identified this as the best place to stay during wartime. The Pentagon and the British Ministry of Defence had told the senior management of the major news organizations in off-the-record briefings that the Al Rasheed Hotel, where journalists had stayed during the first Gulf War and which had that unforgettable mosaic of Bush Senior in its lobby, had a series of fortified bunkers beneath it and was therefore a legitimate target.

They said the same of the Ministry of Information, even though at first the Iraqis would not permit us to work anywhere other than the ministry. As journalists looked for other possible hotels to stay in, the Palestine became the obvious choice because from the eastern side of the river it had the best views of the main government buildings and palaces in the heart of the city. It was on the opposite bank of the Tigris and was located in a largely civilian residential area where there were no legitimate military targets and, perhaps more importantly, the Pentagon and the Ministry of Defence had the exact satellite co-ordinates for the hotel and would therefore – or so we thought – not single it out for attack. I never imagined I would come to have a grudging affection for it.

In those last hours of peace, the hotel had a forsaken, dismal atmosphere. Many security and intelligence officials, and virtually the entire staff of the Press Centre, including minders, also came to live there with those journalists who had elected to stay in Baghdad. In my more claustrophobic moments the place began to feel like a cell where the condemned were forced to live alongside their jailers. The corridors of the hotel were crowded with the constant flurry of journalists ferrying containers of water, satellite equipment, food rations and first-aid boxes. From every room you could hear the familiar sound of ripping tape as strips of masking tape and sticky plastic blast-proofing material were torn off and stuck over exposed glass doors and the windows of the hotel balconies.

Saddam Hussein's demonstrations on the streets of Baghdad took on a different tone. Where they had once been unconvincing displays of undying loyalty to the Iraqi leader and the Ba'ath Party, on the eve of war they increasingly became, for the people forced to attend them, expressions of hostility to the notion of direct rule by the United States. On 16 and 17 March several gatherings had taken place in the centre of Baghdad. There was the inevitable burning of American, British and Israeli flags and the torching of effigies of President Bush. Among the rather more nervous-looking Ba'ath Party officials were thousands of Iraqi civilians: factory workers wearing boiler suits, office clerks in suits and ties and students carrying their books and course manuals, as well as school children with their satchels still tied to their backs. Some had been given guns to wave in the air. The Iraqi leadership intended these scenes to be a warning of the bloody street-fighting battles that awaited any invading army. The circle of loyalists close to the Iraqi leader, at least publicly, subscribed to this belief.

However, we found a very different truth when we spoke to some people in the crowds. It was as though they had fast-forwarded to the future they knew was not far away, one in which the war had already taken place and where rule by Saddam Hussein had been replaced by the rule of an American general or pro-consul. 'We are Arab people! Muslim people! We don't need USA in Iraq. We don't accept them,' shouted one man. A young doctor, still wearing his white coat, said calmly, as the smoke from a burning Israeli flag swirled around him, 'We will never accept to be ruled by foreigners. This is not the Iraqi tradition. We are a nationalist people and we have a very, very ancient history. No single Iraqi can accept to be ruled by Bush or Blair. We are against this completely.' For once, I thought, I was hearing someone at a rally in Baghdad say what they genuinely believed. These people were far more animated than the men and women I had met during the staged demonstrations of previous months where protesters woodenly pledged allegiance to the government. However, they had also begun to fast-forward to a world after the war and about this world they were far from certain.

It was the first public murmuring of disaffection about the prospect of 'regime change' I had heard from ordinary Iraqis. Everyone could foresee the swift destruction of the Iraqi leadership; few had any idea of what would follow. Those who had monitored international radio broadcasts,★ and there were many in Baghdad, had heard the descriptions by the Bush administration of a transitional period in which the country would be governed by an American civilian official. The suggestion was met with suspicion and hostility. If there was anything that these last demonstrations indicated, it was that Iraqis exhibited a greater passion against the idea of being colonized than they did for fighting in order to preserve Saddam Hussein's regime. For his part, the Iraqi leader appeared on state television, dressed in military uniform for the first time in nearly two years. By his side were the Vice-President and Vice-Chairman of the Revolutionary Command Council. Also at the conference

---

★ Shortwave radios were available in the marketplaces of most cities in Iraq and were not prohibitively expensive. Many middle-class and less wealthy Iraqis owned a set. Most people received news about the outside world through the English and Arabic broadcasts of the BBC World Service and other international stations.

table were other senior ministers, commanders and Ba'ath Party officials, all similarly dressed. Another bulletin showed Saddam Hussein's eldest son, Uday, carrying a gun in a black leather shoulder holster.

On 18 March President Bush's twenty-four-hour ultimatum to the UN Security Council had elapsed without response. He now gave Saddam Hussein and his two sons forty-eight hours to flee the country into exile, as the only means of avoiding war. Unshown on Iraqi television, President Bush's address to the American nation was broadcast into the country by international radio stations and US agencies.

'My fellow citizens,' he began with a sombre expression, 'events in Iraq have now reached the final days of decision.' He emphatically repeated the claims about Iraq's weapons of mass destruction and that the regime was allied to Al Qaeda who could soon gain possession of these materials. 'Intelligence gathered by this and other governments leaves no doubt that the Iraqi regime continues to possess and conceal some of the most lethal weapons ever devised . . . [the Iraqi government] has a deep hatred of America and our friends, and it has aided, trained and harboured terrorists, including operatives of Al Qaeda,' he said, without the slightest hint of doubt. The President continued on the theme of a possible doomsday pact between Baghdad and Al Qaeda: 'The danger is clear; using chemical, biological or, one day, nuclear weapons, obtained with the help of Iraq, the terrorists could fulfil their stated ambition and kill thousands or hundreds of thousands of innocent people in our country, or any other . . . before the day of horror can come, before it is too late to act, this danger will be removed.' He was foretelling apocalypse for an innocent and unknowing people and he swore that he would strike first before this 'day of horror' occurred. It was like hearing an Old Testament prophet arguing the merits of the modern doctrine of pre-emptive action.

'Under Resolutions 678 and 687, both still in effect, the United States and our allies are authorized to use force in ridding Iraq of weapons of mass destruction. This is not a question of authority,' he said curtly, 'it is a question of will.' And then he turned his disdain on the international body which had issued those resolutions. 'The United Nations Security Council has not lived up to its responsibilities, so we will rise to ours . . . All the decades of deceit and cruelty have now reached an end,' he said, speaking with a sense of finality that presented this more as a declaration of war than an ultimatum. 'Saddam Hussein and his sons must leave Iraq within forty-eight hours. Their refusal to do so will result in military conflict, commenced at a time of our choosing.' Just to make it clear that the world was only hours away from a war with consequences that could only be guessed at, President Bush said, 'For their own safety, all foreign nationals, including journalists and inspectors, should leave Iraq immediately.' And with those words George W. Bush heralded the end of an era.

Then he spoke directly to the Iraqi people, saying, 'I have a message for them.' He made them a promise by which, he suggested, the war against Saddam Hussein's government would be judged. 'As our coalition takes away their power, we will deliver the food and medicine you need . . . We will help you to build a new Iraq that is prosperous and free . . . The tyrant will soon be gone. The day of your liberation is near . . . The terrorist threat to America and the world will be diminished the moment that Saddam Hussein is disarmed.'

We were packing up the last remaining essential pieces of equipment from our office at the ministry. We would have to keep our satellite dish at the ministry, so we stored it in two large canvas tents, complete with working desks and generators. The rest we moved to our suite in the Palestine Hotel, where we kept much of our editing and radio equipment. If anyone had any doubt about the Ministry of Information being a target, President George W. Bush's stark warning to all foreign journalists to leave Iraq immediately put paid to it. Those journalists remaining in Baghdad had all decided not to hang around in the ministry after dusk, which was about 4.30 p.m.

Saadoun's eyes were bloodshot and dark shadows had formed beneath them. He had long complained of high blood pressure and he was anxious and utterly exhausted. We had agreed weeks before that, once the war began, he must stay at home with his wife and teenage children. 'You know where I live,' he said to Paul and me. 'If you or your family need anything at all, Saadoun,' Paul told him, 'even if you need to come and stay with us in the Palestine. Just turn up. You don't need to ask or send messages.'

'And to you as well. My house is yours. But don't worry about this talk of being strangled by Iraqi officials. That is nonsense.' He gave us a hug and kissed us on both cheeks. And with that he left to drive home, where he would stay for the duration of the war.

Mohammed had the same responsibilities, and we knew long before this moment that he would also be staying at home with his family. We'd made sure that they had whatever they needed in the way of supplies. He told us that Luai would take good care of us, but that if we needed him for any reason we should send Dylan, our driver, to his house to collect him. We told him that his first priority was his family and that he shouldn't hesitate to bring them to the hotel if he felt he had to. 'We just pray that this nightmare will be over quickly and cleanly. Everyone is really worried about chaos and disorder after the war.' Mohammed said he doubted whether Britain and the United States understood how dangerous and complex the aftermath would be. 'We will see each other soon, Rageh,' I remember him saying, 'but I pray that it does not become a long siege.' Mohammed said goodbye to everyone and left for home.

In the early hours of the morning of 18 March the weapons inspectors finally left the country. They didn't so much depart as slip out of the city. They had arrived with such fanfare, in theory commissioned by the leaders of the world to facilitate a peaceful conclusion to this international tension. Now they left, dejected and consigned to irrelevance by the very governments who had sent them. Hiro Ueki, a Japanese national who gained a reputation for being both bland and highly officious in his position as spokesman for the weapons inspectors, came out to the front of the UN headquarters at the Canal Hotel to speak to the small number of journalists who had waited for some last word. Even in this most dramatic of moments Mr Ueki was as wooden and uninformative as he had always been. Then again, the circumstances required the spokesman to say as little as possible. 'We were here to do a technical job,' he said somewhat ponderously, 'and that's what we did. The political decision' [to pull the inspectors out] 'had to be made by others.' Then a journalist said in a rather bemused voice: 'But you haven't finished the job yet.' Mr Ueki thought about his response for a moment. Then in a dignified manner he simply said, 'Well, the job has not been finished yet, but up until now, we have played our part.'

Buses arrived to take the 150 remaining weapons inspectors and support staff to Saddam International Airport where the last UN jet was sitting on the tarmac, ready to fly them out of the country. Much of their equipment and other personnel had already been evacuated several weeks earlier. Yet, the inspectors had continued to work right up until the previous day. Now they walked through the empty departure lounges of the airport with their suitcases and shoulder bags, some still wearing their blue UN caps. Many of them looked disconsolate and humiliated. 'We had a purpose being here and a job to do for the international community,' one of them told journalists, 'we would have liked to continue our jobs here in Iraq, but we've been ordered out by the UN. I wish the best to all my Iraqi colleagues at the UN and I hope to see them again one day.' Geoffrey Beaumont, the deputy director of the inspectors, was quoted as saying: 'People are sad because they have put their hearts and souls and blood and tears into this. They worked bloody hard, and let's face it, no one wants war.'*

They boarded the white plane, marked with the black UN logo, and it lumbered up the runway and then out of sight. Quietly, and almost unnoticed by most Iraqis, the UN inspectors withdrew from Iraq, their mission of peaceful disarmament at an end, pushed aside by Washington and London's desire for regime change. Their boss, Hans Blix, was preparing to give his last testimony to the UN Security Council in New York. Dejected and now powerless, he

* Suzanne Goldenberg, *Guardian*, 19 March 2003.

said, 'I naturally feel sadness that three and a half months of work carried out in Iraq have not brought the assurances needed about the absence of weapons of mass destruction . . . [and] that no more time is available for our inspections and that armed action now seems imminent.'

The Foreign Minister, Naji Sabri, hastily arranged a press conference. Sitting behind a raised desk lined with dozens of microphones, he spat out his contempt for the invaders and his indignation. 'How can an ignorant, idiot man become the President of the United States?' he asked the assembled journalists. 'A man who doesn't know whether Spain is a kingdom or a republic. How come he can become the President of such a clever people like the American people?' He didn't wait for a reply, but quickly got up and walked out, flanked by three bodyguards.

The remaining French diplomats gathered at the front of their embassy with their Iraqi staff, many of whom had arrived with their wives and children to say goodbye. A young Iraqi woman in her twenties cupped her face in her hands as she wept, while her father was hugged by one of the French diplomats, who was trying to maintain his composure. He said nothing, but instead held his Iraqi friend tightly, before pulling back to look at him, and then slowly walking away. Once all belongings had been packed in the cars for the drive out of Iraq, the metal embassy gates were banged shut and padlocked. In the chaos that followed the fall of the city, the French Embassy and the French Cultural Centre were ransacked and vandalized by looters.

By 19 March the trappings of war had appeared on the city's streets as Bush's forty-eight-hour ultimatum for Saddam Hussein and his sons to leave the country drew to a close. Traffic police at the main roundabouts and intersections now wore metal helmets and carried AK-47s. Trenches had been dug by the side of roads and sandbagged positions and bunkers could be seen throughout the city. For the first time there were long, anxious queues of cars and lorries at virtually all central petrol stations. We returned to our office at the ministry to strip everything that we could from the room which had been our base for six years: tables, bookcases, hundreds of archive tapes filmed in Iraq and endless yards of cabling. The officials of the ministry were doing the same thing. Near the entrance of the Press Centre dozens of computers, hundreds of boxes, files and computer disks were ready to be taken out of the ministry building.

By late afternoon Baghdad was a ghost town, a city without people. The last frenzied moments of stocking up on bandages, painkillers, candles, kerosene and diesel, biscuits and water had passed. Doctors at the main hospitals reported that the wards had been cleared of all but the most urgent cases. Paul, Killa and I drove up and down Saadoun Street on the eastern bank of the Tigris, past the lines of chemists, electrical shops and food stores. None was open. We were the only people along a road that would usually have been filled with thousands of evening shoppers, people returning from work, children going home. Doors had been pad-locked, and some shop owners had placed wooden boards across them in the hope that they might deflect a bomb blast. I counted about four or five cars in the space of fifteen minutes, speeding past and not stopping for the traffic lights – a sight rarely witnessed before in the tightly controlled busy Baghdad roads. Three Ba'ath Party militiamen, easily identifiable by their distinctive green uniform without the epaulettes or regimental insignia of regular soldiers, were standing in the doorways of an office block on the other side of the street, clearly using the building as a lookout post. Darkness was approaching, the last light of Baghdad's final afternoon of peace ebbed away. I finished recording my piece to camera and we packed up the equipment in silence. We drove down Saadoun Street into Firdoos Square, opposite the Palestine Hotel, the shuttered and locked shop fronts gliding past.

It was hard to know what to say. Even harder to think of what to do. Malek and Killa had set up their cameras along the balcony of our suite. Duncan had done the same thing in his room four storeys directly above us on the seventeenth floor. Throughout the night they would get up to inspect their cameras, peering through the viewfinder, adjusting the framing and exposure of the Baghdad skyline. The satellite radio, tuned in to the BBC

World Service, had now been given over to round-the-clock broadcasting. 'With a little over seven hours to go until President Bush's ultimatum for Saddam Hussein and his sons to leave Iraq expires, Germany's Foreign Minister, Joska Fischer, says . . .' I can only describe it as an empty feeling. There is little to feel as you wait for a war to start. We watched the final seconds disappear before the spell under which the city had existed for so long was shattered.

The radio reported that American armoured divisions had already entered the demilitarized zone between the Kuwaiti and Iraqi borders, that columns of tanks and armoured personnel carriers were pouring through huge gaps along the wire fence marking the strip of no-man's land which had been cut the previous day. Paul checked the antennae for our satellite phones and made sure their batteries were fully powered. A row of dark-blue flak jackets and helmets hung from pegs on the wall of the suite, each with a strip of tape bearing our names and blood groups. Paul Wood sat in the next-door room with his computer on his lap, typing out a dispatch for Radio 4's news bulletins, a torch lamp strapped around his forehead in readiness for a power failure. Tiredness began to drain us. By midnight some of us tried to get some rest, for an hour or so. I slumped on to a sofa in the suite and closed my eyes. I slept for about twenty minutes.

It began a little after 5 a.m., a long melancholic note that fluctu-ated in pitch and intensity. Baghdad was still swathed in darkness, the first glimmer of dawn yet to show itself. The deadline had passed an hour before. Across the west of Baghdad, the orange and white street lights illuminated the desolate streets of the city. If a city could speak, if it could cry out 'Stop! Do not do this!', this cry would come in the form of the mournful lament of air-raid sirens. It is a dreadful sound that turns the marrow in your bones to ice. The sirens seemed to be coming from several points across the capital. Each one would begin with a single blast of sound that would climb slowly like the howl of a dog, before falling, only to rise again. Seconds later came the metallic clatter of anti-aircraft guns. The tracer fire leapt into the air from their barrels, slowing down as it arced across the sky. It seemed to hang there like tiny stars before burning out. The batteries across the river joined the assault – the gunners nervously firing staccato bursts, more to overcome their fear, one felt, than because they thought they would hit something.

Within a few short minutes the first specks of daylight broke on the horizon. To the horrible wail from the sirens was added the plaintive call of the muezzins, as if the very city was beseeching God for help. For about ten minutes the loudspeakers from the mosque in Firdoos Square nearby carried the voice of the imam. The same phrase was repeated again and again: '*Allahu Akbar, Allahu Akbar, la illaha il Allah.*' God is Mighty, God is Mighty. There is no God but Allah. It was a call for salvation as well as an act of defiance, telling the city's people that the war had finally begun.

From the outskirts of the capital we could hear a distant thudding sound, muffled and irregular. It must have been about 5.45 a.m. when we saw the first explosions. One came from the far south-west of the city. A dark blue column of dust rose up and then burst into a ball of bright orange flame. As the fiery glow subsided, a dark mushroom plume grew and ascended into the cold air of dawn. Killa and Malek scanned the horizon with their cameras, lenses gliding from left to right and back again. Then we heard a familiar voice through the speaker of the satellite radio. It spoke softly and deliberately, dwelling on each word: 'My fellow citizens, at this hour American and coalition forces are in the early stages of military operations to disarm Iraq, to free its people and to defend the world from grave danger.'

Paul shouted for everyone to remain quiet for a moment, as he turned up the volume to hear George W. Bush's voice from the Oval Office. The American President sounded calm in his effort to reassure his countrymen. There would be no going back now. He said that selected targets were being attacked in the 'opening stages of what will be a broad and concerted campaign'. He warned that war could be longer and more difficult than some had predicted, but added ominously that it would not be fought with 'half measures'. The sound of two more explosions burst into the room. Closer this time and not muffled. The hollow cracking of the detonations lingered for a few seconds.

President Bush's voice, as clear as if he were in the next room, continued, 'We come to Iraq with respect for its citizens, for their great civilization and for the religious faiths they practise. We have no ambition in Iraq, except to remove a threat and restore control of that country to its own people.' He repeated his claim that the United States had chosen to go to war 'reluctantly' against what he called the 'outlaw regime' – pronouncing the word 'outlaw' with particular Texan relish – because, he argued, this regime threatened the peace enjoyed by America and its allies with 'weapons of mass murder'. He tried to embolden the American people. 'We will pass through this time of peril,' he told them, 'and carry on the work of peace.' And then, bizarrely, nothing. Just silence and emptiness. We waited for the thunderclap, the unleashing of the fury that the Pentagon had promised in the form of hundreds of cruise missiles in the first forty-eight hours of the war. Nothing. Dawn had given way to day, and save for the wispy clouds of smoke from the earlier explosions, the Baghdad skyline looked unchanged.

I went downstairs. The lobby of the Palestine Hotel was buzzing with journalists and ministry officials. I stepped out of the lobby with Duncan and Luai and walked towards Abu Nuwas Street, which ran along the side of the river, across from the Republican Palace. One car drove by, then another, as I recorded a piece to camera. Looking back at the tape my puffy eyes betray my bewilderment. It didn't feel like a city in the eye of a firestorm. Was Saddam dead? Had the regime been 'decapitated' in an 'opportunistic strike on a leadership compound' as the radio reports from Washington were telling us? The Shabab channel, controlled by Saddam Hussein's eldest son, Uday, was still on air, playing non-stop footage of the Iraqi armed forces and commandos. The newsreader read out a statement that could only have come from the mouth of Uday. In a voice full of portent he reported his condemnation of the 'offspring of whores and bastards' who had come to 'pillage the wealth of noble Iraq'.

The television screen cut from the announcer, dressed in military uniform, to a close shot of Saddam Hussein, also dressed in uniform and with a black beret on his head, sitting in a chair in a windowless room, with nothing but a dark curtain behind him. He held a document in his hand, and most surprisingly was wearing a pair of large black-rimmed reading glasses – surprising because he had never been seen in public in glasses before and it seemed an odd moment to choose to wear them for the first time. He may have been a hunted man, but his swagger had not disappeared. He left no doubt that he had survived the attempt to assassinate him. To prove this point, in his opening remark he referred to the exact moment when the bombardment had begun. 'With the dawn prayer today,' he said, 'the reckless criminal, Bush Junior, and his henchmen carried out their crime with which they had been threatening Iraq and humanity. Bush's criminal deed is supported by those who sided with him. Thus, he and his followers have perpetrated further crimes to be added to the series of their despicable crimes against Iraq and humanity.' As was usual for such an address, he spoke in high classical Arabic, which at this moment seemed to mirror the self-important style of his opposite number, the American President. 'These days will humiliate the infidels, the enemies of God and humanity. You will triumph, O Iraqis, and with you the sons of your Arab nation will also triumph.' He depicted the battle as though it were part of an ancient struggle being fought with sabres and cavalry, rather than satellite-guided munitions. 'Unsheathe your sword, fearless and intrepid,' he bellowed. 'Unsheathe your sword so that Satan might witness it. Unsheathe your sword because the enemy has massed his forces.'

Then he spoke to the outside world, particularly to Arab and Islamic nations who had overwhelmingly opposed the war: 'O friends and those who resist evil in the world, peace be upon you. You have noticed how the reckless Bush disregarded your positions and views that you voiced against the war and disregarded your true calls for peace. He has perpetrated his macabre deed today. We pledge to you in our name, the name of the leadership and the name of the Iraqi people and Iraq's heroic army, in the Iraq of civilization, faith and history, that we will resist the invaders. God is great. May the lowly ones be accursed. Long live Iraq. Long live Iraq. Long live jihad and Palestine.' He was not gone, and he would fight to the end. Or so he clearly believed.

6. Siege

Before the war, I had presumed that Baghdad would become a vast armed camp, ruthlessly controlled by the regime's enormous array of military and intelligence agencies who would smash any murmur of dissent. The reality from the first put paid to this notion, and in the throes of the war there were no tanks on the streets, no checkpoints, no curfew or blackouts after dark. Baghdad remained a remarkably open city.

Abu Nuwas Street, by the side of the river, took us down towards the Joumhouriya Bridge to the western side of the capital. We had the windows of the car open so that we could listen out for anything in the sky above us. Khalil kept a steady speed, as we scanned the road ahead. Tahrir Square, a vast roundabout in the commercial heart of the city, was entirely empty save for the small flocks of plump pigeons sitting on the wide billboards advertising Turkish-made TV sets and great tubs of household paint. Three policemen, wearing pathetic, flimsy tin helmets, the sagging pouches around their waists holding magazines for their old AK-47s, sat smoking on stools in the doorway of a barricaded shop. We waved, and they waved back. One of them smirked, as if to say 'Those crazy westerners. Not only do they stay behind in Baghdad, they start driving around the city as soon as the war starts.'

Unsurprisingly there wasn't a single person to be found in the area by the gate of the Republican Palace, and without any prompting from us Khalil sped up as soon as we got close. This was not a safe place to hang around. We passed the public park in front of the Iranian Embassy, where a few more policemen peered out of the foxholes they had dug by the makeshift football fields where young boys used to congregate in the evenings before the war. The policemen were more animated now that it was daytime, no doubt not looking forward to what the night would bring.

Like the port of an island in the middle of a quiet, empty sea the Ministry of Information was noisy and full of life. The small number of remaining journalists rushed about, searching for information on a rumour that the authorities were laying on a guided bus trip around the city. Some were clutching video tapes to be taken for editing or transmitting, others were scribbling notes. The senior officials of the Press Centre no longer donned their suits and jackets, but instead, like their military counterparts, now dressed in the green uniforms they had been ordered to wear once the war started. The minders seemed pleased that this directive was limited to their bosses and that they weren't forced to abandon their usual attire.

By mid-morning life tentatively began to emerge on to the streets. One car. Then a little later several more, and even a few people, walking warily down Haifa Street in front of the Ministry of Information. Everyone in the city seemed similarly baffled; the pummelling that had been predicted had so far not materialized.

This fact was not lost on the Minister of Information, Mohammed Said al Sahaff. A few hours into this first day of war, after the air-raid sirens had signalled the all clear, we were urgently marshalled into a press conference. Al Sahaff, a short and stocky man with a long jowly face, had been Iraq's Foreign Minister for much of the 1990s, a role which he had clearly relished and which he had much preferred to the post he now occupied, which would make him an international celebrity, though not in the way he would have liked. He had a deep suspicion of journalists, which at times bordered on loathing, and which was just about the only thing he shared with his western political counterparts. Very direct and usually aggressive, he had an unpredictable temper and his expression was permanently tense, his fuse about to blow at any moment. As the world was to discover, his bulletins to the daily press gatherings were idiosyncratic to say the least.

We shuffled into the atrium of a building adjacent to the Press Centre where a podium had been set up for the minister. About a hundred reporters and cameramen pushed and shoved and took up every inch of space along the stairwell, balcony and floor. The

minister appeared before us in his black beret, green uniform
tightly stretched over his gently rotund paunch, a leather holster
prominently displaying the handle of his handgun. He started as he
meant to go on, full of bluster and spitting scorn for both the British
and American governments. Although he spoke English reasonably
well, it could not do justice to all he wanted to say, and so his
speeches were delivered in comically mangled grammar that I
suspect reminded most British viewers of a character from a 1970s
sitcom. He made some bizarre observations and spoke, in this age
of political spin, in a way that few modern politicians do. For us
then he was – as he is now – a figure of amusement. But for many
people around the world he appeared very differently. While he
spoke in broken English to a bemused western audience, he'd
speak Arabic to the Arab TV stations in Baghdad as he addressed
sympathetic Middle Eastern audiences who were overwhelmingly
opposed to the war. His performances were being seen from two
opposing perspectives. Were we just laughing at his poor English?
What if it had been Tariq Aziz who had said these things – with
his flawless English and knowledge of how the western media
worked? Would we have been laughing then, or would we have
found it just a little unnerving?

Al Sahaff was asked if the first missile strikes had indeed been an
attempt to assassinate the Iraqi leadership. 'I am sure that they are
stupid,' he said, 'and that they will never succeed. But it proves
that they are criminals and killers, and that they believe in assassina-
tion. They are stupid and criminals.' He came across as remarkably
self-assured. No wonder. It had been predicted, after all, that his
government would implode within a matter of days after the first
onslaught. He betrayed the self-satisfaction which must have been
spreading within the regime at that point. In the first Gulf War they
had survived more than a month of aerial bombardment and the
Iraqi leadership were clearly beginning to think they could with-
stand the same again, if the first night of attacks was anything to go
by. Al Sahaff was asked a question about what Iraq could do in the
face of a superior military force. 'Our reaction has not started yet.
You will see,' he said. 'In 1991 we saw a much larger scale of

military action than we have seen now. We can absorb all the
military threats.'

The chasm between the perception of the threat and the reality
of the dangers facing the Iraqis was clear in this speech. This chasm
seemed only to widen when about forty reporters, cameramen and
photographers, accompanied by four officials from the Press Centre,
were taken on a tour around the city in a bus identical to a tourist
sightseeing bus – 'to see that everything is normal and under
control', as the director of the Press Centre put it. The destinations
had been pre-selected by the Ministry of Information to show only
the effects of the bombing on civilian targets. The streets were
empty and there was little evidence of the ancient, rusting cars and
lorries which used to line the roads; no sign of the woodsmoke that
usually drifted from the dingy kitchens of the roadside restaurants;
no sound of screeching, tinny music from the electrical shops and
ladies' fashion houses. All of that was gone. War had robbed
Baghdad of the things that had allowed it to reveal its true identity
beyond the image of it that was tied to the regime. It was like a
different city. This wartime Baghdad looked like a Stalinist nirvana
of wide avenues and stark utilitarian apartment blocks resembling
vast concrete pill boxes. Like a group of mesmerized western
tourists visiting an historical ruin, we gazed out of the windows
and pointed when we saw ordinary Iraqis on the streets, or a group
of desultory middle-aged civil defence guards sitting behind hastily
built sandbagged positions.

The bus came to a stop outside the entrance of the Al Kindi
Hospital. The doctors and nurses courteously escorted us through
the corridors of the hospital, which at first seemed worryingly
quiet. We all trooped into one of the wards, where a young woman
lay on a bed. Both her legs were heavily bandaged but blotches of
blood still seeped through the white gauze. The doctor told us that
she had been wounded by shrapnel but that she would be okay.
'We know this is just the beginning,' he added. Several photographers and cameramen stood close to her bed, trying to take her
picture quickly to avoid prolonging her embarrassment. She looked
at us, and returned the gaze of the camera lenses with a dignified

stare. It was hard not to feel uneasy as we stood around her bed. All of us had been in this kind of position too many times, in other places around the world where we had witnessed what war does to innocent civilians. Once the pictures have been dutifully taken and the words spoken by doctors and relatives recorded in notebooks, there is very little you can say as you walk away from a hospital bed. But in this instance what was most surprising, and further deepened my sense of unease, was that nobody there said anything recriminatory to the many among us who were British and American journalists. Nothing at all. Neither the doctors nor the wounded nor the other patients in the hospital addressed a single word of anger towards us.

It was to be this way throughout the war. Most of the Iraqis we met had this same extraordinary capacity to distinguish between individuals and their government. Perhaps they recognized the difference in themselves and this was a silent acknowledgement of their desire for an end to the tyranny that had blighted their lives for decades. I briefly shook the doctor's hand as I left and thanked him for his time. He smiled gently and said, 'Welcome, please!'

Now the war had begun, the city felt truly isolated. With no access to satellite television we had no idea how the war was going elsewhere, even if, when I called my wife and children in South Africa, the powerful satellite phone made them sound as though they were only in the next street. Psychologically, they felt a million miles away. I listened to the reports and descriptions of colleagues embedded with British and American forces in southern Iraq, or on the very battleships from which the cruise missiles hitting Baghdad had been fired, with only a vague picture of what was happening in the southern deserts of the country. We were trapped in this city under fire and had no way of seeing the picture in Iraq as a whole. If this made us feel nervous and claustrophobic, it made the people who lived in Baghdad even more so, particularly as many of them had homes and family outside the reaches of the capital. Like the rest of the city, each day we could only wait for that night's onslaught, while all the time we imagined the force of an army a quarter of a million strong, with the most destructive weapons at its disposal, hurtling towards us.

As dusk was drawing in on that first day of the war we began to pack up our equipment in our tent on the roof of the Ministry of Information. We had moved much of our equipment into the Palestine Hotel, but the Press Centre would not allow TV news organizations to take their satellite dishes there. It was also stipulated that we could not take our satellite telephones to the hotel either, but most journalists ignored this and hid phones in their hotel rooms. No reporter dared stay in a government building after dark. By late afternoon, the front of the Press Centre was clogged with vehicles, their side doors and boots open as journalists crammed themselves and their equipment inside before driving nervously back to the hotel. The lobby of the Palestine had become a make-shift extension of the Press Centre and housed a row of desks, on one of which a handwritten placard read 'Press Centre Information Desk'. The director of the Press Centre had taken over one of the offices near the hotel's restaurant, which used to belong to a travel company in the days when tourists rather than British and American soldiers wanted to visit Baghdad. The thick haze of cigarette smoke had shifted from the Press Centre to the lobby's atrium as the minders lolled about on sofas, cigarettes permanently dangling from their fingers. Behind the concierge's counter, four reception-ists darted back and forth between the pigeonholes handing out room keys.

It was odd to see the Palestine functioning like a normal hotel in these extraordinary circumstances. Some journalists handed their keys in to the concierge every morning before setting out for a day's work, just as they might have done on holiday. Until the very last days of the war, the hotel staff would appear each morning at the door of our hotel rooms to inquire whether we needed the beds made up. On one occasion I'd left the door of my room open while on air with BBC radio. I had begun a live broadcast when there was a knock at the door and I turned to see one of the hotel staff waiting on the threshold. I was halfway through describing the overnight bombing of Baghdad and couldn't stop, so I beckoned the man over but gestured for him to keep silent while I finished. He dutifully waited until I had stopped talking, then offered me the crisp white towel he was holding and said, 'We have some clean towels, but only a few because the laundry machines aren't working very well. Would you like one?'

The first strikes of the morning had been light; we worried about what the night might bring. When darkness fell the street lights came on all over the city – as they had done on the first night of the first Gulf War. Looking out from our balcony we saw the wide roads and avenues, government buildings, presidential compounds and bridges shining clearly in the night as thousands of street lamps lit up the city in a blaze of orange and white. This may have been merely an attempt by the regime to keep up appearances. But it may also have been the realization that a blackout could be used as cover by small teams of coalition forces to drop secretly into the capital. And also, if, as was expected, the allies bombed electricity supplies, the regime could then accuse the coalition of targeting the civilian infrastructure.

Shortly before 9 a.m. the air-raid sirens wailed their dreadful sound across the city again. It was hard to believe that only twenty-four hours earlier I had driven through the empty streets of Baghdad on the last night of peace in the city. It was the end of the first full day of the war, and yet it felt much longer. Then the anti-aircraft guns started up. The rounds burst in the sky, pricking the darkness with their bright sparks. The Iraqi gunners again seemed to be firing more for effect than anything else. Their salvoes were followed by a momentary stillness. Like us, they must have noticed the absence of the roar of jet engines. They unloosed another aimless barrage. Then came the first massive detonation. I was standing behind Malek, who was filming from the balcony. As I turned to walk back into the room I felt the blast, as if someone had pushed me hard from behind. There was a deafening crack. 'Jesus!' I heard someone yell. About a mile away, on the western side of the Joumhouriya Bridge, the Ministry of Planning, a wide, purple, flat-fronted edifice, was engulfed in thick smoke. Flames lashed out of the windows of a smaller building in the same compound. A huge black mushroom cloud rose above the wreckage before drifting along the bank of the Tigris.

As more bombs exploded, fire and smoke smashed through the streets across the river, where the most important buildings of Saddam Hussein's state were located. This central government area stretched for about three miles along the western bank of the Tigris and was about two miles deep. It was now overwhelmed by torrents of heavy smoke. An ambulance raced across the Sinak Bridge, about half a mile further down the river from the Joumhouriya Bridge, the light on its roof flashing red and white. Minutes later there were two further explosions that seemed to come from the far western edge of the enormous compound that housed the Republican Palace. By now the thick black smoke had almost completely enveloped the western bank of the Tigris, obscuring all the buildings on that side of the river. All the while the anti-aircraft gunners continued their nervous and disjointed firings into the air against an enemy they could neither see nor hear, nor reach with their weak, old weapons. It must have lasted about forty-five minutes and amid it all, from the loudspeakers of the 14th of Ramadan* Mosque, on the other side of Firdoos Square, came the unbroken melancholy chant of the imam. Over and over, his undulating tenor voice cried out: 'Allah is mighty, Allah is mighty.' After the explosions from the bombing had ended, the sky was still intermittently lit by tracer rounds from distant anti-aircraft guns. I don't remember hearing the all-clear air-raid siren. The air war had finally come to the heart of Baghdad.

In the early hours of the morning the city seemed remarkably peaceful, at first showing no trace of what had happened only a few hours earlier. The palls of smoke had dissipated and were transformed into a line of smog, so familiar to the skies above cities in the developing world. The streets were completely deserted and

---

* Ramadan is a month in the Islamic lunar calendar. The 14th of Ramadan Mosque, its dome distinctively inlaid in a green and blue mosaic, became a familiar feature of international broadcasts from the roof of the Palestine Hotel.

the people who huddled in their homes knew that the bombardment could only intensify. All the initial talk of 'limited opportunistic strikes' was now meaningless.

From my notebook – 21 March 2003

The first Friday of the war. No chance yet to meet/talk to Iraqi conscripts
or soldiers. Probably anathema to such a regime especially during war.
May be possible during Friday prayers. Very weird thinking of those
pilots flying overhead – and conscripts manning anti-aircraft guns. Can't
see each other but are attempting to kill each other. Driving back to hotel
from Ministry at dusk worst bit. Relief amongst all when we reach car
park of Palestine. More spooks in hotel, the real gangster types, snappy
suits & creepy manner – checking rooms of journos to see who has
satphones stashed away.★ Already starting to lose sense of time. Seems
like 4 days but today is only second full day of war. Bound to get heavier
now after last night. Everybody anticipating this.

I was eager to meet ordinary Iraqi conscripts, if only to be able to
see their faces. I wanted to talk to the men who had to man those
hopelessly inadequate guns each night, looking up to the sky and
wondering whether that night would be the one that would mark
their end. What did they think they were defending? Their city?
The regime? Or just themselves? And I wanted to see if in their
faces there was any sign of the strange process they were living
through; engaging other young men in a horrifying yet faceless air
war over the skies of Baghdad. There was something disturbing
about the notion of young men confronting the awful intimacy of
death without being able to see who was attacking them.
    We decided to go to the small mosque opposite the ministry,
beside the Sinak Bridge, to film Friday prayers. There were several

---

★ The Iraqi authorities were obsessed with satellite telephones as they were the
one form of communication that was difficult to control or monitor. Many of
them feared that journalists were talking to intelligence contacts in the West and
thus helping the coalition in their war strategy.

anti-aircraft batteries in the vicinity and a group of soldiers and policemen had been billeted in the government-run shopping arcade across the road from the mosque. I assumed that some of them would attend Friday prayers, so we walked there about half an hour before the main prayer at noon. The mosque was a modest place and could not have been much more than fifty years old, despite the ornate blue and yellow painted tiles on its dome in imitation of the mosques in the older parts of the city. The entrance from the street led into a small concrete courtyard and on the right was the mosque itself, which could probably hold about 150 worshippers. It was already full by the time we arrived, and the staff had laid out four long rows of rush matting in the courtyard to accommodate the overspill. There were lines of dark green uniforms, with the occasional splash of colour from the shirts and jackets of civilians among the congregation of soldiers. All the space along the steps from the courtyard to the entrance to the mosque was taken up by soldiers. The imam was giving his sermon before the main prayers and the men sat close together wherever they could find room. On the steps a middle-aged soldier propped himself up against a pillar and looked warily at the sky as he listened to the preacher's words. At the back of the courtyard a younger soldier, still wearing his gun in his holster, sat cross-legged, his arms resting on his knees. The small red triangle on the lapels of the uniforms indicated that most of the young men were from the Republican Guard.

The sermon did not stray beyond officially sanctioned guidelines as it called on the faithful to fight and repel the infidel invasion. But there was no bombast either. It was a sermon intended for those who had come to seek reflection and hope for some kind of salvation. 'God will not abandon you,' the imam told the worshippers. 'He is just and strong in fighting for those who believe. Those who fight for their land and their faith will not be abandoned by Him.' He called them to prayer, and they stood as he read the first lines of the Fatiha, the opening verse of the Koran: 'In the name of Allah, the beneficent, the merciful. All praise is due to Allah, the Lord of the Worlds, the beneficent, the merciful, the master of the Day of Judgement. We serve Thee and we beseech Thee for help.' At the end of the worship, the imam led them in their prayers to God. The congregation held their hands aloft and, with their eyes closed, they repeated the words of the preacher calling on God: 'Show us the path of courage and strength . . . provide protection and sustenance to the people of Baghdad, the Iraqi people and Muslims everywhere . . . strike down the criminals who have attacked and invaded this Muslim country . . . Amen!' The worshippers brought their cupped hands to their faces in the traditional gesture of offering their prayers up to God.

As they rose from the ground at the end of the service, I approached some of the soldiers to ask if they would speak to me. Many of them walked past, shaking their heads, eyes fixed on the dusty ground. Finally a short young man, in his mid-thirties agreed. His name was Mwafiq Dhiab, a member of the Republican Guard and an anti-aircraft gunner, 'but of course I cannot tell you where', he said. Other soldiers began to crowd round to listen to what he had to say. I asked him about his experiences during the nightly attacks. At first he sounded like a pre-recorded propaganda tape issued by the regime: 'We welcome the chance to die for our country and our mujahid leader President Saddam Hussein . . . death for one's country is an honour deserving of paradise.' He began to look unnerved by the increasing number of people who were gathering around us – other soldiers and officers, a French TV crew who wanted to listen to what he had to say – and he was no doubt also unsettled by the presence of Luai, who he knew was a minder. His eyes darted round the crowd of faces and I could see that his hands were shaking. He touched the red triangle insignia on his shoulder. 'You see this badge? The words on it say "Allah is Great". All of us manning the anti-aircraft guns [during the bombing the previous night] chanted "How sweet victory will be with the help of God".' I ended the interview by thanking him and began to walk out of the courtyard.

As the crowd around us melted away, and he headed slowly for the door, I went over to him again and said that I wanted to get the correct spelling of his name. While I was writing it down, I asked him how his colleagues were coping with the bombardment. 'They are strong,' he said, then looking down, he muttered softly, 'but many of them are young. This is their first war. God willing we will all be safe.' He cut off mid-sentence, not wanting to draw attention to himself any more. Then he smiled weakly and said he had to go.

When we arrived back at the Press Centre we found senior officials pacing up and down the car park. 'Hurry, there is a press conference with His Excellency the Minister and another senior minister. You must come!' one of them barked. As Luai had told me before the war began, the regime desperately wanted and needed western journalists to stay and report the war from Baghdad. They knew there would be civilian casualties but they also knew that no one would believe their reports of civilian deaths if there were no journalists to verify them. The authorities were also keen to show they were still around and to refute the idea of 'regime change' by their daily appearance on television. As a result, at eleven o'clock each morning, whether there was anything to report or not, there was a press conference at the Ministry of Information which we were all strongly encouraged to attend. The conferences became known to western journalists as 'the eleven o'clock follies' – a reference to 'the five o'clock follies' of the American military briefings of the Vietnam War.

I had been at the mosque only an hour before and the scene at the Press Centre was a jarring transition. The Minister of Information, Mohammed Said al Sahaff, was standing behind the podium. By his side was the Minister of the Interior, Mahmud Dhiyab al Ahmed. The post he held in the regime said it all, and the way he conducted himself in front of the cameras, some of which were broadcasting his antics live across the world, confirmed that, as his title suggested, he was one of the regime's real gangsters. He shouted into the microphones, as if threatening the journalists and possibly even the viewers thousands of miles away. As he did so he waved a silver-plated Kalashnikov rifle in the air, occasionally casting its barrel in an arc in the direction of the stunned crowd of journalists, some of whom were looking down in an attempt to conceal their laughter. He never took his finger off the trigger. The minister also carried a hunting knife and wore a vest with special compartments for magazines for his rifle. 'The Iraqi people have sworn that they will not give up their guns to the invaders,' he yelled. 'I have a son who is eighteen, and he is also armed, and we will sacrifice ourselves for President Saddam Hussein and his family, I tell you.' For once the Minister of Information had to take second place in this bizarre display.

Paul, Killa, Luai and I headed across the Tigris to the northwest of the city by an elaborate route which took us across the Sab'atash Tamuz Bridge by the side of the Ministry of Defence. The brown-brick maze of buildings which made up the ministry looked intact and had not yet been bombed – it lay in a densely populated civilian district. Close by was Rashid Street, home of my favourite teashop, shuttered and virtually empty now, save for the few clusters of policemen sitting on rickety chairs in front of the barricaded shops beneath the colonnades. Killa set up his camera down a side alley which was shrouded in darkness. I couldn't see what had grabbed his attention. One of the policemen came over to us, but only to ask if we had any cigarettes. Dylan gave him the remainder of his packet and without a further word he walked back to his friends. At the end of the dark alley, silhouetted against the light, was a row of thick metal bars. Beyond them on the other side of the street stood a large statue of Saddam Hussein, proudly resplendent in his Field Marshal's uniform. Dylan saw what Killa was filming and chuckled. He put his wrists together in imaginary shackles. '*Mahabiss*,' he said quietly in Arabic. Prisoner.

We filed our report and Paul instructed me, Paul Wood and Andrew Gilligan not to accept any more requests from London to do further telephone interviews because we needed to get off the streets quickly. 'I want to pack everything up from this roof and get back to the hotel,' he said. The BBC's foreign news desk had told him there was a lot of attention being focused on RAF Fairford in Gloucestershire, from where B-52 bombers were taking off to fly to Baghdad. 'The desk mentioned that Nick Childs [the BBC's

Pentagon correspondent] was saying that Pentagon briefings were hinting at a new shift in the bombing strategy,' Paul said, adding that it would take the B-52s about six hours to reach Iraq, and so they were only a couple of hours away. The planes could easily have been heading for targets outside Baghdad, but it focused our minds, as B-52s – infamous since being used in the carpet-bombing of Vietnam – were bad news and there was no point in taking any chances. Word of the planes had reached all the other journalists and there was a more urgent quality to that afternoon's evacuation of the Press Centre. We left for the hotel to wait nervously for the attack.

That night I was walking down the hotel corridor talking to John F. Burns of the *New York Times*. When we reached his room, he opened the door, then stopped. 'What was that?' he said with a startled look. 'It's started.' I ran down the darkened stairwell counting the landings to the thirteenth floor. The anti-aircraft batteries were firing ferociously. The blasts from the batteries were incessant, altogether different from the nervous faltering barrages of the previous nights. Barely inside the door to our suite, I felt the first massive explosion from the other side of the river. The sliding doors to the balconies and the window panes rattled violently as the whole room shook. Crouching behind the balcony wall I saw the mighty black cloud of ash and debris cascade through the air, the bright red embers from the explosion mingling in the smoke. Across the still brightly lit horizon of Baghdad there was nothing but a rush of tracer fire from the anti-aircraft guns. The Republican Palace, the titanic structure that was at the heart of Saddam Hussein's symbols of power, had already been hit. The black smoke drifted across the vast complex of heavily protected and reinforced security buildings and the even larger number of lavish residential compounds. The Republican Palace was less than half a mile from my balcony on the opposite side of the Tigris. To the north of it, in an area stretching for perhaps two miles, was the heart of Saddam's regime. We gazed out at the ministries, intelligence and security offices, leadership installations and Ba'ath Party compounds as they were hit again and again. Buildings that had been erected at such great expense, with such vainglory, and that represented a quarter of a century of insufferable cruelty were being destroyed in seconds in front of our eyes.

I tried to describe what I was witnessing as I stood and sometimes crouched on the balcony gripping the satellite phone that was connected to the BBC in London. The footage from that night cannot hope to capture the extent of the destruction. For even Baghdad, a city more accustomed to air strikes than almost any other in the world in recent years, had never experienced anything like this before. Three ear-splitting explosions ripped into a compound behind the Ministry of Planning. Moments later I watched four brightly shining dots hurtling in a straight line from the sky. A surge of adrenaline hurtled my senses into a heightened state. Then came a series of blinding flashes as the fireballs obliterated everything in their range. I felt my body tighten in anticipation of the waves from the blast. They arrived seconds later with a terrifying wall of noise. It was the noise more than anything else. A shattering roar that makes you afraid to move. A few miles beyond the Republican Palace, out towards the west, I saw the crossed swords of the Hands of Victory monument and the tall thin Baghdad clock tower silhouetted against a huge column of smoke that flickered with a deep orange glow from the fires below it. The whole city was swathed in a canopy of smoke. Mushroom clouds were everywhere. Building after building ablaze, disappearing in cauldrons of fire and ash. Such was the ferocity of it all that within one five-minute period I counted at least thirty strikes. I kept talking to the BBC news presenters in London, who were watching live, trying as hard as I could to convey the sheer violence, the thunderous noise which rumbled through every street and avenue of the city, and the terrifying sight of plumes of debris being hurled at least 300 feet into the air. The fury was so spellbinding that it defied instant description. The ramparts of the main edifice of the Republican Palace were crowned at their apex with a series of huge bronze busts modelled on Saddam Hussein, in the guise of Saladin, the ancient conqueror of Jerusalem. The busts were lit up by another series of ferocious explosions that threw a wall of smashed concrete and masonry hundreds of feet above the roofs of the city while Saddam's sullen face, immortalized in bronze, looked out at the destruction of all that represented him. The windows of our hotel rooms, even though we had reinforced them with blast-proofing tape, shuddered.

The architects of this night of 'Shock and Awe', as it was described, knew full well that many of the buildings they had selected for such punishment had long been evacuated. They were the last places on earth that Saddam Hussein and his commanders would stay during the war. But the targeting owed more to political factors than military considerations. This was meant as an act of humiliation to show Iraqis and the rest of the world how easily the symbols of Saddam Hussein's power could be obliterated. The destruction was so spectacular, so infused with rage, that it could only have been meant to show the world that the regime was being offered no escape.

As swiftly as this firestorm had rained down from the sky, suddenly it was over and the heart of the city fell into a stunned trance. Car alarms shrieked through the stillness – the only sound, apart from the occasional cold clatter from an anti-aircraft gun. My ears whined. We stood staring blankly at each other. Paul told us to take it in turns on one of the satellite phones to ring our relatives. 'They don't know where the Palestine Hotel is in Baghdad and they may have just seen all that on television and are probably feeling fucking petrified about us,' he said. The screaming of car alarms continued as Baghdad's night air choked on the dust and smoke.

I found it hard to sleep that night, convinced that the bombing would start again. Morning couldn't come soon enough. The following day, contrary to what many of us expected from the Iraqi regime, there appeared to be no attempt to present a wildly inflated official assessment of civilian casualties from the previous night's ferocious bombing. The Minister of Information, Mohammed Said al Sahaff, said three civilians had been killed and over 200 injured, a figure the Red Cross said they believed was accurate.

Journalists were taken to the Yarmouk General Hospital, where most of the injured were being treated, a significant number of them women and children. It was clear to all the journalists that the wounds and severe burns they saw were consistent with injury from bombing. One young boy, his head swathed in a large bandage, screamed with fright as he stared out at the banks of television cameras. A young and beautiful girl, no more than thirteen years old, had both her arms and one of her legs wrapped in thick strips of white gauze. Her mother lovingly and gently swept back a lock of her thick black hair that had fallen in front of her eyes. A man in his mid-fifties was panting quickly, as a large bandage was wound round the middle of his stomach. 'There are multiple shell injuries,' one of the doctors said in a loud voice so that all the reporters could hear. He gesticulated with both hands to emphasize the point. 'There are multiple traumas: to the chest, abdomen, skull and limbs.' If the twenty floors of the Palestine Hotel shook and swayed in the face of the blast waves from those munitions, what chance did those people have who lived in the flimsy mud and brick houses close to the targets that had been blown to pieces?

By late afternoon, something odd had emerged across the skyline. At first I thought it was the result of smouldering buildings from the previous night's attack. Long columns of jet black smoke were emerging from the edges of the city, climbing into the sky like the thick black branches of a tree. They appeared from every direction: three in the south-east, two from the north, four out to the west. The columns twisted upwards until they were dispersed by the gentle breeze into a greyish fog. 'Trenches with oil,' Khalil said as we got into the car, 'for the aeroplanes.' So this was to be how Baghdad would defend itself from the laser- and satellite-guided bombs. The burning of the oil-filled trenches was a pitiful response. Nothing could so have revealed the defenceless and hapless plight in which the city found itself: besieged by an army which professed its desire to liberate it, but still in the grip of a regime that had no way of responding to the aerial onslaught except to unleash these acrid fumes across the capital.

The newsreader on state television looked decidedly uncomfortable in his military uniform. A pen was hanging from one epaulette. His eyes kept flitting back to the statement written out on the sheets in front of him. It seemed that there was no teleprompter to help him deliver the evening news, which meant that he must have been working from a makeshift secret studio. Further proof, if it were needed, that the regime had moved all key instruments of control out of the main buildings and into secret locations. The image cut from the newsreader to show the man at the centre of it all. He looked slightly thinner. An unfamiliar loose clutch of flesh hung from beneath his chin. He was in a dark empty room with a low ceiling – no doubt part of the vast network of underground bunkers he'd obsessively built over the decades. This was now his life. A fugitive living a hidden existence beneath the earth of the city he ruled. How much did he know of what was going on above him? What could he know of the noise and fury being endured by the 4 million other inhabitants of this ancient city? Had he smelt those bitter fumes of the blazing oil trenches? Had he seen the hospitals, the ruined hulks of his cherished buildings?

Some of Saddam's most senior officials, including his son Qusay, the anointed defender of Baghdad, sat with him around a table covered with an enormous map of Iraq. It was supposed to be a scene of military power: a leader in his war rooms, laying sophisticated traps for the invading armies. To Saddam Hussein's right sat the Deputy Prime Minister Tariq Aziz. The screen showed him laughing uproariously. Next to him, somewhat improbably, sat our old friend, the Minister of Information, Mohammed Said al Sahaff. He smiled too, sharing in the joke. As did the Defence Minister, General Sultan Hashim Ahmed, who sat next to al Sahaff.

It was all supposed to have been over for Saddam Hussein by now. It was day four of the war and few Iraqis or outside observers had believed that the regime would survive this long. Perhaps that was why state television had chosen to show Saddam Hussein's ministers grinning around their conference table. They were at the very centre of this war, yet, looking at them on television, they could have been miles away. Iraqis, too, would be watching these images, as they faced another night barricaded in their homes, wondering whether their stocks of masking tape would last them throughout the coming days and weeks.

These attempts to manipulate the viewers of Iraqi television were almost as ineffective as the regime's efforts to control the information broadcast by the international media. The idea of a highly sophisticated and efficient media censorship machine inhibiting our broadcasts and controlling what we saw was laughable. The Ministry of Information certainly did *try* to control what journalists reported, and it was a propaganda machine. But sophisticated? Efficient? I hardly think so. It was an inefficient blunt instrument that relied on threats. Luai had given up the pretence of trying to see what we were filing. Each night as we returned to the hotel, he would inform us that he was going to his room, say a cheerful 'Good night' and we wouldn't see him until the next morning. Paul once asked him if he was all right in those evenings, particularly during the bombardment, when the boredom of waiting for the attacks could eat into your nerves. 'No, it is okay,' he replied. 'Khalil is staying with me and he has found some beer from a Christian shop. We are fine.'

There was only one occasion when an Iraqi official saw one of my reports before it went to London by satellite. It was on the first day of the war, when the director of the Press Centre informed Paul and myself that 'We are now under attack and at war, so there will now be war censorship.' He instructed one of his deputies to accompany us to the satellite transmission point to view what we were about to send. He checked that we had not filmed key sensitive installations because the Iraqis, rightly, feared that the images would provide western military planners with data showing how accurate their targeting had been, which could be used for what is known as 'bomb damage assessment'. He looked at the film once and paid no attention to the accompanying script, said, 'Okay, thank you,' and walked away. We broadcast our report in full. That was the first and last time that any Iraqi censor had a preview of the reports filed by me or by Paul Wood or Andrew Gilligan throughout the war. Luai was instructed to check our reports, but he told us, 'If anyone asks you if I have checked your reports, say yes.' He never asked to see anything.

Luai was a man who did nothing to hide from us his disillusionment with the system. Like the vast stifled and silent majority of Iraqis, he wanted an end to the cruelty and thuggery that were the hallmarks of the regime he had found himself serving. Once, as we headed towards the Ministry of Information, one of us wondered aloud how long it would be before one of the presidential compounds we had just passed would be home to the new American governor of Iraq. Luai, sitting in the back of the car, laughed and said, 'And the day that they come, I will stay close to you,' and threw his arm round Paul's shoulders. We all laughed but there was a serious point beneath Luai's joke. He would never be loyal to the regime he feared and hated and was not worried about the impending arrival of American troops. But he was an exception. There were many other people working within the Ministry of Information for whom regime change threatened their privileged status. Whereas Luai could foresee exactly what fate lay in store for the regime and was looking forward to its demise, other officials, in a sort of inverse Pavlovian reflex, showed greater zeal in their work as they followed the edicts of the dictatorship even as American ground forces drew closer to Baghdad each day. These were the diehard senior intelligence and secret police officials, the kind of men who feared the wrath and vengeance of ordinary Iraqis once the regime had collapsed, a retribution they knew would not be visited upon lowly minders.

Senior intelligence officials were attached to a small number of journalists of whom the ministry was particularly suspicious. CNN had been assigned one as a minder several weeks before the war. He rarely left their side and was always present whenever I visited CNN's office, watching their every movement and transmission. Fearing that the Ministry of Information would be bombed the CNN team understandably refused to set foot inside it, and tried to file their reports from the Palestine Hotel where they had stored broadcasting equipment. As soon as their pictures were shown they were ordered out of the country. This proved how closely the authorities were monitoring the broadcasts of international channels like CNN, BBC and Al Jazeera, and once CNN had flouted the Ministry of Information's rules their fate was sealed. The Minister of Information and his deputies had a personalized hatred of anything to do with CNN, and they took much delight in expelling them. CNN was the last remaining American TV network in Iraq, and their expulsion gave the Iraqi authorities the opportunity to vent their disdain for what they saw as American superiority and jingoism. After their broadcast was exposed, Nic Robertson, the experienced and well-liked CNN correspondent, who had remained in Baghdad during the first Gulf War, had to sit through a tirade from one of the ministry officials. 'We don't want you here,' the official screamed. 'CNN must get out! Go! Leave immediately!'

After CNN's expulsion, we were told that their extremely assiduous minder would be assigned to us. We were all appalled at the idea but in the event he followed us only once, when he rather pointlessly insisted on accompanying me on one of the coach trips around the city organized by the ministry – a trip that would hardly allow for breaches of security anyway. We talked as we were driven through the shattered city. We passed the pummelled remains of the huge, extravagantly built Sujood Palace and the wreckage of a large Ba'ath Party office in the Mansour district, before arriving at Al Dora, the main oil refining and processing terminal in Baghdad. He was full of the same fantasies that so gripped the regime: ordinary Iraqis would fight and die for their President; the Americans and British would be humiliated in a bloody and prolonged battle for Baghdad. He expressed a deep-seated resentment at the thought of this most ancient of Arab countries being invaded and effectively colonized by western armies.

During the following days, we didn't inform him when we left the hotel in the early morning, but instead travelled around the city with Luai. This, we calculated, would make it difficult for him to report on us to his bosses. After all, Luai was, on the face of it, also a security official. The first time this happened, he came up to me when we entered the hotel lobby after a long day's filming. 'BBC! Mr Rageh, where were you today, you did not call me!' he said, looking agitated. I told him I had had to leave quickly and besides Luai had accompanied us. Luai was standing beside me and interjected in Arabic, saying that the nature of our work meant that we often had to travel into the city quickly and there was no room in our car for more than one minder. The security man didn't pursue the matter, and from that moment on he never bothered us. Luai had saved the day again.

As the war settled into a predictable routine, Baghdad began to resemble its pre-war self. People slowly started to emerge from their homes. The roads were once again busy with traffic during daylight hours, a few shops and markets began reopening. Luai had an explanation for it. 'Maybe it is because the American army did not expect that so many of the party and the militias would fight this strongly,' he said coyly. 'Even I am surprised. Until now Basra and Umm Qasr did not fall. You know Umm Qasr, Mr Rageh, it is a very, very small place. How come they cannot capture this yet? And even in Nassiriyah, they say they are going around the town but not inside. What is this?'

An Iraqi colleague who worked for a western news agency and had lived in Britain for some time put it more succinctly. 'I wish they would just fucking finish this,' he whispered furtively. 'The longer this goes on, the more hostile ordinary Iraqis become. Now my friends are beginning to think that this could last months and those bastards [the Iraqi government] will prepare a bloody siege. It will be a bloodbath if this happens.' He paused, before adding, 'I don't know how much more of this the people can take. We just want an end.'

The siege was beginning to create a kind of unreal daze in the city. It is a well-known phenomenon and has been written about extensively of other cities that have endured a similar ordeal in modern times, albeit in different circumstances. 'Siege mentality' had taken over as anxiety and nervous exhaustion transcended into a form of crowd hysteria. A single rumour could throw Baghdad into panic. I had just finished a live report on the roof of the ministry, when Killa noticed a group of people gathering on the Sinak Bridge. About ten of them had hoisted themselves up on to the metal balustrades on the side of the bridge so as to peer into the waters below. A few cars driving along the bridge slowed down to have a look. We thought someone might have fallen over the side and people were coming to help.

By the time we had collected our television equipment and walked to the other side of the ministry roof, there was a growing commotion among journalists. Police sirens could be heard now, and the crowd on the bridge had swelled to around fifty, and rising by the minute. I peered down at the street below by the side of the ministry and saw a number of reporters running towards the bridge. About ten minutes had elapsed since we had seen the group of people looking into the water. Paul had run down there to find out what was happening and returned, out of breath, shouting: 'People are saying that a pilot's been shot down and has landed in the river with his parachute, we've got to get down there.' One of the car park attendants in front of the Press Centre was yelling at us, waving his arm frantically, beckoning us to join in the rush. 'Quickly, quickly. There is an American pilot hiding in the river.' How could he know this? How could anyone know this? We joined in the charge down the main road towards the river about 300 yards away, looking like the stragglers at the end of a city marathon.

Three police cars had parked on the northern side of the bridge. Four young men in plain clothes, carrying Kalashnikovs, emerged running from the embankment down to the water's edge, out of breath and confused. I spoke to them in Arabic as they jumped into their cars as if auditioning for a part in *Starsky and Hutch*. 'Is there a pilot in the river?' I asked. The young man nearest to us nodded vigorously. 'British or American?' I asked inanely, as though he would be able to tell. 'Yes, American,' he replied, and with that his colleague sped off. We rushed after the car as it raced along the riverside dirt track, passing beneath the bridge. By now there were several hundred Iraqis by the riverbank and the atmosphere was frantic. Speed boats carrying soldiers had been launched and they peered into the cracks in the concrete feet of the bridge. More soldiers, plain clothes police and Ba'ath Party militia arrived. Along-side them came the ever increasing number of bemused Iraqis: street hawkers, shoe-shine boys, students, mothers with their children in tow. All of a sudden, on a whim, one of the soldiers standing by the edge of the river began firing into the water. Two other soldiers joined in. They were trying to look tough and it seemed an act for the benefit of the gathered civilians more than anything else. It was as if the soldiers were engaged in the same charade that Saddam Hussein and his ministers had played on television the previous night: an illusion that they were fully in control, that they knew what they were doing and that they could outwit the forces of the western powers, either real or imagined.

There were shouts from the reeds and bulrushes that lined the riverbank 200 yards away. Some of the soldiers and militiamen ran towards the area, starting a stampede of journalists and onlookers. Had they found him? About five men, carrying knives, had waded into the thicket, swiping, hacking, trampling the plants as they strode thigh-deep into the Tigris. Nothing. No sign of an airman, nor his torn canopy nor discarded helmet. A man appeared with a burning piece of cloth, and the riverbank was set ablaze. Thick smoke began rising from the reeds as they cracked and hissed amid the flames. The security officials marched back and forth, issuing orders and speaking urgently into their walkie-talkies. Yet the onlookers seemed to be curious rather than frightened or angry. There was the same peculiar fascination and sense of welcome distraction that characterized the pre-war rallies and neighbourhood marches the regime had organized. Whatever the regime chose to believe about its citizens, the people I saw on the riverbank did not look as though they had any wish to tear apart an American or British airman with their bare hands. The scene at the river did, however, reveal something of the mood of Baghdad, a city under siege, barely coping with the claustrophobic conditions. People were beginning to look for any sign – real or imaginary – of how close the invading armies were. Had some forces already been secretly infiltrated into the city?

The fevered scenes by the Tigris inevitably led to a series of other rumours. The next day, a close Iraqi friend told me that his wife had returned from the school where she was a teacher in the south-west of Baghdad, saying that her colleagues had been told that the American Air Force was dropping mannequins dressed up as US soldiers over key Republican Guard positions on the outskirts of Baghdad, and that many of the Iraqi troops had fled their positions. 'She asked me to ask some of my friends in the western media if this was true.'

By the end of the first week of the war, the air-raid sirens had lost the plot too. The first sign that they had broken down was when the night-time attacks were heralded by the all-clear sound. As the anti-aircraft guns began firing into the air, the long single note of the sirens declaring the all clear would pipe up, rather than the swelling scale of notes that was the signal for impending attacks. Later on, as the Iraqi army's radar systems were bombed repeatedly, the sirens barely worked at all. Another, far more haunting, sound came to herald the night-time bombings. Just minutes before the missiles and bombs began raining on their targets in the city, the stray wild dogs in the empty streets of Baghdad would begin to howl. We could see them sometimes, walking quickly and aimlessly in packs along the riverbank. Night after night, the same thing happened. Dogs are able to hear sounds on a much wider wavelength than humans and there was a story that they could pick up the sonic waves of incoming missiles long before we could. Their long, mournful wailing reverberated around the streets – followed ten or fifteen minutes later by the first explosions.

Our own technology also began to forewarn us of impending bombardment. Half an hour before the first wave of attacks each night it became virtually impossible to make a connection on the satellite phones. Something that was almost instantaneous during the day would take at least eight attempts. The British and American forces seemed to be narrowing the available bandwidth on satellites in the area ahead of the attacks, which were using satellite-guided munitions.

It's not just people reading about war from miles away who begin to feel immune to its dangers and horrors. Even within it a strange sense of routine began to dull our fear. We learned to internalize the sound of howling wild dogs, and, suddenly, what had been an unsettling warning signal became almost reassuring. We learned to adapt to the frustrating inability to maintain the emotional lifeline of speaking to relatives on the phone because of satellite jamming, by calling at different hours. In the first days, every detonation, every anti-aircraft barrage made me jump out of my skin. The seismic shock from heavy penetration bombs was even more harrowing. I remember the first time one was dropped close to the hotel. It was like the distant, thunderous footstep of a dinosaur, smashing into the ground. Seconds later the hotel was moving, swaying gently from side to side – all twenty floors of it. But slowly it did become easier and more natural to get more than a couple of hours' sleep at night. The noise, the shuddering windows, even the pre-dawn call from the muezzin, issuing out the familiar invocation for God's help – all of this was subsumed and accepted by our numbed senses.

But the war was eating into the city's consciousness. The night-time bombings started to extend into the day, and it was hard to escape the sense that a noose was being tightened around Baghdad and all who lived in it. The heavy shadow of black oil smoke which hung over the low houses was now lined with the clear vapour trails of British and American planes.

7. Civilians

A week suddenly began to feel like a very long time. In 1991 it had taken only four days for the coalition ground offensive to break the back of Saddam Hussein's army and drive it out of Kuwait. Five days of war had now passed and Saddam Hussein's position seemed astonishingly rosy. Iraqi television had broadcast pictures of captive or dead American soldiers on the battlefield and paramilitary forces around Basra were fighting advancing British forces that still hadn't penetrated the city, even though its fall had already been announced by the British government on more than one occasion. Even Umm Qasr, a tiny port town, had not fallen. I'd visited the town many times over the years. Apart from the large port there was not much more to it than a loosely scattered group of villages and hamlets that were home to a farming community of about 5,000 people. The Iraqi regime was delighted.

So on 24 March, when Saddam Hussein emerged from his subterranean existence to take to the airwaves in a televised speech, he appeared genuinely convinced that he and his regime had a chance of surviving. His image popped up on the screen just after 11 a.m., wearing his green military uniform, and again he had recorded his homily in some sort of reinforced basement. He seemed more focused, less fidgety and disconcerted than on his appearance on the first day of the war. 'This war has produced these decisive days,' he told his forces, before urging them on, 'O Iraqis, these are your decisive days. Strike now as you are ordered by your God. Strike over the necks, strike their fingertips . . . exhaust the enemy to the point where it becomes unable to continue to commit further crimes against you, against your nation and against humanity . . . The enemy wanted to make the war short in order to extricate itself from its predicament but we hope, God willing, to make it long and heavy for it. It will be bogged down in the quagmire until it is stifled and until it is defeated in panic.' The word from Washington and London over the previous days had it that Saddam Hussein had been mortally injured. Or that, at the very least, he was out of the loop and no longer in effective control. That wasn't the way it looked in Baghdad that day. This was an altogether different performance from the faltering and indecisive one he'd given only hours after the first attack of the war. His speech would set the tone for the rest of the regime in the coming days.

However, Saddam Hussein's confidence would be short-lived as the American attack entered a new phase. We were six days into the conflict and the cycle of nightly bombardments had begun to feel familiar, if not reassuring. The city had grown accustomed to the frightful bursts of anti-aircraft guns, the phosphorescent glow of the tracer rounds lining the sky and the shattering cracks of the detonations. Airstrikes were a form of warfare that Baghdad was familiar with, having endured nearly a month and a half of aerial bombardment during the first Gulf War, and I suppose this had lulled everyone into believing that a ground attack was not yet close. But it was the notion of an invading army fighting its way through the streets, with all the unknown, unpredictable terrors that could entail, that so haunted the faces of the people we met.

The long, rumbling sound that drew in from the edges of the city at the end of the first week made us realize that a ground attack was not as far off as we had hoped. It resembled a deep drum roll. It built quickly and after a brief climax dissolved into silence. Far off, perhaps thirty or so miles away on the horizon, there was a brief quiver of white light, as B-52 bombers carpet-bombed the positions held by Republican Guard divisions. Then ten seconds later we heard the low muffled roll of the explosions. It was the sound of the American army knocking on the gates of Baghdad. The massed columns of the US military's 3rd Infantry Division and the marines had already crossed the Euphrates river. They were not far away now, and the terrible sound of carpet-bombing was the signal of their approach; the 'softening up', as the military double-speak described it, of Iraqi ground forces that blocked the way to the capital. We wondered who would stay to fight and die for Saddam Hussein.

From my notebook – 26 March 2003

Sandstorms hit Baghdad with a vengeance. Radio reports from embeds★
say ferocious & blinding storms around Nassiriyah make it impossible to
see more than a metre or so. Local Iraqis say these are worst in living
memory. We wake to city completely carpeted in sand. It just keeps
getting worse. Don't know if the equipment will be able to take all
the dust.

It had been another restless night. I kept waking suddenly from
what felt like hours of deep sleep to find it had been only half an
hour. It went on like this for five hours. I could hear the palm trees
on the slopes of the Tigris thrash against the high winds which
howled around the empty city streets. From the sliding doors to
the balcony came a series of long swishing sounds, like the rustle
of paper, as the raging wind threw the fine desert sand against
the glass.

Even nature seemed to be forewarning of the horrors that were
approaching Baghdad. The B-52s had introduced a new and unsettling sound, and now the weather had transformed the city's appearance. We woke to a city completely covered by a blanket of fine
brown sand. The air, the buildings, the streets, the cars, everything
looked as if it had been painted in thick coats of brick-coloured
paint. The desert gripped us as soon as we stepped outside: the
powdery sand filled our nostrils and lined the backs of our throats.
We made our way to the roof of the Ministry of Information,
wondering whether our tent and the equipment within it had
survived. The sight of other reporters coming down the stairs
carrying pieces of mangled metal frames and torn tarpaulin gave us
a clue to what we were going to find. On the roof there was chaos:
tents upended at crazy angles; yard upon yard of awning and tent
fabric wrenched from its moorings, flapping in the now gentle
breeze; solid wooden frames for our cameras broken like twigs. It
was a spring morning, but the cars passing on the main road beneath

★ Journalists embedded with American units and travelling with them.

us had their headlamps on, as drivers tried to penetrate the dark golden fog that shrouded the city.

Luai found his way up to the roof and, squinting against the sand-filled breeze as he tiptoed daintily around this scene of devastation, said: 'There is a bus for the journalists to see some damaged civilian areas.' These organized trips happened sporadically and depended on what the officials wanted us to see. This time we were not told where exactly the bus would be taking us. In actual fact most of the tours concentrated on civilian areas rather than government buildings, which eloquently demonstrated the concerns of those organizing them. Killa and I decided to go on this occasion, and we boarded the coach with about thirty other journalists. We headed to the east of the city, through largely residential neighbourhoods, and at about 10 a.m. arrived in a densely built and largely middle-class district. We were taken by Press Centre officials down a narrow side street lined with shops and small restaurants, a number of which were open. On either side of the lane were dilapidated brick houses with low sunken doors that led directly into the living quarters. A hundred yards down the street one of the houses had been partially demolished. Although the structure was still intact something had smashed into the roof and one of the side rooms had been gutted, opening it up to the sky. Just outside the house was a neat pile of rubble. If this was the result of an American weapon dropped from the sky, where was the secondary damage to the tiny, frail houses on either side? How had the rubble fallen into one small pile, right in the middle of the road, right outside the house? The shop owners sitting drinking tea on the pavement nearby seemed far too relaxed given what had supposedly just taken place. It was a repellent scene, as if all the genuinely tragic images that crowded the city were somehow not enough for the Iraqi administration.

Killa went through the motions and desultorily recorded some footage. He was standing by the pile of rubble, pointing his camera at the roof of the house, when we felt it. The whole side street trembled. Strangely there seemed to be no sound of an explosion. The bomb must have fallen far away and the explosion been muted by the closely packed houses. Killa looked anxiously up at the sky. 'I think we'd better get out of here,' he said. We packed up our equipment and along with the rest of the coach party, some of whom were also becoming anxious, set off back to the Ministry of Information.

Something was definitely wrong as our bus drove up from the Sinak Bridge towards the Press Centre. Journalists and officials were running back and forth along the pavement, buses and cars hooted their horns as they clogged the road by the ministry car park. Cameramen were frantically beckoning to reporters to hurry up and get into their vehicles. Ministry officials were directing journalists to make their way to a district in northern Baghdad. A senior official saw me as I descended from the bus and shouted: 'Rageh, go, go, there has been a big attack. Hurry!' Unusually, the authorities in the Press Centre were urging us to go in our own cars and make our own way there, regardless of whether minders accompanied us or not. There was no attempt at the usual stage management, and this in itself was the first indication that something dreadful had happened.

Khalil drove us to the Al Sha'ab district, a largely working-class neighbourhood in northern Baghdad. Its name in Arabic means literally 'the place of the masses'. It lies on the main trunk road from the capital to the oil city of Kirkuk, in the northern, predominantly Kurdish, part of Iraq. The roads were heavy with traffic, the vehicles occasionally parting to let through a police car or ambulance. By now the sandstorms had plunged the entire city under a blood-red film of light, as day was turned into a perpetual dusk. Rain had transformed the streets into a slurry of slippery mud. Along the side of the road, shops and low stalls hugged the pavements, straddling the tiny lanes that led down to small family homes. Then suddenly to my right, down one of the side streets, I noticed the unmistakable shape of a missile launcher. It was a momentary glimpse but was instantly recognizable. Was this what the bombers had been aiming for? But it was at least a mile from the area that had been bombed and it wasn't as if the launcher was difficult to spot. We had all seen it clearly from the street as we rattled past at twenty miles per hour.

Suddenly the streets were full of people. There were hundreds of Iraqis: men and women of all ages and small children, all in a state of panic. We stopped the car and walked out into a scene of carnage and utter confusion: police sirens, men shouting orders, car horns blaring, women screaming. I stood frozen for a moment, overwhelmed by the chaos. In front of me, in a dark alleyway, was the stump of a tree still burning, the ferocious winds stoking the charred embers. On the corner of the street a row of parked cars had been crumpled like paper by huge hunks of masonry that had been torn from one of the office buildings. A tangle of wires from the street lamps dangled forlornly above the destruction. On the pavement below, as if punched into the earth by a giant fist, were two deep craters. The façades of the blocks of flats and shops were scarred by a spray of shrapnel holes. Beside the larger crater, a row of auto-repair workshops lay in ruins. Wrenches and spanners were scattered across the ground, amid the blood, mud and twisted metal. In front of the workshops stood the eviscerated hulks of cars, inside some of them blackened figures still sat in the drivers' seats. A small crowd of people gathered as I spoke to Ali Abu Haidar, a young mechanic whose car repair workshop had been destroyed in the attack. 'We're just trying to make a living in our shops,' he said. 'What do they want from us? Why are they doing this? Our homes are going, and our livelihoods are gone.'

There was utter bewilderment among the crowd. Most Iraqis had believed that this really was a war aimed solely at overthrowing the regime of Saddam Hussein in order to liberate them, led by a superpower which they regarded as being endowed with almost God-like powers and whose sophisticated weaponry meant that a scene such as this was unthinkable. So why was this happening to them? On the opposite side of the road a family was clambering over the rubble to get to the stairs of a block of flats, desperate to recover what was left of their possessions. A small truck was already partially loaded with mattresses, sheets and blankets and cooking utensils. Eighteen-year-old Mohammed Adnan Abdul Hadi climbed up the stairwell, crunching shards of broken glass beneath his plastic flip-flops as he went. His movements were ghost-like.

He was in such severe shock that he seemed not to notice the carpet of glass beneath his unprotected feet. 'I only heard just one explosion,' he told me, 'which threw me against a wall, then there was just dust and damage everywhere. I began screaming to my two younger brothers and my aunt who were staying with us. I thought they had been killed. The thought of it made me not want to live. But thanks to God, they survived.' His hands were trembling as he spoke.

The sandstorms had delivered a bitter, unseasonal chill to the city, magnifying the cold shock of what lay around us in this forsaken neighbourhood. Mohammed's and other families now had to find somewhere else to sleep that night, and were looking around for places to go, refugees in their own city. As I recorded a piece to camera, trying to compose myself in this scene of pitiless devastation, a man approached and began to speak to me in Arabic. 'Tell them we are just innocent people,' he said. 'We don't know why this is happening to Iraqi people. Why? What does Bush want from us?' He pointed to the spot where moments before I had looked in horror at pieces of brain tissue scattered across the steps – small clumps of pinkish grey mass, stared at in silent horror by the people around me. 'Is this civilization?' he asked. 'Is this the freedom we are to be given?' He didn't expect an answer. He looked contemptuously towards the camera, as though it was representative of millions of ordinary people in Britain and America, and then just walked away.

At least seventeen people had been killed, more than thirty wounded, in an overwhelmingly Shia working-class district. Several eyewitnesses told me that the explosions had been from incoming missiles or bombs. One man said he had heard a plane circling overhead, which was common in Baghdad as by now coalition warplanes were conducting daytime bombing raids.

It was the first large-scale incident of civilian casualties from the war in the city and it took barely an hour for the political shock-waves of this horror to make themselves felt around the world. Brigadier General Vincent Brooks, the coalition spokesman at Central Command in Qatar, said that although 'mistakes can occur' in war it was too early to say whether the strike on Al Sha'ab was the result of an American attack which had gone catastrophically wrong. He vaguely suggested that it could have been the result of some sort of Iraqi suicide bomb attack, but he added that attempts were being made to check if the coalition bore responsibility for the civilian deaths in Al Sha'ab. Virtually every survivor and resident journalists spoke to at the scene said they believed the bomb had come from an American plane.

No war, whatever the promises of military commanders and the fervent wish of politicians, is free from mistakes or civilian deaths. But the stated intentions of this war had focused heavily on the liberation of Iraqi civilians, and so scenes such as this had greater resonance than they might have had in a less controversial conflict. The experience of civilians during the early part of this war would be central to how they would view the invading armies once they arrived in the capital. The people of Al Sha'ab felt that they, the very people in whose name the war was being fought, had become its victims. Many of them were taken to the Al Kindi Hospital, and several of the wounded died in the casualty wards, places that had become brim-full of shock and grief. One doctor encapsulated the feelings that had emerged from the rubble and death that lay strewn on that road in Al Sha'ab. 'This war is affecting the lives of every Iraqi now,' he said. 'There is no safe place in Baghdad.'

That evening the night-time bombardments came back to the centre of the city with a vengeance. In the early hours of the following morning I listened to the satellite radio which was broadcasting the first statement by the coalition on the bombing of the civilian quarter. 'Coalition aircraft used precision-guided weapons to target nine Iraqi surface-to-surface missiles and launchers in Baghdad at approximately 8 a.m. GMT,' it said. 'The missiles and launchers were placed within a civilian residential area. Most of the missiles were positioned less than 300 feet from homes. A full assessment of the operation is ongoing. Military targets − such as the missiles and launchers placed in Baghdad − are a threat to coalition military forces and will be attacked. While the coalition goes to great lengths to avoid injury to civilians and damage to civilian facilities, in some cases such damage is unavoidable.' If the planes had been aiming at missile launchers placed in civilian areas, where was the evidence of a damaged launcher? No journalist reported seeing the remains of the vast green military vehicles that transport such missiles, and surely we would have seen the blasted pieces of twisted metal usually found after machinery of this scale has been attacked?

Another day and another press conference. This one was altogether more grim than anything the Minister of Information was used to serving up. We gathered at the Press Centre late on the morning of 27 March to hear from Umid Mihdat Mubarak, a Kurd by origin and the Minister of Health of Saddam Hussein's regime. I had met him several times over the previous six years, and he, unlike Mohammed al Sahaff, was not prone to theatre even as he tried to serve the propaganda interests of his government. It was impossible to corroborate the dreadful figures he gave us as the coalition was not publicly keeping a tally of the civilian dead or wounded, but they seemed to me to have the undeniable ring of authenticity. He said that since the beginning of the war, a week earlier, over 350 civilians had been killed throughout the whole of Iraq and around 4,000 wounded. I was surprised by the figures, given the ferocity of what we had been witnessing in Baghdad and the ground battles around Basra, Umm Qasr and Nassiriyah, and given that it was in the interest of the Iraqi regime to inflate the figures. He added that in the previous twenty-four hours, thirty-six civilians had been killed in airstrikes on Baghdad, including the bombing of the Al Sha'ab neighbourhood.

I wanted to talk to Mohammed, to try to interpret the terrible atmosphere in the city. A menacing sense of approaching doom hung over Baghdad, and slowly everything that made up the fabric of the city was disappearing, unravelling like an ancient tapestry whose intricate threads have hung together for centuries. Mohammed lived in the far south of Baghdad, past the huge Al Dora refinery, across the bridge where the tides of the Tigris bend round the jut of land that houses the Republican Palace, an area that had seen fierce attacks in recent days. I felt enormously relieved when I saw him in the street outside the hotel and not just because he'd managed to get there safely. I had expected to see an exhausted and traumatized Mohammed, a man who stayed awake through the nights trying to reassure his three children during the explosions. I knew that he had enough medicine for his kidney problem, but the emotional damage of living through the siege must have taken its toll, whatever the benefits of the drugs. He looked remarkably well under the circumstances and after we'd greeted each other he reported that his family were well and although some targets around the area where he lived had been hit, none of the bombs and missiles had come too close to their house. A few broken windows and strained nerves, he said. But his tone had changed.

Gone were the fantasies of a swift decapitation of the regime, and in their place was a deep atavistic distrust of an Iraqi future swathed in the Stars and Stripes and the Union Jack – this from a man whose attitude to the West, particularly Britain, had always been one of benign curiosity. 'Everyone knows that the Americans will be here eventually,' he commented, 'but a battle for Baghdad may not be easy and it may be bloody, that is my greatest fear. But beyond that, Rageh, everyone now realizes that at some stage we will be ruled by foreigners. This is inescapable. This is a very, very difficult thing for all Iraqis to accept.' The reality behind regime change was beginning to sink in. As always, Iraqis saw the future with a prescient clarity that escaped most of us on the outside. It was a clear-sightedness that had emerged from the experience of so many years of oppression.

We went to Shorja market together. Only a few stalls were open, selling basic goods: rice, flour, cooking oil. 'War produce' Mohammed called it. A man about sixty years old stood by one of the stalls. He was dressed in an old light-grey wool jacket which he had clearly looked after with loving attention, as there were careful patches on each elbow and neatly repaired lapels. He wore a pair of spectacles with lenses so thick that his eyes looked like tiny pebbles, and he had the benevolent smile of a kind old uncle. He didn't want to give his name, but instead described himself as a retired civil servant. He spoke reasonable English, but felt more comfortable talking in Arabic. He seemed like someone who was too decent to succumb to feelings of hatred even though he clearly hated what he could see happening around him. And so the conversation came round to questions of what he thought about the British and American governments.

'They have begun a very bad mistake in attacking Iraq,' he said. 'This is a very old country. I have lived through many things, not just the last twenty years,' he continued, alluding to the era of Saddam Hussein without referring to it by name. 'The Ottomans, the British, they were all driven out of Iraq. Who can accept to be colonized? Whatever the cost of this aggression, when it is over, it will end in humiliation for Bush and Blair. The Iraqis will not accept their rule.' And he added, 'And even their own people will not accept it.' The drone of jet engines echoed around the empty sky, as people fitfully cast their gaze upwards. We shook hands and bade him good luck. He responded effusively with the traditional Islamic farewell, '*Fi aman Illah*', Go in God's safe keeping. He walked away with the gait of an aged man pained by bowed legs, rocking gently from side to side.

Darkness was drawing near and I sensed that Mohammed was anxious to get home to his family before night fell. We hugged and I insisted that he take the remnants of our chocolate ration for his children. He set off, a look of tired sadness on his face as he waved goodbye. It would be the last time I would see him until the war ended.

It was lucky that Mohammed got home before dusk because 27 March was the worst night of bombardment so far in the war in Baghdad. Ferocious and unrelenting, it began when we were being corralled into the conference hall of the Palestine Hotel for what would prove to be a chilling and sobering press conference with Iraq's Minister of Defence, General Sultan Hashim Ahmed, a stout, heavy-set man who had represented Saddam Hussein during the ceasefire negotiations at the end of the first Gulf War. Aided by one of his officials who tapped a giant map of Iraq with a long wooden stick each time he referred to the different battlefields and deployments of Iraqi and coalition forces, General Sultan made no attempts to hide the progress of coalition ground forces towards the Iraqi capital. His words were interrupted by the sound of massive detonations that reverberated around the hall. The minister painted a picture of American forces being attacked and harassed by irregular Iraqi forces as they progressed north towards Baghdad. So much so, he said, that they were now avoiding major cities such as Najaf and Nassiriyah, and had chosen instead to skirt round them. The real battle of this war, he said, would be for Baghdad.

He presumed that Iraqis in Baghdad would fight the besieging forces to the death and he drew an apocalyptic vision of what such a siege would be like. He described a blood-soaked struggle for the capital, like some Stalingrad on the Tigris, and added that the Iraqi government had made preparations for this scenario. 'Our defences are set to defend Baghdad, so we won't be surprised if in five or ten days the enemy will be encircling great parts of Baghdad,' he said. I asked him how he could be confident that the city would not fall quickly to the might of the American forces. 'As you know,' he replied, 'Baghdad is the capital of an ancient civilization. We Iraqis inherited this history from our forefathers. Anyone who seeks to deprive us of this inheritance will meet with God's fury . . . Baghdad will be impenetrable for the Americans and British as long as any sons of this city are alive.'

The bombardment became more intense as the night wore on. The coalition must have been using the so-called 'bunker buster' bombs, the massive precision bombs weighing up to 5,000 pounds that burrow deep beneath reinforced concrete and steel before exploding, making our rooms shake alarmingly, windows rattle and the whole building sway.

As the Iraqi regime's 'command and control' capability was ruthlessly bombed, the city's infrastructure was also being ripped apart. The following morning we went to one of Baghdad's main telephone exchanges. The tall brown-brick tower was one of the salient features of the eastern bank of the Tigris river and stood in a busy area of the city, among shops and stalls. At the foot of the tower was a multi-storey car park used by many of the businessmen who had shops in the area. The laser-guided munition had left a large clean hole where it had ploughed down to the very foundations of the building where the telephone exchange had stood. Peering into the hole we could see only a blackened and charred chasm with a few wires reaching into the light of day. Further up, on the seventh or eighth floor, the building had been hit by what looked like two other bombs, leaving huge holes in the middle of the concrete, exposing the floors of the building to the sky. Many Baghdad citizens now had no means of contacting each other.

Just beneath the Sinak Bridge we spotted a row of flat-bed trucks carrying what looked like portakabins on the roofs of which were perched some ghostly white objects shrouded in cloth. Killa looked at them closely, then a smile spread across his face. 'Portable radio studios and transmitters,' he said, pointing towards the trucks. 'That's how they're keeping Iraqi radio on air.'

The nights were becoming ever more vicious; 28 March was even worse. I lost count of how many times I had to re-record the commentary I was sending to London on a satellite phone. I would begin a sentence only for a loud explosion to make the building rumble and jolt my senses. 'Sorry, Rageh,' the producer in the editing suite in London would say, 'I've got to ask you to do that again. Are you okay to carry on?' What should have taken no more than a quarter of an hour dragged on. Then, just as I was in mid-sentence, Paul Wood, my fellow reporter, came rushing into the room. 'Hide the fucking satellite phone,' he whispered urgently, to avoid being heard in the next room. 'There's a group of minders at the door searching for equipment.' Without a mention to the hapless producer in London of what was happening, Paul and I pulled all the wires from the antennae and stuffed the satellite phone under the bed. We were lucky, as they found only one of our four phones, which they proudly carried off as a trophy of their night's work. The sound of the explosions blowing their city apart reverberated down the corridor as they walked away. 'Pricks!' Paul Danahar said, as he shut the door behind them.

Press Centre officials came knocking on the doors of journalists' rooms again later, but not, as we at first thought, to search for more illicit equipment. 'There has been another massacre of civilians in the north-west, in a place called Al Sho'la,' one of them said. 'There will be a trip in the next fifteen minutes to take journalists to the scene.' It was an awful re-run of the nightmare the people of the Al Sha'ab district had lived through. A market square at the heart of another predominantly Shia working-class neighbourhood had been blown apart, its community transformed into a wasteland of carnage. The number of dead and injured was even greater than in Al Sha'ab. Several of the first reporters on the scene said they had counted at least twenty corpses. Doctors and medical staff at the nearby Al Noor Hospital said they had received the bodies of at least thirty dead civilians. The corridors of the hospital were filled with the cries of the wounded and grieving. Many of the women screamed the names of their loved ones as they beat their chests in the traditional Shia act of mourning.

A mosque close to the small square housing the flimsy open-air market stalls and corner shops received a further fifteen corpses, their bodies lying in the coffins in which they would be buried the next day as Islamic law dictates. In an act that spoke volumes about the dignity and civilized nature of the impoverished people whose lives had been turned upside-down, western non-Muslim reporters were permitted inside the mosques and mortuaries to witness the bodies being washed in preparation for burial. No recrimination or animosity was shown towards any of them. The anger, even hatred, expressed by many of the survivors and relatives of the casualties was directed at the British and American governments only.

Hussein Ali Hashim sat by the bedside of his six-year-old daughter, the upper half of her head heavily bandaged, her legs and abdomen peppered with shrapnel marks. You could see on his face the visceral anger exploding inside him. However, when he spoke, he did so calmly. 'We have to take revenge for this,' he said. 'We will kill their children as they have killed ours.' Fifty-five dead was the official Iraqi figure from the bombing of the Al Sho'la district, and there was no reason to doubt the figure. It was the largest single instance of civilian deaths in the war. Virtually all of them were Shia Muslims, the people who the British and American governments had hoped would initiate an uprising against Saddam Hussein once the war began, just as President Bush Senior had called on them to rise up in the wake of the first Gulf War, only to abandon them to their fate once they had heeded his call. Once again, survivors recounted hearing the drone of jet engines overhead. None of them expressed anything other than a belief that this tragedy had been visited upon them by a coalition missile or bomb. Once again, coalition spokesmen responded by saying they were 'still trying to learn the truth of the matter' and still working out whether they bore responsibility for the attack.

The bombardment eventually caught up with the Ministry of Information. In fact many of us were surprised that it had taken this long, over a week into the war. I remember sitting in the office of one of the directors of the Press Centre two days before the war began, trying to impress upon him that we had to be allowed to move our operations to the Palestine Hotel because the ministry was bound to be attacked. 'This war is about regime change,' I remember telling him, 'and regime change won't mean very much as long as the Ministry of Information is functioning. It will be hit.' He looked at me dismissively. 'They said the same thing in 1991 during the Gulf War, and nothing happened,' he said. 'They will never bomb a building which they know is being used by the international press.' But bomb it they did, in the early hours of 29 March.

In the morning we returned to our tent on the lower roof of the ministry to find it looking like a scrapyard, with broken metal and smashed masonry lying across it. On the roof of the central block of the building, about seven floors above, I could see the pockmarks from the missile which had hit one of the ministry's satellite dishes. The damage was extraordinarily localized to the ministry's antennae and dishes, and the coalition had clearly avoided using a large missile which would have completely destroyed the building. But the blast wave had been powerful – we found the wall-mounted clock inside our tent knocked to the floor and frozen at the exact time of the strike, 1.35 a.m. Even this attack was not enough to persuade the Press Centre to change their ridiculous rule that prevented us from evacuating the building altogether and taking our broadcasting equipment to the Palestine Hotel. One more strike, however, finally convinced them that it really was time to abandon their obstinate attachment to the restrictions they had imposed. The ministry was bombed for a second time on 30 March, only hours after reporters had left for the evening. At last we were allowed to move out.

The repeated references in the military briefings of coalition commanders to 'precision bombing' and 'surgical strikes' tried to imply that such bombing somehow did not affect innocent civilians and that the accuracy of the strikes on presidential sites, ministries and Ba'ath Party offices left the population unscathed. It was an attempt to argue that an air campaign affected civilians only when they were casualties. The truth is always more complicated.

The Ministry of Information is surrounded by a large number of residential apartment blocks. No more than fifty yards from the government building are a series of hideous square tenements, similar to the sprawling council estates built in the bombed-out areas of British cities in the 1960s. There is another long row of them on the opposite side of the main road that runs past the ministry towards the Sinak Bridge. Both blocks were decorated with overblown paintings of a youthful Saddam Hussein, dressed in a suit and standing behind a shiny armchair. These Iraqi tenements were built for the families of middle-ranking civil servants and army officers at the end of the 1970s and thousands of civilians lived in them, and continued to do so throughout the war. Their position near the ministry meant that it would be only a matter of time before they were hit. We went to see what had happened to them following the night's attack on the ministry. What we saw there graphically brought home to me the hollowness of the expression 'surgical strike'.

Paul, Duncan, Luai and I walked over to the nearest tenement. We saw a woman standing by a broken window of one of the flats clearing up the desolate mess that lay at her feet. We shouted up to ask if we could come and talk to her and she beckoned us over. There was a small unkempt communal garden at the rear which led up to a series of identical, drab concrete staircases to the numbered blocks of flats. On the second floor the stairwell gave on to a long narrow corridor overlooking the gardens, and the woman was standing outside her front door, ready to receive us. She was in her forties, with a mane of black hair swept back into a ponytail. There was something defiant about her face and the way she carried herself as she greeted us – not unfriendly but a certain coldness in her manner. She introduced herself as Najda Abdallah, and said she lived in the flat with her sister and nephew. We walked into the small living room where books that had outgrown the available shelf space lay in neat piles on the floor, cupboards were crammed full of broken cups waiting to be fixed and pieces of kitchen equipment that no longer worked but no one could quite face throwing out. On the sideboard stood an ancient cassette player and some complicated device for curling hair. On the walls of the living room were faded posters of 1980s pop stars. One poster showed a heavily made-up woman in her late thirties with a great halo of peroxided blonde hair. She wore a pair of tight spandex trousers and her lips were outlined in a thick glistening ring of bright red lipstick.

Luai pointed excitedly. 'That is a very famous Iraqi singer,' he told us. 'She is very well known around the Middle East and performed all over the world.' And then it dawned on him. The name of the singer in the poster was Suad Abdallah, the same family name as that of Najda, who had invited us into the flat. Were they related? He quickly turned to Najda to ask her, and at her reply Luai's eyes widened even further. 'Yes,' Najda said, 'that is my sister Suad who lives with me in this flat.'

The woman who eventually appeared from the kitchen certainly looked thirty years older than the woman in the poster. She was still in her dressing gown from the night before. The gown was shiny, in a print of bright psychedelic flowers and wild illustrations of animals, its synthetic fibres now frayed at the edges. Her blonde hair was dishevelled and seemed dry and brittle. Without her make-up she looked her age, and her eyes were dull and heavily lined with exhaustion. She shuffled into the room in a pair of faded pink slippers with pink tasselled ties, dabbing at her dripping nose and wet eyes with a crumpled up piece of tissue. The family were removing the broken glass and clearing up the damage from the rooms of the flat that overlooked the Ministry of Information. Some of the bookcases had fallen off their supports on the walls, vases of fake flowers lay smashed on the floor, and a thin layer of dust covered everything. Najda excused herself to return to sweeping up the shards of glass, and we sat down to speak to Suad. She was clearly deeply shocked, and was trying hard to hold back her tears.

In her 1980s heyday Suad had been one of Iraq's most famous pop stars, singing modern Arabic love songs. For much of the 1960s and 1970s, the most famous singers in the Arab world had been people such as the celebrated Egyptian chanteuse Umm Kalthoum and her Lebanese counterpart Feyrooz. Their performances and songs were still strongly classical, and were accompanied by large orchestras playing a mixture of western and Arabic classical instruments. Oil wealth transformed many countries in the Arab world in the 1980s and allowed members of middle-class families to travel and study in the West, and this experience was reflected in changes within popular culture in the Arab world. Young middle-class Arabs wanted to experience the consumer culture enjoyed by young people in the West; the same kind of films, pop music, clothes and fast food. Popular Arab singers also reflected these changes, abandoning the tradition of songs with lyrics taken from old poems and set to classical music, and instead borrowing from western pop music and using synthesizers and drum machines along with snappier lyrics strongly influenced by American rap music. It was to this generation of singers that Suad belonged.

Suad had travelled extensively across Britain and the United States to give concerts to expatriate and exiled Arab communities, and the Iraqis in particular in those countries flocked to her shows. She had performed in Detroit, Philadelphia, New York, Los Angeles, London, Birmingham, Sheffield. She had lived in central London for two years, a city she still adored. 'I love Britain,' she said, her voice breaking as she continued to dab the small beads of tears with her tissue. She tried to summon up the English words she could remember from her time in London. 'The Iraqi people like the British people. We want to be friends with British people like us, but why you hate us?' she asked in anguish. 'Ten years we have sanctions. No food, no medicines, then after sanctions, war? This is no good. Why you hate?' The trauma of living under the bombardment had left her terrified, but there was more to her pain than this. It was the kind of pain caused by the cruelty of rejection, personal and raw. This was a woman who could not understand how a country she so loved and cherished and of which she had such fond memories could do this to her. She was a true image of what Wilfred Owen called 'the pity of war'.

These two sisters embodied the two most prevalent emotions felt by the Iraqis of Baghdad at that time. Najda possessed none of the attachment to Britain that her sister did. It was not a place of carefree and cherished exile for her, not the place so beloved of the Arab communities who to this day still wander down the Edgware Road. Instead she saw Britain as the former colonial master now trying to revisit Iraq with a modern-day version of 'gunboat diplomacy'. She had nothing but a nationalist's contempt and loathing for the former imperialist overlords. I asked about her feelings at the prospect of seeing British troops on Iraqi soil. She curled her lips. 'Tony Blair is wrong to think Iraqis will welcome his soldiers with open arms and flowers,' she said. 'Many ordinary people look on them as nothing better than thieves, like robbers breaking into their homes.'

8. The End of a World

A strange new sound was coming from the street. It wasn't the drone of aeroplanes or the crash of falling masonry, it was the noise of traffic. Cars were hooting, there was talking and shouting. Had some demonstration been arranged? Perhaps the legions of Arab volunteer fighters that the Minister of Information claimed were on their way to fight the Americans had arrived for some kind of bizarre photo opportunity? I decided to go for a walk to find out what had caused the people to gather on the pavements.

In the lobby of the Palestine Hotel the usual collection of minders sat smoking. One of them tried to stop me from walking out, but when he saw that I was carrying no equipment he let me go. Outside I could see no sign of a demonstration or of foreign armies. I walked towards Firdoos Square where the bronze statue I had seen being erected a year ago now overshadowed the benches and patches of grass. Cars and pedestrians were swarming round the square. For the first time since before the beginning of the war, the city seemed to have rediscovered something of its old self. The past week had become so defined by explosions and air-raid sirens that the sound of traffic and street life was startling. And it wasn't just confined to the area around Saadoun Street – the bridges across the Tigris vibrated beneath the weight of passing cars and trucks. Further south, in the Karada district, shops and restaurants were opening.

We began to have take-away lunches again, brought from local restaurants brave, or foolish, enough to reopen for business. Dylan or Khalil would scour neighbouring districts in search of them, and return several hours later with thin plastic bags steaming with kebabs, grilled chicken and flat unleavened bread, and pots heavy with rich, thick hummus. The familiar food and the everyday bustle of city life provided some brief but welcome reassurance for those of us who had remained behind. We were reconnected to a fragment of the pre-war Baghdad we had known. We felt calmer, despite the Iraqi ministers' warnings of a bloody and prolonged siege. We could listen more objectively to the Minister of Information's descriptions of Arab fighters and mujahideen coming to 'kill the western invaders'.

But, of course, life around us was not quite what it seemed; there was a very specific reason why Iraqis were emerging from their homes in such numbers. By the end of March the telephone exchanges which had served the civilian population had been wrecked by weeks of bombardment: the Rashid Communications Centre, close to Tahrir Square; the main exchange in Karada; the Mimoun International Communications Centre and many others had been reduced to dust and rubble by the coalition's bombing campaign. Telephones had become useless and so residents had to go on to the streets to make contact with friends and family. But this breakdown of infrastructure alone could not explain why people were emerging from their homes. There was also a clear will to create an atmosphere of normality. The Iraqis I met were determined to take up their daily routine again as a refuge from the reality of what was facing their city. Normal life became their fantasy.

Alongside our tent on the roof of the Palestine Hotel was the tent for Reuters Television. One afternoon, just as we were preparing a report, a young Iraqi engineer who had been employed by Reuters walked over to ask if he could have some sugar. We'd got to know each other over cups of tea on the roof and during quieter moments we'd chat about what was happening in the city. On this occasion I commented on how strange it was to see so many people back on the streets of Baghdad, given that advanced units of the US army had crossed the Euphrates and could not be more than forty miles away. He waved his hand impatiently. 'You know,' he said, 'most of us don't give a fuck about the Americans now. Let them come. Let them bring their puppets,★ let them take over the palaces, everything! We just want the war to be over and to live.'

★ He meant the exiled leaders of Iraqi opposition groups who were supported and were being put forward by the Americans for future government in Iraq.

Disillusionment with the promises of the war was beginning to pervade the city and Jamal Ali Hamid, a 47-year-old businessman who imported cheap consumer and household products from South Asia before the war, reinforced this message, albeit more politely. We had bumped into him when he was making his way to the home of his business partner who had left Baghdad with his family before the war, thinking they might be safer in his family's village on the outskirts of the town of Ramadi. Mr Hamid had reassured his friend that he would check on the vacant house in his absence. We met him not far from the 'Thieves Market', in central Baghdad, an open-air warren of stalls and shops selling everything from sacks of rice to razor blades. He had visited England several times during the 1970s and was pleased to discover that we were from the BBC.

'It is like, how do you say in English? The calm before the storm,' he said in his clipped English accent. 'People are thinking that there will be a very long and difficult battle for Baghdad. The government and the party have organized their forces and militia inside the city and the Americans will find a big and bloody fight in Baghdad. People know this, so they are enjoying their city before the attack.' The people he knew believed they were seeing the old Baghdad for the last time before it underwent an unpredictable transformation. 'Everything will change, for sure, and the future? No one can be sure of it. It will be a very, very dangerous future.' Then he added with a wistful smile, '*Allah karim*', God be generous.

American soldiers were getting closer with each day, and the night-time flashes on the horizon signalled their approach. By 1 April round-the-clock bombing of the city had already lasted a week. There truly was no safe place in Baghdad, just as the doctor in the Al Kindi Hospital had predicted after the Al Sha'ab market massacre. All the presidential palaces, already blasted by days and nights of attacks, were still being bombed. During the day, the smoke continued to billow from the buildings and compounds in the Republican Palace, mingling with the constant thread of pitch-black fumes from the burning oil-filled trenches around the city. Each night our satellite radio gave a running commentary on the approach of US forces: divisions of the Republican Guard thirty miles outside Baghdad were being bombed; US marines were on the main southern highway only twenty-five miles from the capital.

We dreaded the prospect of a prolonged siege, depressed at the thought of being trapped in the city. We wondered what we would do if the Iraqi authorities' predictions of a long and pitiless urban battle came true. We thought about the possibility of hiding, finding a 'safe house' belonging to Iraqi friends, such as Mohammed or Saadoun. But we soon realized that this was an unworkable idea. Carloads of foreign pressmen with their hi-tech equipment and luggage would be rather conspicuous in a residential neighbourhood and it would not be long before local party officials reported us. One prospect did seem more hopeful. Among the journalists we knew in Baghdad was a veteran Indian former BBC correspondent called Satish Jacob. He knew Paul well and had worked with him at the BBC Delhi bureau. Satish was accompanied by a young Indian cameraman, and we often helped them out when they had trouble filing their reports. Satish had been a long-time acquaintance of the Indian ambassador to Baghdad and, just before the war as India's diplomatic staff prepared to leave and close their embassy, the ambassador had given Satish a set of keys to his house should he need to take refuge.

The embassy would be an ideal bolthole if the situation became just too dangerous; it was not in a residential neighbourhood and thus the chances of going undetected were greater there than in the houses of Iraqi friends. The unfair treatment of Indian Muslims by India's government had not penetrated the consciousness of the majority of the Iraqi population, and Iraqis viewed India as a neutral country and were particularly fond of Bollywood films. Most Iraqis also saw India as a poor country and the embassy would therefore not be an attractive target for looters if the city descended into chaos. Gangs would be more likely to go for the embassies of wealthier countries or the offices of the UN, where they believed greater riches would surely be found.

As we discussed the possibility of using the embassy as an escape route, we felt reassured by having a contingency plan, even if we dreaded the circumstances that would drive us to use it. However, this option still meant that we would have to remain in Baghdad throughout the siege. The most difficult question to contemplate was how long the siege could last. Weeks or months? What conclusions could we draw from recent historical events? The siege at Sarajevo which lasted three years? The Russian army's siege of Grozny, the Chechen capital, which lasted two years? We began to realize that in these circumstances we would have to take our chances and attempt to drive across the desert to Jordan. If we decided to take this route then there was the very real threat of 'friendly fire' from American aircraft. After all, what would a pilot see on his radar? A fleet of expensive four-wheel-drive vehicles driving in convoy at great speed out of Baghdad and heading into the desert as his fellow soldiers attempted to take the city. The pilot would have only a few minutes to decide whether to engage this target or not. Deciding whether to risk driving out of Baghdad would be like playing some modern wartime version of Russian roulette – there was no way of knowing whether it would be safe. As the Russian ambassador to Baghdad would find out, when his diplomatic convoy was shot at by US forces when it attempted to make exactly this journey out of the city on 7 April.

All of us in Baghdad were living in a terrifying limbo, aware of what was closing in on the city but finding it hard to imagine how it might affect those who remained within it. And it was far, far worse for our families. I was able to speak to Nina every night on the satellite phone but it was almost unbearable to talk about how much longer the war could last; about when the end might be. Instead I spoke of how that day had not been as bad as the day before; how we had managed to eat more than one meal of freeze-dried self-heating army rations; how the previous night's bombardment had been relatively quiet and not too close to our hotel. But of course our families could not know what it was really like to live and work in a city under fire. What they did see were the two or three minutes of each night's report – the casualties, the explosions, the buildings on fire, the grieving relatives – and they could only imagine that that was what was happening everywhere in the city, every day. None of us in Baghdad knew what the coming days held, and this made it even harder to reassure our wives and families of our safety.

Before the war, many western leaders had hoped and believed that British and American soldiers would be welcomed ecstatically by ordinary Iraqis and that the conflict would last no more than a week. But after two weeks of war in the capital they could see that this was not going to happen, or at least not on the scale that they'd hoped. There was now a palpable fear of American troops, which grew as they came ever closer to the city because their approach brought forward the likelihood of a bloody siege. The last two weeks had shattered the people of Baghdad. Even in a city that was only too aware of the ferocious capability of the American military, the harrowing tide of destruction and upheaval brought by the invasion and siege had shocked everyone. Many of the journalists in Baghdad were experienced war reporters, but even the most jaded among us at times were left struggling for words to convey what we were witnessing.

Modern history is full of examples of cities besieged by invading armies where the toll of slaughtered innocents was far greater. Yet the American-led bombardment of Baghdad was extraordinary in its expression of sheer power. In a dispatch on 4 April in the *New York Times*, John F. Burns described how the 'Shock and Awe' campaign of the US airforce had truly lived up to its name:

Since the war began two weeks ago the people of Baghdad have been exposed to a reality so stark, so astonishing, so overwhelming, that those who have witnessed it have struggled to find words adequate to express what they have seen . . . American air power, as the twenty-first century begins, is a terrible swift sword that strikes with a suddenness, a devastation and a precision, in most cases, that moves even agnostics to reach for words associated with the power of gods. Along with this, life under the bombing has continued to roll forward with an everyday nonchalance that, in its own way, has been as hard to adjust to as the bombing.

At times it was hard to believe that such destruction could be the work of mere mortals. The thunderclaps from the explosions, the eruption of fire, ash and smashed concrete and the towers of smoke seemed beyond human scale. How could all this come from young men and women sitting in some control centre at a coalition base, staring into computer screens and selecting targets thousands of miles away? The military planners guided the air war from quiet, air-conditioned bunkers in secret bases in rural England and from a specially built command centre in the Gulf state of Qatar. The banks of computers in these command centres were more reminiscent of a dealing room in an investment bank. Could the officers or their senior commanders look beyond the screens and appreciate what 'Shock and Awe' really looked like to the ordinary people who were forced to endure it? It seemed to me naïve at best to believe it was somehow possible to strike shock and awe in the hearts and minds of the few hundred men who made up the government, while the rest of the 4 million citizens of Baghdad would remain unmoved, quietly biding their time until it was all over, to emerge jubilantly from their homes, psychologically and physically unaffected.

On the night of 3 April, the war finally entered every home in the capital. We stood on the balcony of our room and watched it happen. It was around 10 p.m., and Killa was filming the brightly lit horizon of western Baghdad, expecting another bombardment. Then, suddenly, the lights went out and total darkness fell across the city. It began in the south-west, and then spread quickly as each street and home was plunged into darkness. In seconds the whole city was pitch black – as if someone had flicked a giant switch. Within minutes the richer neighbourhoods resounded to the hum of diesel generators. 'They can't be far now,' Duncan said, looking out across the darkness, pricked here and there by candles and lamps. 'The Americans are bound to try to send some units in now they've cut the electricity in the city.' In fact, unbeknownst to us, they had already opened their offensive against the capital.

Reports had begun to circulate that afternoon that Saddam

International Airport had been taken by the US 3rd Infantry Division. The Minister of Information responded by calling the reports 'silly'. 'They are nowhere in Baghdad,' the minister told the western media gathered at the Press Centre. 'Their allegations are a cover-up for their failure.' Then he turned to the officials by his side and said, 'Why don't you take them to the airport, to see how big these American lies are?' And so I and about thirty other journalists were driven the twelve miles out to the airport that lay on the south-western edge of Baghdad. We found it entirely deserted, save for about ten lightly armed security guards who lolled about looking bored, like rather odd passengers waiting for a flight. There was nothing but ghostly silence in the departure halls and three tired and ancient Iraqi Airlines planes sitting forlornly on the runway. Yet only two hours after we returned to the Palestine Hotel, the first reports by the embedded journalists showed them walking around the very same concourses and terminal buildings where we had just been. We realized then that we can't have been more than 500 yards from the US soldiers. Months later, a BBC cameraman, Peter Gigliotti, who was travelling with the 3rd Infantry Division and was at the airport that day, said that American units could see us through their binoculars as we walked around on the edge of the runways.

That evening, once the power had been cut, the bombardment began again in earnest, much of it in the south-west. It went on throughout the night, an unrelenting series of devastating explosions which ripped apart government buildings and compounds across the western skyline of Baghdad. Only this time there was also the distinct sound of artillery fire. Out to the far west, behind the titanic new headquarters of the Ba'ath Party, a series of intense orange balls lit up the grey-blue sky, filling the horizon with light, like an accelerated sunrise. It ended with a ponderous swirl of smoke that twisted into the air. The ground war had finally come to the city.

The grounds of the Yarmouk Hospital in central Baghdad were oddly deserted. A couple sat waiting by the gates in an old rusted saloon car. Two dilapidated ambulances were parked inside the courtyard with no sign of a driver. An elderly couple and two women in their long black *abbayas* sat on benches near the main entrance waiting to visit patients inside. They looked at us wearily but without a trace of animosity. The emergency wards were crammed with the wounded lying on beds and stretchers: young men in fake football strips; old men in their sixties, the cloth of their dishdasha gowns speckled with blood and holes from flying shrapnel; and young children, their spindly arms and legs swaddled thickly with bandages. The hospital had its own generators that were just sufficient to keep the emergency wards operational; the rest of the hospital was forced to remain empty.

A junior doctor approached us in the corridor outside one of the wards. Although we had visited many hospitals throughout the war, the situation was now different and extremely tense. The fighting had come to Baghdad and now, more than ever before, we needed to seek the co-operation and blessing of the medical staff and patients to film the casualties of battle. The young doctor agreed to our request, but added, 'Please do not take much time. Relatives of militiamen wounded fighting the Americans were in the hospital in the morning. This is a sensitive situation, maybe they can come back, so please be aware of this.' We followed him into the ward and he headed first to a bed occupied by a young man, no more than twenty years old. His uncle sat by his bedside. Along the length of his left leg a deep gaping wound had been freshly stitched, and the side of his chest was flecked with tiny shards of shrapnel that left a cluster of black dots on his skin. The young man grimaced and clenched his teeth as the doctor undid the swathes of bandaging to dress his wound. I tried to ask the doctor for more details of the cases he and his colleagues were dealing with, but he didn't want to be interviewed or appear on western television. He directed us instead to the senior surgeon who was in his office in the next building.

We found Dr Jamal Abdel Hassan, the director of the hospital, sitting with two other doctors on a wooden bench outside his small rudimentary office. They all looked exhausted, their eyes hollow and glazed, as they drew heavily on their cigarettes. Dr Hassan had an oddly detached, faraway look as he talked. He said that 230 patients had arrived at the hospital since the early hours of the morning, all from the area around the city airport. Many of them, as the young doctor in the ward had earlier intimated, were soldiers or irregular fighters. But there were many civilians, too. All of them, he told us, had been wounded in the fighting that had taken place there during the previous twenty-four hours. He said forty-two patients had died. 'I can say that the American forces have been using cluster bombs in the fighting near the airport,' he said. 'Several of the civilian casualties have wounds which are typical of cluster bombs.' With these words he became more animated. 'The patients are civilians. The Americans are using these deadly weapons in areas where civilians are living,' he said angrily. 'This is against international law.'

The mortuary stood behind the main blocks of the hospital's clinics and outpatient departments. Alongside the mortuary a narrow path led round the perimeter of the grounds into an empty courtyard laid out in front of a row of small concrete outhouses. These were the homes of the hospital guards and caretakers and their families. A thin and battered metal door, riddled with rusty holes, was all that separated the outhouses from the breezeblock sheds of the mortuary's refrigeration rooms. We were led by one of Dr Hassan's assistants to view the grim pile of cadavers slumped in the forsaken darkness of the sheds. The bodies had been laid on metal trays that lined the sides of the rooms. I stopped counting the number of dead after the first three rooms. I felt an inexplicable emptiness. The journalist in me said I should be asking how they died, how they got there. But instead I just felt blank incomprehension, mesmerized in the presence of so much death.

Suddenly the silence was broken by voices from outside, the sound of women and young children talking in front of the caretaker's house on the other side of the mortuary door. I left the shed and walked towards where they stood. I could see two young boys, six or seven years old, peering through the holes of the door at the group of westerners gathered on the other side. Two women looked out from the dilapidated house and shouted at the children to come away and get ready to go to the shops. But the boys were eager to see the strangers with the cameras and they tried to get past me and get close to one of the mortuary sheds. I was seized by a panicked determination to stop them from seeing what was on the other side of that door. I spoke to them gently in Arabic, trying to discourage them. 'Why?' one of them asked. 'What are they doing? Are they American?' 'Just wait a second, they are journalists and they are filming a report about the war,' I said. 'They'll be finished soon. It's better not to disturb them.' I stood in front of them, blocking the doorway and trying to keep the flimsy door shut. Eventually the two women emerged from one of the dwellings, scolding the children and telling them to come along. They took the young boys by the arms and led them away down a path towards one of the exits at the back of the hospital. As they walked past the open door of one of the sheds, they saw the BBC team still filming inside. The two women and the children turned to look back at us. I heard one of the women say: 'They are filming the dead people. What will they gain by it?'

Rocket fire and the unmistakable crackle of machine guns could be heard from the south-western edge of town, which until now had witnessed only the grand boom of missiles and 'bunker buster' bombs. We drove back through the city without seeing any evidence that Saddam Hussein was managing to maintain any control over the capital. There were no blockades on the main arterial routes into the city; hardly any checkpoints; those hastily dug, rudimentary fox-holes we had seen in the first days of the war were empty, the frightened civilian guards with the pot bellies having long since gone to find safety at home. We saw only a few young fighters from Saddam's Fedayeen★, lurking on street corners or careering around in the back of pick-up trucks, showing off their

---

★ *Fedayeen Saddam*, Saddam's 'Men of Sacrifice', was founded by his son Uday in 1995. The Fedayeen, with a total strength reportedly between 30,000 and 40,000 troops, was composed of young soldiers recruited from regions loyal to Saddam.

ancient rocket-propelled grenades and AK-47s. They were hood-
lums and ex-convicts, recruited into the Fedayeen by Saddam
Hussein's psychotic elder son, Uday. Were these to be the saviours
of Saddam's regime? Were these the 'sons of Baghdad' who the
Defence Minister had told us would make this city of ancient
civilization impregnable to American forces? Were these petty
gangsters the young men who the Interior Minister, with his
silver-plated Kalashnikov, said would sacrifice their lives to defend
Saddam Hussein and his family? These young thugs of Saddam's
Fedayeen were fitting symbols of the regime. At the very point of
its destruction, when all its defences had crumbled, the frailty of
the regime's façade was exposed. Its lies, its fragile mythology, its
false grandeur and ruthless power had all collapsed to expose what
it really was: a chaotic, desperate cabal of violent gangsters. When
ordinary Iraqis passed these militiamen hanging about on street
corners, they glanced at them suspiciously.

It felt as if the city was falling apart, the grim past giving way
to an uncertain and dangerous future. The rapid capture of the
international airport by US troops – barely twelve miles from the
city centre – with little effective opposition, enhanced the fear and
uncertainty. In everyone's mind there was nothing but questions.
What will the Americans do next now they have captured the
airport? Where are the thousands of fighters the regime says it has
prepared inside the city? Will anyone fight for the regime? Whom
should we fear most? Where is the regime? Does it still exist? And
most of all, where is Saddam Hussein?

The man at the centre of it all must have realized that these
questions were being asked. And so he re-emerged for one last
piece of theatre. Late on the evening of 4 April Iraqi television
showed a hunted leader on the streets of his besieged capital. As
ever he was dressed in military uniform, as were the eight or so
guards and advisers who accompanied him. It was vintage Saddam,
the leader who suddenly surprised his people by arriving unannounced among them. He loved the idea of appearing like a prince
among his subjects, a chilling fantasy given how frightened his
subjects were of him. The pictures on the screen showed Saddam

being mobbed by a couple of hundred adoring fans who thrust their way forward to kiss and hug him. One man held his young child above his head for the great leader to bless with a kiss, while the guards and advisers tried to hold the crowds back. He was loving every minute of it, grinning broadly as he jumped on to the bonnet of a car and punched the air. As the camera panned round, it briefly revealed a landmark which showed that he was at the main roundabout of Liqa Azahour, in the Mansour district, at the beginning of the main highway to Jordan. As the camera angle changed, distinctive thin black plumes of smoke from the burning oil trenches appeared in the background. The oil fires meant that the film had to be fairly recent, if not contemporaneous, but there inevitably came the question of whether this was Saddam Hussein at all or just one of his doubles. Such was the Iraqi leader's paranoia and obsession with his own security that the regime employed a number of Saddam 'lookalikes', who were trained in his manner-isms and dressed to look identical to him. These 'doubles' would take his place at minor state occasions such as military parades or receive less important visiting delegations.

There was no doubt in my mind or, more importantly, in the minds of most Iraqis we met that this was Saddam Hussein. The man on the screen was accompanied by some of the most powerful figures of the regime, including Abed Hamoud, Saddam's feared personal secretary. It is extremely unlikely that he would personally accompany a double out into the streets of Baghdad with American forces no more than twelve miles away. The occasion had a desper-ately hollow ring to it. It was an attempt to perpetuate the illusion that the regime remained in power, but it signified nothing. The regime seemed to believe that as long as senior figures and ministers continued to appear on television and in press conferences this would somehow make the Iraqi people and the outside world, including even the American military commanders on the outskirts of the city, believe that they were 'in control'. The regime had relied on deception and public assertions of strength for so long that even at its death it clung to its own extraordinary self-belief. The Minister of Information appeared before us. 'Don't believe them, they are big liars,' he bellowed in his usual cocksure manner. 'We are pounding them . . . those criminals . . . those villains . . . we are surrounding them and bombarding them mercilessly.'

Mohammed al Sahaff had become the face and voice for the bizarre world that was Baghdad on 5 April. But no sooner had he cheerfully described the American forces suffering catastrophic military humiliation, than we heard the first news of an American incursion into the centre of the city. We heard from radio reports that it was a limited exercise aimed at probing the strength of Iraqi defences. US forces had reached several key points in the heart of the capital.

We wanted to drive around the city to try to find these American soldiers, but Press Centre officials refused point blank to let us out of the hotel with our cameras. We could only drive around the city 'not to film' we were told, 'but to go and see with your eyes'. Of course we had no intention of going out without coming back with pictures. Luai was nervous and we could see that he was trapped between us and his bosses, who were clearly getting edgier with every passing day. We had an idea. We would go out with our camera and film what we saw, but before we returned to the hotel, Duncan would remove and hide the valuable cassette from his camera and replace it with a fresh one on which he would record some harmless, inoffensive footage, just in case the authorities confiscated our material. Luai agreed to the idea reluctantly and pleaded with us to 'take care about this matter' and 'be very careful'.

We went north along Saadoun Street on the eastern bank of the Tigris, down through the commercial and shopping districts that took us past Rashid Street. There was an Alice in Wonderland quality to this side of the city which seemed almost oblivious to what was happening across the Tigris river. Here shops were open, flames roasted columns of meat behind the front windows of kebab stalls, there were cars and buses on the streets as well as commercial lorries. People were going about their business. A row of shops near the Shorja market openly sold receivers and dishes for satellite television – utterly unthinkable before the war when these devices were banned by the regime. This was the first clear indication that the authority and control of the Iraqi regime and its security apparatus had completely broken down. Now they couldn't even prevent people from watching foreign TV stations, whose coverage was dominated by news of the war.

We crossed a bridge to the western side of Baghdad towards the grand buildings and compounds of the regime. It was like another world as the calm of Shorja market on the eastern bank of the Tigris was replaced by the complete destruction wrought by over two weeks of merciless bombing. The front of the Sujood Palace had been sheared off, cleanly cut away as if by a surgeon's scalpel. The reek of smoke and burning buildings was everywhere. Bands of young militiamen hung around the streets in faded, dirty football jerseys, jeans and checked keffiyehs swathed around their faces so that only their eyes could be seen. Luai's nervousness grew as we snaked our way through the monumental heart of Saddam Hussein's Baghdad, and every time our car came close to militiamen or soldiers he urgently pleaded with Duncan to put the camera away. Duncan would take it from his shoulder and place it on the seat next to him, resting his arm on the body of the camera so it would not be so visible from the street, but continuing to film the whole time.

Beneath a motorway underpass close to the Baghdad railway station, a regular army unit had positioned two artillery guns, their barrels pointing directly down the expressway that led to the south-west of the city. The road was empty, save for a few birds that picked at the flattened remains of a dead animal lying in the middle of one of the motorway lanes. There was still no sign of the American forces and no clue to their presence in the centre of the city; no sound of gunfire and no civilians clogging the streets in an attempt to flee from neighbourhoods which had suddenly become front-line positions. We swung back across the river and followed its course south towards the Al Dora district, past the huge oil terminal that served the city. The ring of burning oil trenches that encircled the south of Baghdad was no more than two miles away and the huge columns of black smoke towered above us like skyscrapers. Even here, as we gradually approached the edge of the city in the direction of the airport, there was the same air of unreality. A few teenage members of the Fedayeen, in black combat trousers and proudly clutching machine guns to their chests, inexpertly tried to command a rudimentary checkpoint at a roundabout. They looked uncertainly out at the approaching traffic, and most of the Iraqis who passed by in their cars glanced at them scornfully. What little respect ordinary Iraqis did show was more for the guns hanging round the youths' necks than for the baby-faced defenders of Saddam Hussein.

As we arrived at the residential district of Al Dora we saw an enormous fire 500 yards in front of us, its flames spitting and licking the sky, black smoke obscuring the road and houses behind. The burning trench was set in an empty field on the side of the road and the heat penetrated through the metal and glass of our car, right into the carriage, and we felt its sudden rush against our bodies. Our car headed into the thick soot that straddled the road. Even though the windows had been firmly rolled up, the acrid stench of the fumes came through, burning the backs of our throats. Darker and more claustrophobic than any tunnel, it was as though day had been turned into the blackest of nights. It lasted for about five seconds and, as suddenly as it had come, the darkness was gone.

We joined another road leading from the airport. We could see fires ahead of us where the blackened hulks of vehicles lay sprawled amid broken glass and twisted metal. Further ahead an American tank which had presumably broken down had been abandoned and was in flames, its barrel pointed back in the direction of the airport. Rather than allow it to fall into their enemy's hands, the Americans had destroyed it. The ruined pick-up trucks a little further down the road had clearly belonged to Iraqi fighters. I could see the makeshift turrets which they had used to mount heavy-calibre machine guns on the back of the vehicles. The cars had been shot to pieces as they had tried to get near the abandoned tank. Riddled with hundreds of holes, their side doors and engines had been blown from the bodywork and on to the road. Here was the first evidence we had seen with our own eyes of an American military presence in Baghdad, outside the airport which they controlled.

Once we had got these pictures, Luai asked if we could put our camera away, and change the tape as we had agreed.

As we passed the American tank we noticed that the soldiers who had been manning it had inscribed their own motto along the side of the barrel. Some of them must have been Hispanic because the word written in black stencilled capital letters was in Spanish: 'COJONES'. Balls.

When we finally returned to the hotel we heard that the director of the Press Centre had been looking for us. I caught his eye when I entered the conference room near the end of a press conference being held by the Minister of Information. The director glared at me, pursing his lips and shaking his head ominously from side to side. I feigned surprise at his apparent indignation, and stood close to the door where I could be certain he would be able to get hold of me as soon as his boss had finished his assessment of how the 'villains' and 'big international criminals' were being 'slaughtered' by the 'heroic Iraqi Republican Guard and tribal fighters'. When the minister left, the director came straight up to me. 'You have been filming out in Baghdad,' he shouted, his eyes bulging with rage. 'Bring me your cameraman and the tape immediately. I told you precisely that you could not film but only go out to see how everything is normal in the city with your own eyes. Bring the tape. This is unacceptable and it is dangerous.' He yelled instructions to several of his assistants to find the cameraman who had been with me.

Knowing that we were wanted by the authorities, Duncan had swung into action as soon as I had gone off to the press conference. He had hidden the first tape with the footage of the Fedayeen militia and the destroyed Iraqi vehicles near the American tank and had replaced it with another tape, of an innocuous piece we had recorded in the back of the car. Duncan appeared at the conference hall with the new tape and a shocked expression on his face. 'If you have been filming around the city the whole BBC team will be on their way to Trebil★,' the Press Centre official said before walking

★ The border crossing to neighbouring Jordan.

away to view the tape. Luai too had been called in and was forced to wait with the officials while they watched the footage. At the end of the viewing and to Luai's great relief, they acknowledged that he had done his job and apologized for the mix-up. We later learned that some militiamen had reported that they thought they had seen journalists filming scenes on the road to the airport from inside their vehicle and had taken down the number of our car registration and radioed the information to the local party office, which in turn had passed it on to the Press Centre.

Not content with keeping the truth from its own people, the Iraqi regime tried desperately to hide reality even from itself. On 6 April Iraqi television said that all fighters and soldiers who had been 'separated' from their units had been ordered to join 'other units'. Order among the Iraqi armed forces was clearly breaking down and these instructions gave a clue as to just how many soldiers were abandoning their positions and going home with their guns to defend their families against the disorder they feared would follow the overthrow of the government. The regime had to resort even to bribing their soldiers. In the same broadcast it announced that £400, an unimaginable sum of money to an Iraqi conscript, would be given to any soldier who killed a soldier from the coalition. It was clear that the American forces were now pushing at an open door.

For the first time in weeks I slept deeply through the night that followed. Like the rest of the city, I felt that it was merely a matter of waiting for the Americans to come. Just after seven o'clock on the morning of 7 April, the phone by my bed rang. It took me an age to wake from the groggy exhaustion of a proper night's sleep and answer it. It was Paul. 'Rageh! Are you awake?' I mumbled a reply. 'Look outside your window, your window! It's fucking incredible. Get down to the suite, we need to record this moment and do a piece to camera.' I stumbled, still half-asleep, over to the balcony, opened the glass door and stepped out. A crackle of machine-gun fire was the first thing I heard echoing through the cold, foggy air. I looked across the river to the Republican Palace, less than half a mile away, and there they were. Two American armoured personnel carriers had parked on the road running along the side of the palace by the riverbank.

It took me at least five minutes to come to terms with what I was seeing. Not since British generals entered Jerusalem at the end of the First World War had a western army smashed its way into a Muslim Arab capital with the intention of conquering it. I stared transfixed at the armoured vehicles that had been left in full view of the whole eastern bank of the river. They were unprepossessing for such a momentous occasion. But those two armoured vehicles by the side of Saddam Hussein's Republican Palace signified the first moments of an event that would have profound effects on the most volatile region in the world.

I don't remember getting dressed or running down the four flights of stairs to the BBC suite on the thirteenth floor. Duncan and Killa were filming from the balcony, not taking their eyes off their viewfinders, and the expression on Paul's face said it all. It was a mixture of shock and relief that this terrible ordeal that we had feared would mean several more weeks of ferocious fighting was about to come to an end. They are just the other side of the river, less than half a mile away, I remember thinking; it won't be long before they arrive to take control of the areas around the Palestine Hotel. Then a loud crash of gunfire and explosions came from the western side of the city. In the distance we could hear the deep thudding of artillery. We saw a group of American soldiers emerge from one of the armoured vehicles. About six of them, in tan combat clothes, flak jackets and helmets, shuffled towards the outside wall of the palace as they crouched with their weapons at the ready. It was extraordinary to be able to see them so exposed and yet so in control. They disappeared behind the palm trees and bushes that lined the palace wall. About 200 yards from their vehicles mortar rounds and rocket-propelled grenades exploded along the riverbank. The machine-gun fire was almost constant and small puffs of smoke hovered and drifted along the river's edge. The battle continued for about an hour, while the vapour trails of American fighter planes criss-crossed the skies overhead. Gunfire and explosions could be heard from the districts to the north of the

Republican Palace, close to the Al Rasheed Hotel. Yet the American armoured personnel carriers didn't even bother to move from their positions.

Mid-morning, as we watched the fighting around the Republican Palace, we suddenly saw a line of figures appear from the palace compound. The Iraqi soldiers who had been guarding the palace were running for their lives. At first there were about six of them, dressed in black uniforms. They frantically scrambled towards the river, throwing themselves down the dusty embankment. There was a burst of gunfire and then a series of tiny puffs of sand as the hail of bullets ripped into the dried earth of the embankment. Two of the men started rolling down the escarpment as they tried to escape. Then we saw the other Iraqi security guards and soldiers fleeing en masse from the palace grounds. These were Saddam Hussein's elite troops, the Special Republican Guard, to whom he had entrusted the security of his family and regime and whom he had handpicked for the task. These were the men who had been at the heart of the Iraqi leader's concealment strategy and who had led UN weapons inspectors a merry dance for eight years. They were men who struck dread into the hearts of most Iraqis, made people disappear, kept tabs on the movements of citizens. They had been caught completely by surprise. Several of them were dressed in nothing more than a pair of large white Y-front underpants, socks and shoes. Utterly terrified, they tripped and limped away from the palace without any idea of where they were headed. Some ran towards the embankment, others in the direction of the nearest bridge and many of them just followed the man in front. One of them tore off his uniform and threw it into the water, clearly anxious that he would be lynched if he was caught by Iraqi civilians in the clothes of a Special Republican Guard. One of the semi-naked men could only hobble, occasionally clutching his right knee in pain, before another soldier ran up behind him and grabbed one of his arms to help him move more quickly away from the American forces.

We left the hotel and drove along Saadoun Street on the eastern side of the river, directly across from the buildings and compounds being stormed by the 3rd Infantry Division. American fighter planes screamed overhead on another bombing run to destroy what was left of Iraqi positions on the other side of the city. Empty of its people and any semblance of normal life, Baghdad had taken on the appearance of an urban battleground; its streets had become the domain of groups of Fedayeen fighters. The young men were dressed in civilian clothes and held AK-47s and rocket-propelled grenades. Bizarrely they gave us 'V for Victory' signs as we drove by, as if this were just an afternoon's adventure, and they were only acting out scenes from a war film. Everything felt unreal: the bravado of the militiamen in the face of the brutal firepower that awaited them on the other side of the river; the empty streets of eastern Baghdad that seemed a million miles away from the battles erupting only a few minutes away across the Joumhouriya Bridge. The militiamen were erecting barriers across the bridges using concrete blocks and lorries in the vain hope that this would be enough to stop American armour from crossing over. But further along Saadoun Street, close to Tahrir Square, cafés were open and street vendors were plying their trade. It was as if they had just stopped caring, and had already accepted that the regime's predictions of a Stalingrad-like battle for Baghdad had been nothing more than one last hollow lie by a now non-existent government.

No one, it seemed, had told the Iraqi Minister of Information what was going on in the city. Either that, or he had decided to entirely ignore it, as well as what he could now surely see with his own eyes. He appeared before the assembled journalists, many of whom were eager to hear him describe the situation in which his government found itself. He surpassed everyone's expectations. In a bizarrely courteous manner, he chided us in the way that an older uncle might address his excitable nephews. 'Don't believe them,' he said with a confident smile, 'they are big liars. They said they entered with sixty-five tanks into the centre of the capital . . . this story is part of their sickness. The real truth is that there was no entry of American or British troops into Baghdad at all.' Then he proceeded to tell us that we actually hadn't seen what we *had* seen, that somehow we had succumbed to a sort of mass hallucination.

'Don't repeat their lies . . . Don't believe these invaders . . . we are slaughtering them . . . we will finish them.'

He then turned his attention to the pictures broadcast around the world by embedded journalists travelling with the US troops who had captured the Republican Palace. They showed American soldiers lying out in one of the palace's secluded gardens which had hitherto been for the exclusive use of the most senior members of the regime. Another image showed the troops staring up in amazement at the ceilings of the palace conference halls and wandering open-mouthed through its gilded bathrooms. 'They are just cheap liars,' al Sahaff said as he waved his hand in the air. He went on to claim that the pictures of Saddam Hussein's gold and marble bidets had actually been filmed in the arrivals hall of the airport where he said the American forces were still holed up. He then advised us to 'Report the accurate truth, don't be fooled by their tricks and lies.'

I was standing no more than two feet from him, and I shouted to get his attention. He turned round and looked me straight in the eyes with a slightly nervous smirk. 'Mr Sahaff, just on the other side of the river there is a battle going on in the Republican Palace, and we can see the armoured personnel carriers there, and yet you have come, a senior government minister, to talk to us. How do you feel personally as an Iraqi minister, with American forces less than half a mile away?' He squinted at me and bellowed, 'They are nowhere. Don't believe them. As for me, as usual! As usual. Those invaders, their tombs will be here in Baghdad.' And with that reply, he was gone. It was to be the last time I would see him in the flesh.

The larger hospitals in Baghdad began to bear witness to the bloody cost of the battle for the city. Throughout the day, civilian dead and injured were brought into the Yarmouk and Al Kindi hospitals in a seemingly unending procession. They came in battered saloon cars, taxis, ambulances and pick-up trucks. Occasionally young militiamen were also brought in, their shirts and trousers soaked with blood. Fatima Abdel Hamid was writhing in agony in one of the casualty wards of the Al Kindi Hospital, groaning from the wounds across her chest and face which had become horribly swollen. She said she had been hit by shrapnel as an American armoured personnel carrier fired on two vehicles driving on the road from the Al Muthana airfield towards the Al Rasheed Hotel. 'They were just shooting everything. God help us! They were only families in those cars trying to get away from the fighting. They were driving towards the Americans but on the other side of the road. But now they are dead.' Doctors said they had received seventy badly wounded civilians on that day alone. There were similar testimonies from other hospitals which described how American troops, still battling their way through the centre of the city and fighting small groups of Fedayeen resistance, were destroying anything in their sights of which they were uncertain.

The battle continued throughout the night. American forces, realizing that any effective resistance in the face of their over-whelming firepower had crumbled, were tightening their grip throughout the central government quarter in the west of the city. As they did so, US marine units were beginning an advance on the city from the north-east, while further infantry units spearheaded an advance from the north-west. We wondered when this agony would be over. Even amid the far greater suffering of others, and after witnessing the horrific loss and injuries to ordinary Iraqis who, unlike us, had no choice but to remain in Baghdad, it was hard not to think about when the ordeal might end for us.

We talked about it a lot that night. Duncan was pessimistic. 'I think they're just going to sit it out and wait until all the Fedayeen in the centre of the city have been killed or have run away,' he said. 'They're not going to come over to secure this hotel. I don't think it's even a consideration for them at this point.' Killa, like me, was just frustrated and exhausted. 'They don't need to send a whole regiment. They're just across the river, just those two APCs★ would be enough. I just wish they'd get here,' he said. I called Nina in South Africa that night. She was thinking the same thoughts and asked the question which none of us could answer. 'When will the

★ Armoured personnel carriers.

American forces get to the Palestine Hotel?' 'I don't know,' I said, 'soon.' She asked me to promise that whatever the circumstances, however secure or safe I felt, I would not appear on television without a flak jacket and helmet. I promised.

Just after 9 a.m. on 8 April, I switched on the satellite radio. At first I thought the newsreader must have made a mistake. 'Al Jazeera say their compound in the centre of Baghdad was hit in an air raid . . . it is believed that their correspondent Tariq Ayoub was killed in the attack.' I felt my hands go cold. I tried to see out across the river to the western embankment where Al Jazeera's office was located but a thick cloud of smoke obscured the view. I had been in Kabul in November 2002 when the Al Jazeera office there had also been bombed by the United States airforce after the staff had been given a short warning to leave the premises. How could this have happened when before the war had even begun the Pentagon itself had been given the exact satellite co-ordinates of the Al Jazeera bureau? How could they have made this mistake – if that was what it was? Tariq Ayoub, a Palestinian journalist usually based in Jordan, and his team had been wondering the previous day whether they should leave the riverside villa which served as Al Jazeera's Baghdad office. It was isolated and stuck in the middle of what had become a frontline, caught between the Republican Palace to the south and the Ministry of Information to the north and with other key security buildings nearby. Tariq was killed almost instantly, right in the middle of a live broadcast. He was thirty-five years old, married with one child. His death signalled a warning note to a day that was going to get considerably worse.

The A-10 Warthog Tankbuster, to give it its proper name, is a terrifying thing to see in action. Slow and heavy, it has none of the supersonic agility of jet fighters, but it carries an even more menacing instrument of destruction: a cannon that fires several thousand rounds a second of bullets tipped with depleted uranium, and it was coming back in our direction. It banked steeply before descending along a line parallel with the Tigris river, and once again it poured a hail of fire on to the Ministry of Planning, the flat-fronted purple block adjacent to the Joumhouriya Bridge. The whole front of this twelve-storey building disappeared behind a wall of bright flashes, sparks and dust as hundreds of rounds smashed into it. Again and again it would come, until the pilot was satisfied that no sniper who had taken up a position inside the already bombed building could have survived. By mid-morning, the way was clear for American tanks to position themselves on the Joumhouriya Bridge and we watched them, less than a mile away and in full view as they prepared to cross to the eastern bank of the Tigris. Paul Wood was filing a dispatch for BBC radio as this was happening. 'We are not sure, of course, whether these are the final hours,' he said, 'but it certainly feels like it.' It was the beginning of the end, an end that would come quicker than we could have imagined. Any idea that Saddam Hussein's regime still existed in any form disappeared on that morning.

On the edge of Firdoos Square, where the hand of Saddam Hussein's statue stretched imperiously over a city he no longer controlled, I saw several senior Press Centre officials wandering about. One had his hand on the shoulder of a colleague, trying to comfort him. The friend in turn held his hands over his face and seemed to be crying. The minders in the lobby of the Palestine were frantic now. Some of them were trying to persuade the drivers to take them to a district on the eastern edge of the city, but the drivers did not want to, and they knew there was nothing the minders could do to threaten them now. This was the moment that Luai had feared for so long, and he was talking about leaving. Several days earlier Paul Danahar had urged him to stick close to us when US forces entered the heart of the city, but now that the Americans had arrived he was terrified. To reassure him, Paul had written him a note on BBC letterhead in English and Arabic stating that he was a locally hired employee. But that morning, even this was not enough. Paul pleaded with him not to do anything reckless. 'Luai, you are just a badly paid minder. The Americans want to get their hands on the senior officials and ministers of the government. They're not going to come and round up every single one of the 4 million members of the Ba'ath Party. Look, if you try to drive or walk across the city, Luai, you'll be killed, you know that! You've seen what all the injured people in the hospitals have been saying about the Americans shooting everything in their way. Just stay here,' he urged him. Luai didn't respond. He just walked away. That was the last time I saw him.

At noon I was on the lower roof of the Palestine Hotel with Paul Danahar and Killa, preparing to do a live broadcast from our satellite position. Meanwhile, Malek and Duncan were on the balcony of our suite on the thirteenth floor filming the American Abrams tanks on the Joumhouriya Bridge. The BBC studio in London could already see me on their monitors. Killa had hurriedly helped me to plug in my earpiece as it was only a few minutes before we were due to go live. He had just turned from me and was about to take up position behind his camera when it happened. A thundering blast threw me to the floor. I opened my eyes as I lay prostrate in terror and saw Killa lying on the ground four feet away. At first I thought he was wounded, but his eyes had the same wide look of shock, and I realized that he too had been hurled to the ground by the force of the explosion. A fraction of a second later, as we gazed across at each other in stunned disbelief, there was the clatter of thousands of tiny pieces of stone and masonry cascading on to the asphalt roof like a burst of hail from the sky. Then I heard people screaming as horror gripped the journalists on the roof. An engineer ran out from one of the tents and pointed up towards the top floors of the hotel. 'Oh Jesus, they're just killing people now,' he said.

I lifted myself up and looked in the same direction and saw that something had struck the hotel side closest to us. Two wires ran from the balcony of the suite that had been hit, down to the lower roof where we were. I knew instantly that it was the Reuters Television office, as the wires ran from their fifteenth-floor offices down to their satellite dish next to ours. Paul Danahar came rushing out of the BBC tent to see if we were okay, then he told us to get off the roof. He grabbed a large medical trauma pack from the tent and ran towards the fire escape which led into the main building of the hotel. There was panic and confusion in the lobby. People were screaming instructions to clear the area, and I saw a limp body being carried in a bedsheet out of the front door. I took the trauma pack from Paul and told him that I wanted to go to the Reuters office to see if any help was needed. There was a trail of blood stains running along the corridor to their suite. The door to the main room was open and I saw the Reuters TV Bureau Chief, Ahmed Seif, screaming into the satellite phone to their head office in London, trying to explain what had happened. He saw me running towards him and urgently waved me into the next-door room.

There was nothing but a gaping and blackened hole where the doors to the balcony had been. Shrapnel and blast marks had shredded the wallpaper and ceiling. Taras Protyusk, the Reuters cameraman who had been filming the American tanks on the Joumhouriya Bridge, lay flat on his back, in a pool of blood. The flesh of his stomach had been ripped apart. There was hysteria and anger and everyone was shouting. 'Tear the fucking bedsheets off, he's going to bleed to death!' 'No! No! We have to get him to hospital now, for God's sake . . . Jesus Christ, somebody get a car. Lift him! Lift him!' I tore at the straps enclosing the trauma pack: bandages, saline solution, surgical gloves, painkillers. And then I looked at Taras again. His stomach wasn't there. Just a dark and blood-stained cavity and the unspeakable horror of what had been torn out from inside him. A small number of photographers and cameramen were in the corner of the room, recording the scene. With hindsight one can understand what they were trying to do – it was, after all, no different from what we had been doing in the city throughout the war. But at that moment it was too much for many of us and someone shouted at them to get out. We all quickly recognized that there was nothing any of us could do for Taras, and that whatever faint hope remained for him lay in the hands of Iraqi surgeons. I stepped away from a group of people who were frantically creating a makeshift stretcher out of a disused blanket they had found in a hotel cupboard.

I stumbled down to the BBC office. We just sat there, unable to understand what had just happened. The attack on the Palestine Hotel by US forces had been beamed live around the world and

Paul Danahar told us to phone our families immediately. I waited until I had gathered myself before calling Nina. It was just after lunchtime in Johannesburg and she was about to leave the house. Thankfully she hadn't been watching the television. I just kept saying to her that everyone in the BBC team was fine and well, that there had been 'an incident close to the hotel' but that we were all okay. I kept repeating it. We talked briefly about everyday things: how she was, what she was doing, how our credit cards had been blocked because I had forgotten to pay the bill. Then I said goodbye, and repeated again that we were all fine. Fifteen minutes later one of our closest friends, who had been watching the attack live on television, phoned Nina. 'Nina! He's okay, he's okay. Don't worry,' she said. 'I've seen Rageh on the TV where journalists were trying to help the others who had been wounded in the attack, but he's fine, he wasn't hurt.' It was only then that Nina realized why I had been repeating myself with such insistence.

This is not the place for a detailed examination of why three journalists were killed and two seriously wounded by American forces that day, but some points need to be made for the record. The statement given by the Coalition Central Command following the attack stated: 'Commanders on the ground reported that coalition forces received significant enemy fire from the hotel and consistent with the inherent right of self-defence, coalition forces returned fire . . . Sadly a Reuters and Tele 5 journalist[*] were killed in this exchange. These tragic incidents appear to be the latest example of the Iraqi regime's continued strategy of using civilian facilities for military purposes.' There was no fire from the hotel or anywhere near it. At least five television networks recorded continuous footage in the half-hour before the American tank fired its single round into the hotel, the BBC and Sky News among them. I and at least twenty other reporters were on the lower roof of the Palestine Hotel at least fifteen minutes before the tank fired, and there was no trace, either in our personal recollections or on the audio footage, of the sound of gunfire in or near the hotel.

[*] José Cousu, a cameraman for the Spanish TV station Tele 5.

That night was one of the longest of my life. We continued to do live broadcasts from the lower roof of the hotel until it got late, but it was difficult to concentrate. In the middle of the reports I would look around me into the still darkness of Baghdad's streets and the pitch black sky, imagining I could hear the sound of a tank engine or aeroplane. I felt more vulnerable than ever and I couldn't wait for those broadcasts to end. The atmosphere among us that night was one of aching sorrow and deep guilt. For twenty minutes dozens of pressmen gathered for a brief candlelit service to remember our colleagues who had died that day. There was very little to say. Many of us had simply come to the end of our emotional strength. Before I went to bed I frantically rearranged my room, moving the bed into the far corner, as far away from the balcony as possible. The only time I took my flak jacket off was when I finally lay in bed, unable to sleep. Even then I kept it by my side.

From my notebook – 9 April

Press Centre has simply evaporated. No minders, officials or spooks in hotel. Lobby entirely empty – strangest feeling. Full of apprehension. This is most dangerous moment. No authority. Feeling that anarchy and civil chaos just round the corner.

The system of control that had governed our lives as foreign journalists in Iraq had not merely collapsed, it had completely disappeared. There was no trace of the officials, minders and clerks who had made up the Press Centre; their papers, the desks which bore the placards of the various departments, everything had gone by the next morning, 9 April. There was complete silence in the streets around Firdoos Square, along the boulevard of Saadoun Street and the side alleys by the eastern bank of the river.

Just after 9 a.m. an unnerving scene outside the Palestine Hotel caused panic among the reporters. About twenty Arab mujahideen from countries outside Iraq, who had volunteered to come and fight British and American forces, were approaching the grounds of the hotel. Many of us assumed they were coming to kill foreign journalists in a last desperate act. Malek went down to talk to them and discovered the real reason why they had come. Tired, hungry and frightened they wanted to seek refuge among us. They asked for some water and cigarettes and said they had run out of money and were stranded in the city which was falling to American troops. None of them was armed and none of them had any possessions other than the ragged and dirty clothes they wore.

By 10 a.m. Saddam Hussein's rule had ceased to exist in Baghdad. Government stores and warehouses were being looted in the north-west. The sprawling Shia districts of Khadimiya in the northern part of the city, where I had talked to Luai before the war about whether to stay in Baghdad, provided one of the most extraordinary scenes of that day. About 2,000 men of all ages gathered in front of a mosque in one of the poorest neighbourhoods, beating their chests in unison in the Shia ritual of sacrifice and martyrdom, filling the air with a pounding beat as they strained their voices in a single chant: '*La illaha il Allah, Saddam Hussein adow Allah!*' There is no God but Allah, and Saddam Hussein is the enemy of Allah! This ritual had been banned under Saddam Hussein, and the words they were chanting would have cost them their lives. Now they shouted them out with unfailing energy, for they knew that there was no one to stop them. There was no mention of America or Britain or the United Nations or Bush or Blair in the voices of those Shia men; they spoke only of Allah, and the end of the dictator who had brutally repressed them.

As the hours passed the city was filled with scenes of Iraqi civilians throwing out the vestiges of the world that Saddam Hussein had created. The mood spread across whole swathes of Baghdad which were suddenly given over to people who hardly knew how to express themselves in a world without Saddam. Whole families crammed into the backs of their cars and drove through the main streets, honking their horns, the children in the back seats staring out as their mothers wound down the windows and shouted in delight at passers-by.

Groups of men began looting the buildings that most symbolized the fear and hatred they felt for the regime – chief among them the

21. Armed with guns and knives, Iraqi soldiers and militiamen hunt for a reportedly downed US pilot in the reeds along the Tigris river

Market bombing
22. Sala Izit sits dazed outside his electrical repair shop after the bombing of the Al Sha'ab district where fourteen civilians were killed

23. Filming with Killa in the Al Sha'ab district after the bombing

24. An Iraqi mourns a relative killed in the market bombing

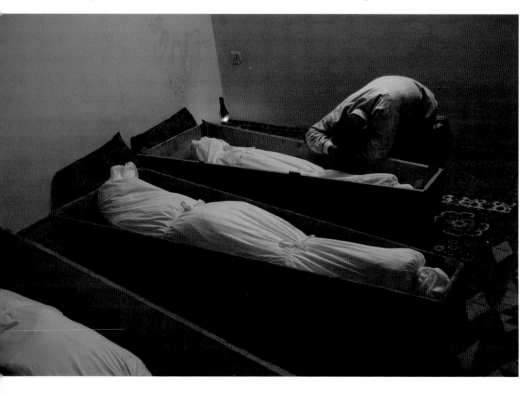

The fall

25. The television crew on the roof of the Palestine Hotel provides the only light after the city's grid was destroyed by the approaching US army

26. American forces close in from the other side of the Sinak Bridge as the fedayeen attempt to hold them off

27. The 3rd Battalion, 4th Marines Regiment arrive. The Palestine Hotel is on the right of the picture

28. American soldiers mask the head of Saddam Hussein in the US flag before the statue is toppled

Looting
29 and 30. Baghdad residents enjoy the spoils of the regime

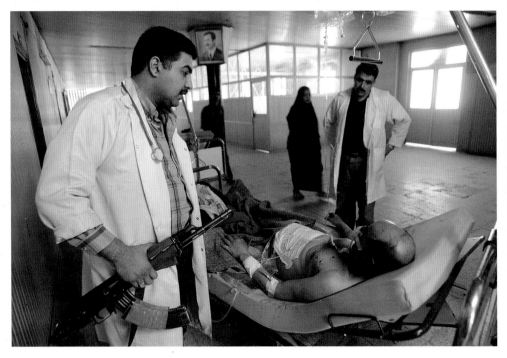

31. A doctor in Al Karh hospital defends one of his patients from prospective looters

32. Saddam Hussein in front of burning offices of the National Olympic Committee run by Uday Hussein

33. I took this photograph from my hotel balcony on the day before I left Baghdad

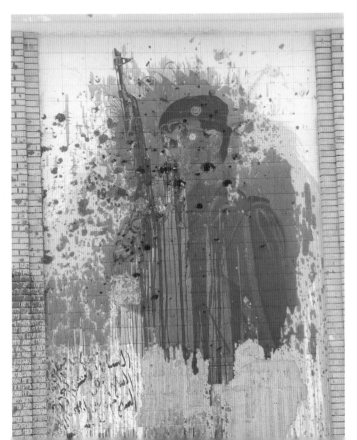

Return
34. A mural of Saddam
Hussein defaced with
paint and cowpats
outside Basra city

35. The identity cards of people tortured and beaten by Saddam Hussein's regime in the central prison in Basra, discovered as British troops rolled into the city

36. Abdel Jawad Tamimi and his wife Aliya hold up pictures of their children, killed by cluster bombs during the coalition bombardment around Hilla in April

building of the National Olympic Committee in eastern Baghdad. This was the headquarters of Saddam Hussein's loathed elder son, Uday, who controlled his fiefdom of business rackets, militia groups and torture chambers from it. Hundreds of men emerged from the building clutching whatever they could carry: Chinese vases, electric fans, carpets and armchairs. Outside its main gate, an old man was unfurling a large painting on canvas of the deposed dictator. As people drove by and honked their horns, he struck the image with his shoe. Another man on his way in to loot the building walked past the picture, bent down and spat on it.

By midday, American marines were just over a mile south of the Palestine Hotel, on the main road from Firdoos Square to the Karada district. The street was almost entirely deserted, with just a few confused and startled Iraqis tentatively beginning to emerge from their homes to look at the tanks and military vehicles that had parked on the road. Going to meet the US forces was for me the most terrifying moment of the entire war – especially as I had only just witnessed the attack on the Palestine Hotel and the death of one of my colleagues. Paul, Duncan, Dylan and I all wore flak jackets and helmets. We took white pillowcases and bedsheets to wave from the car as we drove up the road, holding our hands open outside the windows to show that we were not armed. Our vehicle had been plastered with the letters 'TV' and Dylan kept his foot off the accelerator.

Just before one o'clock, we saw them. Never in the past six years of reporting from Baghdad had I been able to imagine American soldiers on the streets of the city. They looked so out of place, so peculiar in front of the familiar shop fronts with the small portraits of Saddam Hussein hanging over the doors. They seemed unsure of their next move. Three of them were crouching behind a Humvee, scanning the rooftops for snipers. They all looked so young. One of them still had faint wisps of adolescent hair covering his chin. One or two young Iraqi boys approached them awkwardly and tried to say hello, staring in amazement at the soldiers, some of whom could only have been about eight years older than them. 'Mister, mister! Hello, mister,' they said. The marines acknowledged them briefly before turning back to stare down the sights of their guns.

Two cameramen hovered around one of the tanks, where a young marine protruded from its turret. He didn't know what to do. Should he smile and give a thumbs up, or remain serious and focused on the job in hand? He nodded towards the cameras with a brief smile. 'How does it feel to be in Baghdad?' one of the reporters asked. 'We came here to do a job,' the marine said in a thick southern drawl. 'It's still a dangerous place, but we're here to bring freedom to Eye-raq.' 'Thank you,' the journalist said, grateful for the succinct soundbite. 'My pleasure, sir,' replied the young American. Ten minutes later, the thunderous noise of tank engines rumbled through the street as the unit prepared to move on. It sounded the death-knell of a regime that had come to power before many of these young marines had even been born. A few more Iraqis began to emerge on to the street. Several youths started to smash and pull down the pictures of Saddam Hussein that adorned the shop fronts. 'Saddam down, Saddam down!' they shouted.

We followed the marines on the ten-minute drive into Firdoos Square, where for the next two hours the world's attention would be focused. Banks of television cameras had lined up along the edge of the lower roof of the hotel to broadcast live pictures of the US entry into the square. The American forces realized that the images would be seen in every country around the world, and so one of the Humvees, with a marine standing on its roof holding aloft the US flag, drove as close as possible to the TV cameras trained on it from above. Journalists rushed to grab hold of the nearest marine to ask him to say a few words live on air. We asked one if he would agree to be interviewed on the satellite phone. He lifted his Rayban sunglasses, and with a polite and innocent smile said, 'Sure, I'd be glad to do so. What station's this for, sir?' I told him it was for BBC television news in London and that it was a live interview. 'Oh okay, so I guess I shouldn't say "wanker" or anything like that, right?' He giggled at his very British joke before putting the phone to his ear. 'Err, yes, ma'am, I can hear you loud and clear.'

By now about 100 Iraqis had emerged from the apartment blocks on the edge of the roundabout into Firdoos Square. Some were delirious with excitement, others walked around in a daze. I wandered over to one group. It was the first time ever I would be able to speak to ordinary Iraqis and they would be able to answer without fear of retribution. I asked one man, Salman Abbas al Sultan, to describe how he was feeling. 'Very anger, very anger,' he said. 'Saddam destroy Iraq. He kill us. Now finish. We want Iraqi government, Islamic government. After Saddam, American and British leave Iraq. Thank you, Mr Bush. Thank you. But after Saddam, Iraq must be independent.'

The centre of the square where the statue of Saddam Hussein stood was ringed with American armour. One young man climbed up the plinth, and clutching the statue by the ankles shouted down to the rest of the crowd. They whistled and yelled up at the effigy in voices full of hatred. The young man began beating the statue with his fist, and the catcalls grew louder. Fifteen minutes later a man emerged from the crowd with a rope. It wasn't clear where he had got it from, whether it was from one of the American vehicles or whether he'd obtained it from a flat or shop across the street. He threw it up to the youth at the foot of the statue who had now been joined by two others. With the small crowd urging them on, they tried to tie it around the statue but couldn't manage it. I was beneath them with Killa and Dylan, trying to talk into the satellite phone and describe what I was witnessing.

At first the Americans didn't join in. But then something happened to change their minds: as several Iraqis were urging them to help pull down the statue, the marines, surrounded by a throng of cameramen and journalists, realized they might be missing an important photo opportunity. A commander signalled for a large vehicle used to transport battle tanks to move into the centre of the square to help pull down the statue. A cheer rose from the crowd as its metal tracks churned and crushed the concrete steps leading up to the plinth. There was a brief argument when one of the marines barked instructions to the driver to back the vehicle away from the crowd. The driver was angry. He took his helmet off and confronted his fellow marine: 'This operation is going out on network TV and I'm gonna make sure I do it fucking right!' he yelled. A huge metal chain was dragged out of the belly of the vehicle as the mechanical crane on its nose was raised towards the statue. Then, incredibly, the first thing one of the marines did was to climb up the crane whose tip was positioned in line with the statue's neck, and there, in view of the whole world, he unfurled the American flag and draped it over the face of Saddam Hussein. It was a breathtakingly ill-judged act, and yet it was an honest reflection of what these soldiers had been a part of: a war in which the United States, by sheer wilfulness, determination, ideological belief and force of arms, had smashed its way into an Arab capital to destroy a regime it did not want to survive in the post-September 11 world. Dylan, standing next to me as we looked up at the Stars and Stripes fluttering across the face of the statue of Saddam Hussein, gripped my arm, amazed and shocked. 'Unbelievable, unbelievable, I will never forget this,' he said. It took the marines a few minutes to realize that this was an act of triumphalism that few in the Muslim world would appreciate.

Miraculously – and again, seemingly out of nowhere – an old Iraqi flag dating from the era before the Ba'ath Party took power appeared. The hapless marine who had unfurled the Stars and Stripes climbed the crane again to replace the US flag. A loud cheer went up from the crowd. The tank transporter revved its engine as the marines tried to hold people back. With a shudder it started to reverse, the metal noose around the statue's neck becoming taut as it did so. The vehicle heaved back, its engine straining against the tension, the rumbling of its tracks mingling with the loud screams and cheers of the 200 Iraqis who were there to witness the moment. Then Saddam Hussein's metal legs buckled. Ten young Iraqis broke through the cordon of marines towards the statue, hurling their shoes up at the face of the dictator. One last pull and it came crashing down, bouncing and scraping along the concrete floor as the crowd surged around it.

I tried to cling to the phone as I was pushed and crushed in the mêlée, shouting out descriptions of the wild ecstasy around me. I lost sight of Killa, who had disappeared along with his camera behind a sea of flailing arms, as one of the symbols of twenty-five brutal years of hatred and rage was toppled. Two young men jumped on the statue's face, throwing their hands above their heads as they bounced up and down. Others spat at it or hit it with their shoes. It was a fleeting, blissful moment in which many who had known nothing other than Saddam Hussein's cruelty and deceit finally allowed themselves to believe that he was gone.

The imagery of events in our history is significant, even if it can never give us the whole or, in some cases, the real story. The image of Nelson Mandela emerging from prison to walk to freedom did not inform us about the long and painful process of burying apartheid. The fall of the Berlin Wall, which involved hundreds of thousands more people than the pulling down of Saddam Hussein's statue in Firdoos Square, was not an accurate reflection of the difficulties of reuniting Germany. As with these other historical moments, what I witnessed that day was a snapshot, a reference point of a complex, dangerous and uncertain historical process that has changed our world. Yet the only reason why the toppling of the statue came to be that reference point was because it took place under the gaze of television cameras. It was not the most important statue of Saddam Hussein in Baghdad. It wasn't even the oldest – after all, I had seen it being erected only a year before. Its prominence came about because of where it stood, across the road from the hotel where the international press was based. The passionate demonstration by the Shia Muslims earlier that morning in the Khadimiya district, which was also far larger in terms of numbers, spoke more eloquently of the aspirations that many Iraqis shared in a world without Saddam Hussein. But the falling statue was the first real image that allowed the British and American governments to believe that their predictions and hopes of an ecstatic welcome for US forces had at last come to pass, and that all the fears of lawlessness, anarchy and a breakdown in civil order were behind them. They were soon to discover that this was only the beginning.

9. 'Freedom's Untidy'

Four hours after the statue of Saddam Hussein had bounced down to earth, the US Defense Secretary, Donald Rumsfeld, told a press conference at the Pentagon that 'the Iraqi people are well on their way to freedom'. The following morning, 10 April, the skies over Baghdad were darker than ever, as the acrid fumes from burning buildings overwhelmed the houses and the streets in a way that hadn't been seen before, even when the bombardment of the city was at its most intense. The looting had begun. Government buildings and ministries cowered beneath the smoke that signalled the dawn of the new Iraq.

The destruction began with the pillaging of the lavish riverside villas of the most senior members of the regime. On the edge of the Arrasat al Hindiya district in southern Baghdad, as the Tigris river bends east, the streets were clogged with the cars and trucks of hundreds of Iraqis queuing to carry off their loot. We stopped first at the vast house of Watban al Ibrahimi al Hassan, a half-brother of Saddam Hussein and a former Interior Minister. What had been an unsavoury monument to excess had been transformed into a stark and barren pile of bricks. In the front courtyard a man sat proprietorially in a leather armchair, his body dwarfed by its enormous arms and plump cushions. A clock, two table lamps, a stack of plates decorated in gold trim, saucepans and a ceiling fan still caked in clumps of concrete from the ceiling it had been pulled out of, were piled up at his feet. He gave us a cheery wave. 'Hello, mister, Saddam finish. Good, good.' The entrance hall was a sea of shining broken glass. Children tagged along after their mothers through the endless rooms, looking in every direction to see if there was anything left to take. The marble spiral staircase to the first floor was crammed with people fighting to get past each other; there were those on their way down the stairs, stumbling beneath piles of booty, and those on the way up, trying to get to the rooms as quickly as possible before everything was taken. Two men were hammering at the hinges of one of the doors while everything that could be carried was dragged out of the building. The goods under people's arms or on their heads displayed the awful taste of the previous owners. Shiny cream sofas with ornate golden arms in imitation of Louis XIV went by. Paintings were carried off: first the crude erotic oils featuring Arabian damsels in distress in thin, wafting veils alongside cartoon-like lions and wild horses; then the military pictures of Iraqi soldiers on horseback charging into battle beneath black skies lit up by the bombs of hundreds of jet fighters.

We left the villa and drove along the riverside, passing an enormous generator scraping along the road behind the tiny truck that was towing it. By the time we got to one of the many villas belonging to Saddam's son Uday the place was empty. As a parting gesture, someone had defecated in the middle of the now empty sitting room. All the old homes of party officials throughout the city were receiving the same treatment as the people who had been so brutally deprived for so long managed at last to get their hands on the spoils of the regime. For those who had lived through the poverty and hardship that sanctions and Saddam Hussein had created, the opulence of these homes and palaces was particularly shocking. With outrage and glee they sought to make up for all the years of dispossession.

However, what began with the looting of the homes of Saddam Hussein's wealthy and corrupt relatives and henchmen – something that few would look upon with much regret or remorse – quickly developed into a sinister programme of meticulous and orchestrated destruction. The failure to prevent or discourage this devastation was not only outrageous but would prove to have catastrophic long-term results. It is hard to know exactly where it began, so swift and sudden was the wave of vandalism that was unleashed. Embassies, UN humanitarian offices, ministries crucial to the reconstruction of Iraq and its essential infrastructure were all torched within hours of the events in Firdoos Square. The attacks on *these* buildings went far beyond the comparatively petty acts of self-enrichment which lay at the heart of the pillaging of the houses of members of the regime. The destruction of the ministries and foreign diplomatic and humanitarian missions was so swift and so focused that it must have been organized. It was clearly part of a strategy to deny the new rulers of Iraq, whoever they might be, the capacity to govern the country. I believe it was a scorched earth policy on the part of Saddam Hussein's regime, many of whose Fedayeen fighters were still at large in Baghdad in the first days after the city fell.

Tariq Aziz once spoke contemptuously of how Iraqi opposition groups would like to be brought into Baghdad 'on top of an American tank', echoing the thoughts of many of his colleagues in the government. However, with or without an American tank it was going to be difficult to administer the country in the absence of any ministries or offices to speak of. The process of establishing order and the structures of civil society after the strain and upheaval of conflict was not going to be helped by the complete lack of any central authority in Baghdad. Behind the tanks of the American marines and infantry soldiers that rumbled into the capital there was little sign of the political personnel needed to start co-ordinating the reconstruction of city life. 'Regime change' had become a mysterious process. The regime was gone, but there was not much sense of what was to follow, certainly among the inhabitants of Baghdad. The only people 'in charge' after the city's fall were the detachments of US troops – and they were in charge only of the areas where they were positioned.

At four o'clock on the afternoon of 10 April, 200 yards from a branch of the Central Bank of Iraq on the eastern side of the Tigris, the man 'in charge' was Sergeant Timothy Funk of the US marines, whose unit was manning a checkpoint which was mostly on the look-out for 'remnants of the regime'. Up the road groups of looters were trying to break into the Central Bank. I asked Sgt Funk if he didn't think that this kind of destruction of state buildings and offices should be stopped. 'It's disgraceful and it shouldn't be happening, I agree with you,' he said, 'but we just don't have the manpower to prevent it, and to be honest with you, the looters just aren't a military problem and they're not a direct threat. This ain't a job for us, getting the bad guys that are still out there is.'

The lack of planning for the immediate aftermath of war was not just a military disaster, it was a political one too. It is hard to provide incontrovertible evidence, such was the lawlessness and chaos at the time, but it is my belief that when it came to the destruction of state institutions the looters and 'the bad guys' were one and the same. There was a general belief among politicians and commentators that the looting was an exhilarated response to the end of years of tyranny; that not only was it understandable and to be expected but that it would ebb away and order would quickly take its place. This view provided a perfect cover for those bands of young Fedayeen fighters who had dispensed with uniforms long ago and were instead dressed as civilians in T-shirts and jeans. US soldiers stood aside and looked on as buildings were ransacked. For how could they tell if the hundreds of ordinary people making their way into banks, ministries or offices were civilians or Fedayeen? These elements had a free hand to burn down government ministries, which were being specifically targeted not for general looting but for wholesale destruction.

British and American politicians criticized journalists reporting on the breakdown of civil order and the inaction of coalition forces for their exaggeration and negativity. On 11 April US Defense Secretary Donald Rumsfeld expressed his frustration. 'Freedom's untidy,' he told a press conference in Washington. 'Free people are free to make mistakes and commit crimes and do bad things. I don't think there is anyone in those pictures or any human being who does not prefer to be free and recognize that you have passed through a transition period like this and accept it as part of the price of getting from a repressed regime to freedom.' He had missed the point. It would be the transitional government of Iraq being created by the coalition that would have to pay the price for all this devastation, and of course the Iraqi people too would suffer, people who simply could not understand how the most powerful military force in the world could stand by and allow the infrastructure of their city to be ransacked.

The scenes at the main hospitals in Baghdad, which had continued to function throughout the war, were scandalous. A few hours before Mr Rumsfeld would stand up at the Washington press conference and make his comments about freedom, we visited the Al Kindi Hospital. We saw four young men standing behind the front gates, wearing blue surgical gowns. A doctor's mask hung round the neck of one of them and each man had an AK-47 machine gun in his hand. It was a strange world where young doctors had to carry guns to protect their patients, and – despite the Hippocratic oath they had sworn – would use these weapons if they had to. Two hundred yards away a crowd of young men, also armed, had gathered and looked ominously towards the gates of the hospital. Bursts of gunfire filled the street and a place meant for saving lives was turned into a battlefield.

Ten minutes later a Shia cleric appeared. He had been summoned urgently by the medical staff to help prevent the pillaging of the hospital. At this time clerics were the only people who commanded genuine respect from the Iraqi populace. The priest in his white turban walked authoritatively over to the gangs of youths. He talked to them for a few minutes and gestured for them to move away from the area. Slowly they began to shuffle off. Meanwhile the hospital staff had barricaded themselves into the building. The city was now a dangerous, lawless place. Doctors did not want to use ambulances to transport the dead to cemeteries for fear that the vehicles would be hijacked, and so corpses had begun to pile up in the wards and many were buried in the hospital grounds. Journalists who had remained in Baghdad throughout the war reported similar scenes from other hospitals that day. Suzanne Goldenberg of the *Guardian* wrote on 12 April: 'At Yarmouk Hospital, once the city's main casualty centre, the unclaimed corpses were so badly rotted that volunteers wearing chemical warfare masks buried them in mass graves. Sixteen corpses were heaved into the ground . . . there was no time for anger . . . only the sad, sickening work of burying the dead. Rifle fire crackled, and the volunteer burial committees stolidly dug on.'

That afternoon we drove to the Ministry of Trade on the eastern bank of the Tigris. It was on fire and black smoke swallowed up the roundabout in front of the tall, grey block. Small groups of Iraqis stood on the opposite side of the roundabout, looking on in disbelief. One woman who spoke a little English said she wanted to be interviewed. 'We want tell the world,' she said, 'Iraq need help. USA say they want bring freedom to Iraqi people,' she paused, lifted her arm from beneath her black gown and pointed to the burning ministry, 'but this no freedom. Why this happen? Why American soldier do nothing? Very bad. This no freedom.' Two men in the small crowd that had gathered around us tried to interject in Arabic. I asked them in Arabic to wait until the woman had finished and then we would interview them. They said they did not want to be interviewed. 'Anta Arabi?' one of them asked. Are you Arab? I said I was. 'La sawir, ya habibi, eeb.' Don't film the burning ministry, it is shameful. I said that I felt it was necessary. When we walked through the choking smoke and ash we could see the outlines of the offices, mere blackened shells. If this was really the work of a civilian population desperate for any sort of material wealth, then why hadn't the large desks in the building's lobby been carried off? This wasn't looting, it was arson.

We turned round to see a convoy of six US military vehicles driving past on patrol. They didn't stop at the Ministry of Trade. As the soldiers drove by we heard the muffled sounds of a man screaming. They came from a dilapidated car parked by the corner of the building. A middle-aged man sat at the steering wheel, screaming at the top of his voice. Next to him sat a woman, who must have been his wife, clutching a baby. In the back seat were two young boys who looked about seven years old. The man kept yelling, pointing to the burning building and to us, but I couldn't hear what he was saying. What was wrong? He just kept screaming. Killa, thinking that the man was angry because he was filming the torched ministry, looked up from his camera to show that he had stopped. Then suddenly the man got out of his car. He walked to the passenger side where the woman was sitting. He wrenched the baby from her arms and held up the child who was now wailing from the shock and the choking fumes. The man, tears pouring down his face, continued screaming and we could now hear what he was saying. 'Look what we are doing to our country,' he cried. 'Our history and honour is being raped. Shame on us. Shame on all Arabs. Oh God! Oh God! Iraq is being destroyed.' I couldn't bear to watch and Killa was frantically trying to do whatever he could to make him stop. In desperation, thinking that the man wanted to be filmed, Killa turned his camera towards him and pretended to film. The two men with us pleaded with him to calm down and put their arms around him to try to comfort him. The woman had run from the car and was trying to wrestle the baby from his arms. His outburst of fury now spent, the man walked back to his car, still crying, got in and drove away.

One of the men who had helped to calm him walked over to me. He was called Adnan but didn't want to give his full name. He said he owned a shop selling watches not far from the ministry, and had come to check that the looters had not been able to get through the metal shutters which protected the premises. 'I can't believe this,' he said. 'To steal from the houses of government ministers is understandable. Why not? But this,' he said pointing to the still burning remains of the Ministry of Trade, 'this is criminal. They are not Iraqis, these people. Where is their patriotism? They are destroying their motherland.' He had a point, and he had realized immediately that this was more than just ordinary Iraqi families helping themselves to the sofas and ceiling fans of their former oppressors.

What transformed the wrecking of Iraq's state institutions from a tragedy into an astounding act of political folly, though, was the decision of US forces in Baghdad to protect and safeguard some ministries while ignoring the fate of others. Here is an incomplete list of ministries and government buildings that had been wrecked by 12 April: the Ministry of Trade, the Ministry of Industry, the Ministry of Foreign Affairs, the Ministry of Information, the Ministry of Culture, the Ministry of Education, the Ministry of Irrigation and Baghdad's National Archaeological Museum. We had been told that there were not enough American troops to prevent the widespread looting, but two buildings were protected from the outset by US tanks and soldiers: the Ministry of Oil and the Ministry of Interior. This strategy was a grave political miscalculation which began to have an effect almost immediately. The joy that millions of Iraqis in the capital felt as they saw the collapse of the regime which they hated unreservedly soon became mingled with bewilderment and anger.

The people of Baghdad had waited for over two decades to see their city without Saddam Hussein; to live freely in it, to love it, to delight in its ancient heritage. That moment came, and ended, on 9 April – a fleeting moment of blissful freedom. On that day Iraq began its attempt to heal the wounds that the cruelty and psychological trauma of a quarter of a century of Ba'ath rule had inflicted. And then the moment was gone, replaced with a new age of insecurity and a different sort of fear. The tenth of April saw the first act of a planned vicious war of insurgency by former members of the Ba'ath Party, Saddam's Fedayeen and the groups of radical and violent Islamists who had made their way to Iraq to attack coalition soldiers and to destroy the institutions which the country's new occupiers would need to be able to govern. It was the beginning of an era that quickly came to be seen by many Iraqis as an occupation.

All our moorings were gone. Baghdad was a place that we no longer recognized. Our points of reference had been shattered, our Iraqi friends were either out of reach or had disappeared. There was utter chaos on the streets. As the structure of the city crumbled so did our sense of certainty. We began to feel that we should leave before our luck ran out completely. We put up small posters in the lobby and the lifts of the Palestine Hotel inviting journalists who might want to join a BBC convoy driving out of Baghdad to Amman, Jordan, to meet outside the hotel on the morning of 13 April. Ten people responded: Americans, Britons, Spanish, Italian and Australian. With phone lines cut and rising insecurity in the city, saying goodbye was difficult. All my attempts to contact Mohammed and Saadoun in their homes ended in failure. Luai, who had disappeared the day before Baghdad fell, could not be found. I did manage to find Dylan, Khalil and Mustafa, and it felt very strange to be leaving them behind. The experience we had just lived through together had brought a great intensity to our relationship despite the differences in our backgrounds.

At dusk on 12 April, I packed the clothes, books and equipment that had lain scattered across my room throughout the war. The chemical and biological warfare suit and mask had never been unpacked, the books I had been able only to glance at, my note-books and diary were full. The sun dipped behind the horizon as I stepped on to the balcony to take a last picture of a city that I had grown to love but which had also been a setting for unimaginable horror and sadness. The waters of the Tigris were perfectly still and the thin clouds were strips of golden light. Plumes of black smoke hovered between the sky and the water. As I took my final pictures, a blaze of fire shook the window panes. Directly below my room, on Abu Nuwas Street, young soldiers parked in an American Bradley fighting vehicle thought they had seen something on the other side of the river. The cannon fire from the Bradley shredded the reeds on the western bank. Other marines ran to the side of the vehicle and joined the attack with their M-16 machine guns. It went on for half an hour. And then it stopped and the marines dispersed. I heard one soldier shouting to another. 'Just saw a flash from across the river in the bushes,' he said. 'It looked like a torch or something, like someone was hiding there.' Baghdad was a place of ghosts and enemies for the young soldiers who now occupied it.

It was 7 a.m. on Sunday 13 April and it was unusually cold. I stood shivering by the side of the car. I could have been shivering with nerves, it was hard to tell. Our convoy of eight cars started to move off, but no sooner had we turned round the corner of the hotel on to Abu Nuwas Street than we came to a grinding halt. There was no way past the row of tanks that blocked the street. We sat in the car trussed up in our flak jackets and helmets. Ten minutes later we managed to snake our way through a narrow corridor which the soldiers had allowed us between their vehicles. There was nothing on the streets. No cars, no people. Across the Sinak Bridge we slowed down to go past two wrecked Jeeps, a van and a saloon car, burnt and riddled with bullets. Inside one of the Jeeps were the hideous remains of two bodies; almost liquefied, the corpses melting on to the floor of the wrecked vehicle. We passed the Ministry of Information which was still smouldering. We needed to get on to the main road that would take us to the Mansour district and the motorway to Jordan.

The driver began heading towards the Al Rasheed Hotel, which was now an American base. We yelled at him to turn back and take another route, so frightened were we that the American troops at the Al Rasheed would mistake us for the enemy. The road was thickly carpeted with empty bullet casings. They covered the street and the pavements and made a metallic crunching sound beneath our wheels. Baghdad was an empty, scorched and barren wasteland and it was the emptiness and silence that shocked me. It felt as if the heart of this ancient city had been torn out. We drove in almost complete silence through the Mansour district, until we got to the motorway. Then the driver suddenly accelerated as if sensing our desperation to escape the scenes of degradation we were finally leaving behind.

Epilogue: Return

The large lorries transporting the tan-coloured battle tanks lumbered down the motorway so slowly that they seemed almost stationary as our car passed. US army Jeeps drove in their dusty wake, heading towards the Iraqi border. The young American soldiers inside wore sunglasses and barely glanced at the vehicles that overtook them. It was August and the desert between Kuwait and Iraq was at its most unforgiving. The car's temperature gauge read 42 degrees Celsius. The clock sitting next to the thermometer on the dashboard reminded us that it was still only seven o'clock in the morning.

The neat and efficient tarmac highway heads north out of Kuwait. Within twenty minutes it transports you from the garish abundance of Kuwait city with its bright neon signs and its billboards displaying advertisements for luxury cars, washing machines and grand hotels to the sand of the desert and an empty pale blue sky. Like a thin strip of black wire the motorway winds its way through the scorching desert into Iraq. If there is a place, or a stretch of land, that future generations of Iraqis will visit when they want to remember and contemplate the ruin that befell their country in the last decade of the twentieth century, it is to this road that many will come. The stretch between Kuwait and the southern Iraqi city of Basra at the mouth of the Gulf is haunted by ghosts. It was along this road that Saddam Hussein sent his tanks and soldiers on a disastrous mission to invade Kuwait on a blistering day in August 1990; it was along this same road that the unfortunate Iraqi soldiers fled in chaos and under fire when they were routed.

As we approached the border I noticed a sign which has painful memories for many Iraqis but means little to most people in the West. In the spring of 1991, on the Mutla Ridge on the highway from Kuwait to Iraq, as they desperately tried to escape in whatever was left of their military vehicles or in stolen cars and ambulances, Iraqi conscripts were picked off by American bombers, helicopters and tanks. Burnt and dismembered corpses of Iraqi soldiers lay scattered in the desert, many of them as if peering out of blackened vehicles. One image from this scene of unspeakable horror was reproduced on the front pages of newspapers around the world. It showed the charred body of an Iraqi soldier still sitting in the driver's seat of the lorry in which he had been attempting to escape. His hair had been completely burnt away along with the flesh of his lips, revealing his still clenched teeth. He looked as if he had been trying to crawl out of the cabin, through the windscreen, his arms raised slightly as he used the steering wheel for leverage.

What was a road of ruin for those Iraqi conscripts in 1991 was also the road which in spring 2003 would witness the beginning of Saddam Hussein's downfall, when the 250,000 strong Anglo-American force assembled in this desert at the start of that year marched into Iraq. In August 2003 as I drove towards the border on my first return to the country since the end of the war had been declared, I noticed that the road sign marking this piece of blood-stained land had changed. Just above the words 'Mutla Ridge' in Arabic, a large black and yellow sticker had been fixed, bearing the message: 'God bless US troops'.

At the point of entry to Iraq changes such as this became ever more apparent. If borders symbolize a nation's sovereignty it seemed that Iraq's existence as a sovereign state was now very much in doubt. There was no Iraqi customs post. There were no Iraqi visas in our passports, no Iraqi officials to examine our documents or search our vehicles. The Kuwaiti border official's only concern was to see that I had obtained an exit stamp. He didn't care what permission, if any, I had for entering Iraq. He handed my passport back with the sort of look you'd give a condemned man on his way to the gallows. I stepped out of Kuwait and on to Iraqi soil without any permission whatsoever.

Walking across no-man's land, I followed a group consisting of three women and a young girl. Less than a hundred yards ahead, a crowd of their relatives were waiting for them on the Iraqi side.

In the last few yards the young girl broke away from the three women and ran into the arms of one of her male relatives. She was sobbing uncontrollably. The women caught up with her and the family disappeared in a frenzied embrace. I could see the women shuddering with tears beneath their black veils as they clasped tightly on to their relatives. For the first time in years exiled families, and anyone else for that matter, could enter Iraq without fear of interrogation.

A short walk across a non–existent border was all it took to bring me back on to Iraqi soil. Within minutes of my arrival it was clear that the country had become a place without any semblance of order. On either side of the main road stood a small detachment of British soldiers who occupied and controlled the southern region around Basra. I saw no more than about ten of them in all, with two manning a gun position behind a turret of sandbags in the middle of the motorway. Not one of them was there to check and control people coming across the border. Their main task was to protect the military convoys that constantly travelled along this route. Known as the 'MSR', the Main Supply Route, it runs from the Kuwaiti border all the way up to Baghdad and beyond, and it had become a lifeline for the 150,000 British and American troops who remained in Iraq after the war.

It was extraordinary, particularly given the stringent security at Iraq's borders in the past and the terrifying violence that was engulfing the country at that moment, that anyone or anything could enter Iraq without so much as a look from the coalition troops. In no–man's land, not far from the small group of British soldiers at the border, was a traffic jam of cars, still with number plates from places like Bahrain and the United Arab Emirates, awaiting collection by their new owners. The smugglers didn't want to leave them unattended on the other side of the border, inside Iraq, where they could be stolen for a second time. Everybody at the border, including the Kuwaitis, knew they had been stolen but neither they, nor the security forces, seemed to care.

Two hundred yards further up the road was a crowd of about 100 Iraqi men. 'Are they waiting for relatives?' I asked a man standing by the border post. 'No, they want to steal,' he replied. I presumed he'd misheard me and so I went on to ask someone else the same question. 'No, they are not waiting for people, they have come to try to get something. Either by begging or, if they cannot succeed, by stealing. Look there at that lorry, you see?' I looked towards the crowd and saw the men surround an Iraqi commercial lorry. Three of them were trying to climb into the driver's cabin and it looked as if they were attempting to dislodge the driver from his seat. In an effort to distract his assailants, the driver threw some bottles of water out of his window and then, in panic, sped off; the men gave up and jumped clear of the wagon. The only people with the power to control the Iraqi border, and regulate Iraqis – or anyone else for that matter – coming into or leaving this country, were the ten or so young British soldiers standing at the border, yet their primary concern was the protection of other British and American soldiers.

After leaving Iraq in April 2003 I had spent the summer contemplating and imagining my return. I sat in the living room of my home in south-western England with my children, with no other sounds to disturb the peace than their voices and the mild notes of birdsong outside. But every evening on the television news the images from Baghdad broke the calm. I sat transfixed as the screen showed plumes of black smoke across that familiar skyline; American soldiers shouting at crowds of Iraqi protesters facing them across the lines of razor wire outside the Palestine Hotel; the horrific scenes of Iraqi civilians being rushed into the city's main hospitals, bleeding from gunshot wounds; convoys of American military vehicles crossing the bridges over the Tigris river. At these moments I was frightened of going back. The journey's sense of familiarity was gone, the confidence of knowing what to expect and whom I would be able to find on my return had disappeared. Since my return to Britain I had been able to speak to Mohammed on only a few brief occasions, and we always left so much unsaid. My last conversation with him had been in late July, shortly before I set off on my journey back to Iraq, and I wanted him to tell me of his experience of life in Baghdad, if only to help me prepare for what

I would find. 'Well, everything has changed, Rageh,' he said in an exhausted voice. 'We will talk about all of this when we see each other.' I had once felt I had a knowledge and, to a certain extent, an understanding of this country. Now there was just a blank slate. The Iraq I had known no longer existed.

The road through the border town of Safwan was packed with traffic. Taxis, stolen cars, lorries and trucks were parked on either side of the tarmac. Men talked on the pavements while others loaded large cardboard boxes of goods into trunks and the back of pick-up trucks. We filmed the scene as we drove by and some of these men, on seeing the camera, pointed at us curiously, wondering what could possibly be of interest. This previously quiet small town had the feel of a smugglers' market – and that is exactly what it was. There were no police around and the occupying soldiers had greater threats to worry about than illegal trading. However, it was clear that it was not only people who could pass unregulated into Iraq these days but goods too. In the weeks that followed, as I saw countless young men with guns hanging nonchalantly from their shoulders in most small towns through which we passed, I began to wonder what might have been in those boxes that were being lifted into the back of trucks that day and how wise it was for the occupying forces not to have been a little more inquisitive.*

The road carried on north past a series of blackened official buildings destroyed five months earlier during the first stages of the ground offensive. But where was all the destroyed Iraqi armour? Where were all the usual relics of the battlefield? Across the fields around Safwan you could still see the ancient, corroded Iraqi tanks wrecked during the first Gulf War. Desert shrub has grown around them over the years and now they sit amid grazing sheep herded by young peasant boys. The absence of ruined or abandoned Iraqi tanks from the recent war meant that for the most part British troops around Basra had had to fight irregular soldiers and para-

* In November 2003 Paul Bremer, the chief administrator in Iraq, was reported as saying that coalition forces had found 650,000 tonnes of ammunition since the end of major hostilities.

militaries from groups such as Saddam's Fedayeen and the Ba'ath Party militia rather than a standing army using conventional weaponry. The smashed and bullet-ridden buildings where many of the militiamen had taken up positions were further testimony of this.

I drove along the motorway towards Basra expecting to see the familiar landmarks of statues and portraits in honour of the country's former ruler. But half an hour later and close to the heart of the city, there was still no sign of them. We passed the local Ba'ath Party branches, the city's university, the intelligence headquarters, now in a state of collapse. The compound was strewn with broken masonry and great lumps of concrete. The roof of the two-storey building had collapsed in on itself, and metal rods poked out from the shattered walls. I remembered the dozens of pictures that used to overshadow every part of this town, but Saddam's image had completely disappeared. They had been torn down, burnt, slashed to pieces or shot so many times that the dictator's features could no longer be distinguished. Some reports would have us believe that, like the looting that had brought Baghdad and many other cities to their knees in the immediate wake of the war, the destruction of Saddam Hussein's effigies was the product of a cathartic outburst of anger. The Iraqi people were just letting off steam before everyone and everything returned to normal. If only this had been true. The reaction was much more than simply an outburst of frustration or even vengeance. The ruler's image had been so completely and insistently wiped from Basra, it was as though the people of the city were practising some sort of exorcism. The thoroughness of the destruction of Saddam's image represented a psychological process, a ritual cleansing. Saddam Hussein was no longer in these people's lives, but – as the stain of blood had done Lady Macbeth – he haunted them. Their attempt to eradicate the memory of him was furious and obsessive, and fuelled also by the fear that somehow he would come back. The idea that there were 'loyalists' to the regime in this part of Iraq was impossible to believe.

For the people of Basra it was necessary not just to destroy any vestige of Saddam Hussein, but to put in his place the image of the men to whom they now turned for guidance and salvation. The local people were using the dictator's own methods to assert the authority of their new power. Pictures of revered Shia clerics and ayatollahs had gone up on walls throughout this overwhelmingly Shia Muslim city, many stuck on to the murals of official buildings which had previously carried the images of Saddam Hussein. In many cases, the dictator's face had been painted over and, if you looked closely, the features of the deposed tyrant loomed beneath the thin coat of whitewash, before being plastered over with the new posters.

The portraits were impressive: clerics in long black gowns, their hair tightly hidden beneath meticulously neat black turbans, their stern bearded faces gazing down on the city streets. Whatever the number of British troops occupying the area with their modern weapons systems, the hastily produced posters left no doubt as to whose authority the people of Basra looked to and respected.

Even by the dilapidated and impoverished standards of Iraqi cities during the years of sanctions, Basra had always stood out. As punishment for the role the city had played as the birthplace of the uprisings that had spread like wildfire through Iraq after the first Gulf War, it had been deliberately starved of resources by Saddam Hussein's government. For it was in Basra that Iraqi troops, exhausted at the end of their long retreat from Kuwait, had tried to overthrow the regime. The first shots in the rebellion which began in March 1991 were fired by the traumatized and humiliated remnants of the army that had been sent to invade Kuwait.

A month into the first Gulf War, on 15 February 1991, in a statement broadcast on several international channels that reached Iraq, President George Bush called on the Iraqi military to rise up against their leader and the 'Iraqi people to take matters into their own hands and force Saddam Hussein, the dictator, to step aside'. The speech was really aimed at the military to encourage them to stage a coup, but, by addressing the Iraqi people and by implying they had American support, he effectively stirred the civilians to revolt. The Shia population, who had suffered for years under Saddam Hussein's Sunni regime, did not need much encouragement. The uprising was amazingly successful and by the end of March the rebels had taken fourteen of Iraq's eighteen provinces. All good so far. However, at that moment, from a town just over the border from Basra a movement was gaining ground, the Supreme Council for the Islamic Revolution in Iraq (SCIRI), and pictures of the deceased Iranian leader Ayatollah Khomeini began to appear on the streets of Basra. This was the moment that the fate of the Shias in southern Iraq was sealed. America was frightened off by the prospect of an Iranian-influenced, Islamic coup in the country and withdrew its support of the rebellion. Saddam Hussein quickly regained control of his territory and, through his Ba'ath Party officers, proceeded to massacre vast numbers of the Shia population. The officers would often film the murders as a way of further frightening the already vulnerable community and to deter them from ever attempting to rebel again.

For years after the Gulf War the constant stench of open sewers hung heavy in the air of Basra. Many cities, including Baghdad, suffered during the sanctions regime from the Iraqi government's inability or unwillingness to repair and maintain the sewerage system and other essential services. Although Basra's plight was far more acute, Saddam Hussein's government always turned their attention to other parts of Iraq, leaving the city to wait and suffer. Saddam saw it as a place of instability, of seething resentment, where people's loyalties would always remain with their exiled Shia religious leaders. He contained and weakened the city by means of violence, deprivation and poverty.

Given the city's recent past, few places in Iraq after the overthrow of Saddam Hussein had greater social and economic expectations from British and American occupation. In the minds of the citizens of Basra, the war to depose the dictator was the starting point from which the occupying powers would rectify not just the destruction of the conflict, but also the legacy of under-development which Saddam Hussein's government had bequeathed them. The belief of people in Basra that the UK and USA were inextricably committed to fulfilling these expectations was reinforced by their knowledge of what lay beneath the soil of this region of Iraq.

Just south of Basra, after driving no more than forty minutes, you leave the city limits, passing a long row of grim utilitarian working-class housing blocks on either side of the highway. The urban sprawl then gives way to the open expanse of flat desert. Oil is evident long before you reach the refineries and pumping stations. When I returned to Iraq in August I drove towards the oil fields and stopped the car before reaching the main Basra refinery. I gazed out across what at first seemed to be a huge pool of shallow still water, the smoke and fire from the factory's gas flare reflected in its surface. But this was not water, it was oil. It was as if the earth could no longer hold the huge reserves beneath it and the precious black fluid had bubbled to the surface. The oil lake was a result of seepage from the pipes running beneath the earth near the refinery and was deliberate. It had been a strategy used long before the war to help clear the pipes and occasionally relieve the pressure. This is the first image that many of those young British and American soldiers who poured over the border at the start of the war would have seen. Securing the oil fields was one of the most important initial military objectives of the coalition which had stated that it wanted to stop the Iraqi army from destroying the oil fields in a last desperate act of economic vandalism. The British and American governments said that their ultimate aim was to preserve them for the benefit of the Iraqi people. For the anti-war lobby, the immediate seizure of these rich resources was only further proof of what it believed was the real motive behind the war.

The offices of the Southern Oil Company lie in a large gated compound on the edge of Basra. It was from here that many of the oil fields and refineries around the city were run during the years under Saddam Hussein, and it still serves as the headquarters of the company that has to run this vital industry in the new Iraq. When I visited it, the main administration building was being repaired and repainted; it had been looted and burnt seven times at the end of the war. Jabar Ali al Lueibi, Director General of Iraq's Southern Oil Company, sat in his large air-conditioned office fielding calls on his portable satellite phone every few minutes. About seven men – engineers, accountants and administrators – sat at one side of the room, clutching folders bulging with papers which they needed to consult him about. He looked exhausted by the multitude of problems he and his colleagues were facing, but he was keen to sound optimistic. 'The Iraqi oil industry is in the hands of Iraqis only,' he said. 'I would describe myself as an Iraqi patriot, but I see no contradiction in working with American oil executives. They can assist us with many technical things that we cannot manage by ourselves, and every oil country needs outside help. Even in America there are French oil businessmen.'

Barely had we finished our interview with him when we were confronted by a large and angry crowd outside his office. The company's guards were trying to enter the management offices, shaking their machine guns above their heads. As BBC cameraman Darren Conway, or DC as he is known, began to film them, some of the guards shoved their hands in front of his camera and screamed at him to stop. They blocked the gates of the compound and prevented anyone from leaving. Armed guards had driven vehicles across the roads to the gates at the facility. It was pay day and they were not happy with what they had been given – £40 for two months' work.

The car park outside the main administrative building of the refinery was full of British and American military vehicles and the armoured four-wheel-drive cars of American oil technicians and businessmen. Four months after the war had ended, many of the facilities on which the future economic development of Iraq depended were still only partially functioning. All over southern Iraq I found petrol queues stretching for several miles. In temperatures of 55 degrees centigrade, many motorists told me they'd been waiting for more than two days to get petrol. The level of anger had reached such a pitch that the British army decided to take control of the filling stations and ration everyone to forty litres. The British and American forces that had taken over the country and the large number of western contractors that followed in their wake had prepared themselves for the reconstruction only of infrastructure damaged as a result of the war. They barely had a sense of the much larger damage, erosion and dilapidation caused by a decade of the most punitive sanctions in United Nations history. This naivety, combined with the uncontrolled looting of government factories and facilities at the end of the war, and the guerrilla warfare and sabotage attacks mounted by Iraqi militia groups opposed to the foreign occupation had resulted in an almost complete collapse of basic services. They hardly knew where to start. Just as the Basra oil refinery was almost ready to resume operations at nearly 60 per cent of its pre-war capacity, the sabotage of local power lines by unknown Iraqi militant groups meant that none of the fuel, diesel or cooking oil produced by the plant could be pumped to the million people who lived in Basra and so desperately needed them.

It was obvious that things were falling apart. We had come to the refinery in order to film a regular weekly meeting between British and American military commanders, American oil executives and Iraqi managers of the Southern Oil Company, the men who had overseen the running of the facilities. A young British military press spokesman courteously told us that he was looking into whether we could film the meeting, but that everything depended on his colonel who had 'a hell of a lot on his plate'. We waited in the corridor, having left the television equipment in our cars, knowing full well that there was little chance of being allowed to film such a sensitive meeting.

After about half an hour the British colonel hurriedly came out of the conference room in the administrative building to where the BBC producer and I were waiting forlornly. He clutched a mobile phone to his ear and walked towards the window to get a better signal. He paid no attention to the people around him and didn't register that we were journalists. 'Look, we've got to get a grip on this situation,' he said sternly. 'These riots could easily get out of control and that can't happen. We've got to start getting fuel to the petrol stations in the city. It's really got to be a priority.' Before we could ask him anything, he'd disappeared back into the conference room. We looked at each other quizzically, wondering what riots the colonel was talking about. We'd driven through the centre of

Basra two hours before and had seen no sign of a disturbance. We decided to abandon the meeting and head back into Basra.

We quickly found ourselves behind a British armoured personnel carrier which was crossing the main route to the city through the fields of oil. At a large T-junction on the outskirts of Basra we saw three men carrying machine guns manning a makeshift roadblock at the first right turn. The British soldiers drove past to the other side and one of the officers dismounted and walked back across the junction towards the men. We had slowed down as we approached the three armed men, who were looking to see who was inside our expensive American-made four-wheel-drive vehicles. DC was in the back seat filming the scene. I told our driver, Abu Salah, not to stop but to keep driving slowly towards the other side of the junction where the British soldiers had parked their vehicle. None of us had thought that the riots the colonel was talking about would involve armed men in the city setting up roadblocks, and this was no time to stop or get out of the car. We drove past the British patrol and my last sight of them was of the British officer trying to talk to the armed men at the junction.

We took a right turn at the next block towards one of Basra's main squares, parallel to the road we had intended to take. It ran in a straight line all the way into town, passing rows of square brown-brick tenement blocks. Washing lines heavy with drying linen were strung across the passageways that led to the crumbling flats. Beyond these blocks were a few small shops by the side of dirt tracks that radiated from the road, across open fields to a series of houses. Three old men sat on a makeshift wooden bench in front of one house. Ahead of us, dotted across the landscape, was a line of twisting fingers of black smoke that shrouded the horizon in a grey haze. It was late afternoon, just before sunset, when the heat of the day has passed. It was a time when you expected people to be heading home from work or elderly men to be walking in their neighbourhoods taking in the brief afternoon breeze. Yet the streets seemed to have become the preserve of young men. Three hundred yards ahead of us in the middle of the road were two small fires. At the base of the fires I could just make out the pile of black tyres that had been set alight and was now belching out the choking soot that shifted slowly across the tarmac towards the houses and shops on either side. Salah slowed down fractionally, his head turning to the left, then the right, then the left again as he scanned the roadside.

'Salah, don't stop for anyone. If anyone tries to block you just go round, or if you have to, go fast, so they jump out the way,' I said. I meant it as encouragement but I think it only worried him more. As we got closer to the burning tyres, the thick black curtain of smoke seemed to part, and out stepped four teenage boys. In their hands they held rocks which they'd collected from the stony desert floor. I only caught a glimpse of the face of one of them as the car began to pick up speed. He was about fourteen, dressed in jeans and a fake designer T-shirt, his mouth hanging open in admiration at our expensive vehicle, and fascination at who could be inside. They must have believed that we were yet another delegation of western businessmen or oil executives returning from the refineries.

They began shouting at us. 'Ay, ay, ay. Stop. Thieves! Imperialists! Get out! We want money, we want our wealth!' I waited for the rocks. I heard the first one land on the window just behind DC, followed by a volley that battered the boot and side of the car. But I heard no sound of glass being smashed. 'It's good they're young,' I said turning to DC. 'At least they don't have guns.'

'Mr Rageh, this is not good!' Salah spoke in Arabic, never taking his gaze off the road in front of him, where more of those fingers of black smoke lay ahead. Salah's main concern was not for his own personal safety nor, indeed, for ours. These were not organized armed militiamen we were facing and his concerns were for his car and that of his father. These two vehicles represented the only means of livelihood for them and three generations of their relatives in a country without a functioning economy. Any damage to the cars would destroy their ability to support their families.

Half a mile down the road came another makeshift checkpoint. But this one had been organized with a level of sophistication and planning that gave it an altogether more menacing quality. There were more piles of burning tyres, arranged at ten- and twenty-yard intervals. The flaming barriers formed a chicane, which was impossible to negotiate at speed. I braced myself, expecting Salah to slam his foot on the accelerator at any moment and crash through. Then I felt the car bank steeply to the right. Equipment and supplies slid across the boot into the side, as DC was thrown next to me. We swerved off the road and sped along the steep pebbly verge, as Salah followed his father's example in the car ahead. The young men at the checkpoint were stunned, their heads turning in unison like spectators at a tennis match as they watched the cars stumble along the embankment. Most of them were too surprised to hurl any rocks. One or two did try but they missed their target.

As we got closer to the centre of town most of the burning checkpoints were on the other lane of the highway heading out of Basra. Our hotel was about a mile away, past a big roundabout. We saw with relief that, in addition to the teenagers, there were older men on the streets, businessmen and traders. As we crossed a small bridge, we noticed a crowd of about a hundred or so protesters running along the street holding banners aloft. We told Salah to park the car, but to keep the engine running, while DC and I stepped out to film the scene. A smartly dressed young man approached and addressed us in English. 'From where are you?' he asked courteously. I explained who we were and why we were filming, and seizing the opportunity he launched into an account of what was happening to Basra. It was at once a searing attack on the occupation and an expression of shame and regret at what some of the youths were doing. 'What you expect? We went through war! We were ready for this suffering because Bush and Blair said they will help us with everything after Saddam is gone. They make this promise and we believed them, that they will change Iraq, change our lives. And what happened? Nothing! Just soldiers and occupation.' He was talking quickly, giving voice to his anger. He could clearly speak English well, but such was the intensity of his grievance that he wasn't wasting time correcting his grammar. 'I know, I understand,' I said helplessly, trying to give myself time to consider what to ask him next.

Men began to gather around us as we spoke. 'What do you do? Are you a businessman?' 'No, I am a pharmacist. I used to work for the Red Cross here in Basra. Look.' He pulled out a small laminated identity card with a photograph of himself and the insignia of the Red Cross and Red Crescent.* 'I am a pharmacist and yet I am doing nothing now. What these youths are doing is wrong. They are ignorant! We Iraqis want peace, we want security and order. But there are no jobs for even educated people here in Basra. What is this, this occupation which brings nothing? Do they expect us to just be like dogs, to wait until each time they choose to feed us with small plates of old food?' Other men joined in, offering their condemnations in Arabic. 'We want them out,' said one of them. 'They are doing nothing here but stealing our oil. Let them go to the Kuwaiti rulers who are the servants of America and who give them their oil for free. This oil is for Iraqis.' A British army truck with about a dozen soldiers carrying guns and wearing helmets with plastic visors drove by. About half a mile further down the road in the centre of Basra was one of the main bases of the British army. We realized we should get back to the hotel. Abu Saleh and Salah were keen to get their cars off the streets.

The main boulevard to our hotel was deserted. In the foyer the few guests, mostly western and Arab journalists and aid workers, were milling about. We went up to our room to view the day's footage. After a couple of minutes we were interrupted by a series of thuds, like boulders being dropped from a great height, followed by the shouting of voices in panic. There was the sound of shattering glass. We ran to the window and from there could see rocks and bricks cascading over the bonnets of the parked cars. Along the corridors we could hear frightened voices and doors being opened. One of the receptionists screamed out instructions from the floor below and out of nowhere came the hotel electrician and janitors carrying machine guns.

---

* On 27 October 2003 thirty-four people would die in the bombing of the Red Cross headquarters in Baghdad. The offices had to close. The Red Cross's offices in Basra were also closed temporarily subsequent to the attack.

We decided to go up to the roof to get a better sense of what was happening. The sounds of breaking glass and panicked shouts were escalating and as we reached the roof we heard the first burst of gunfire around the compound. The name of the hotel stood perched on metal sticks on its roof and through the gaps in the letters we had a clear view down on to the car park. About twenty young men had gathered along the side street in front of the hotel gate. Peering out from the other lanes they let fly volleys of rocks. The gunfire was now more sustained as the hotel's janitors suddenly found themselves transformed into armed guards, firing warning shots in quick bursts. The street in front of the gate filled with a bright orange flash as a bullet hit the electricity cabling that hung loosely from a lamp post. The youths instinctively ducked when they heard the explosion. The sound of shooting filled the neighbourhood, punctuating the melancholy call to evening prayer that rang out from mosques across the city. Against this backdrop of anger on the streets, it seemed like a lament from a different age.

Barely two months earlier the people of Basra had been truly relieved that the British army and not the Americans were occupying their city. The Shia community had bitter memories of having been let down by the American government in the uprising after the first Gulf War. But the people of Basra also drew comfort from the knowledge that Britain was the former colonial power, with a long history in the region, and had a professional army with much experience of peacekeeping in other parts of the world. It bred a belief that British military occupation would at the very least be more sophisticated, deferential to local cultural sensibilities and devoid of the swagger associated with US military power. At first the absence of the kind of daily violence that was blighting the American presence in the rest of Iraq seemed to bear testimony to this. But the failure of the occupation to deliver the basic requirements of modern life – security, electricity, fuel, employment and a functioning healthcare system – was now eroding the sense of comfort and reassurance that the Union Jack had previously generated.

Before sanctions took hold on the Iraqi population the government had been a major employer for the Iraqi middle class. Like
many other oil-rich countries they had the wealth to offer good
wages to civil servants and doctors. Even after the sanctions had
had such a debilitating effect on the country many people were still
paid by the state. Thus, as soon as the state was effectively dismantled
by the war in 2003 thousands of city-dwelling Iraqis found themselves completely unable to earn a living. For those angry young
men holding rocks in their hands on the streets of Basra, the
difference in attitudes between soldiers of the two occupying armies
was of little relevance. They were part of the same project, enforcing
the same occupation.

However, as the days passed, the situation for the British army
in southern Iraq did begin to improve. In many ways the south of
Iraq presented more dangerous and formidable obstacles to the
occupying forces. The Shia Muslim south had suffered particularly
brutal repression and impoverishment by the former regime, and
groups controlled by religious clerics who advocated an Islamic
state were the dominant political force in the wake of the overthrow
of Saddam Hussein. But by abandoning the aggressive and visible
strategy of military occupation adopted by the Americans, which
was underpinned by a doctrine of 'search and destroy' in response
to the guerrilla attacks, British forces have succeeded in convincing
Iraqis in the south of the country that their presence is helping to
alleviate some of the insecurity. Most importantly, far fewer Iraqis
have been killed in British military operations in the months following the war than in American operations in the centre of the
country. However, as I travelled through the south in August, I
met the people who were attempting to live out their daily lives in
a semblance of order at a time of extreme uncertainty, and who
were beginning to feel the strain of the present. One such man was
Ali Sharif.

The doctor's story

The early evening sun bathed the courtyard of Basra Teaching Hospital in rich orange light, as the suffocating heat of the day began slowly to ease. The shadows from the long brightly coloured skirts of the young women flickered and danced on the concrete walls of the dean's office where they had gathered. The women ran to each other in greeting, tilting their heads back as they pressed their cheeks together, kissing the light evening air. The men wore neatly pressed crisp shirts, the young children were in smart shorts or voluminous knee-length dresses. The earnest young men who'd elected themselves photographers for the occasion buzzed around the gathering with their cameras poised. More families arrived. Different generations walked hand in hand, searching out other families whom they recognized.

Even in the places you least expect it, in circumstances that you'd think would make such scenes impossible, the middle classes cling to the habits that render them instantly recognizable. There is the same desire to turn out in one's best clothes at occasions where other families you know will be present. There are always the same annoying individuals who insist on taking charge, the same tantrums and arguments between the children, the same coy looks from the girls, and the same clumsy attempts by the young men to strike up conversations with them. In any other context a graduation ceremony complete with overprotective parents, proud grand-parents and a general air of friendly competition would be deeply familiar and perhaps even slightly comic. But standing there in the grounds of Basra Teaching Hospital, seeing these families come together for a graduation ceremony for young doctors preparing to embark on new lives in this broken city, I felt deeply moved. Relatives gathering to honour the young men and women of whom they were so proud was a simple, even mundane, event and yet it anchored these families to the normality and the stability which they so craved for their country, and which we in the West so take for granted.

As the appointed hour approached and the 200 or so relatives began filing past the dean's building to the student basketball courtyard where the ceremony would be held, the reality of Iraq intruded to remind us of the fragility of this moment of peace. Scattered across the rooftops of the hospital buildings, silhouetted against the sun, were about ten armed guards, hired by the hospital staff – there to ensure that the criminal gangs who had risen so quickly from the streets of this new lawless Iraq did not try to kidnap any members of these middle-class families.

Ali Sharif sat on one of the benches at the side of the courtyard. He had a boyish face, with a faint moustache that stretched into a goatee beard on his slight chin. In a modest, gentle manner he eagerly explained the problems he faced as a general doctor and manager of a rural clinic thirty miles outside Basra. It was he who had invited me to the graduation ceremony, to see his young wife, Maysa, graduate from the same college that he had attended. Maysa stood amid her excited and nervous fellow students in their long black academic gowns with yellow and red ribbons running down the lapels. Her face was bright and pretty, her large round eyes accentuated by long eyebrows and thin lines of mascara. Many of the young female doctors had dispensed with Islamic dress. Their hair was highlighted and their jeans were fashionable. Maysa's hair was hidden beneath a modern headscarf patterned with bold white circles.

Once everyone was seated, the dean led out a small procession, with the two top students of the year walking behind him. One was carrying the Iraqi flag, while the other hoisted up a burgundy flag inscribed with the name and motto of the teaching hospital. A cleric read a verse from the Koran and blessed everyone there. One of the heads of departments then made a brief, rather formal speech, pointing out how well the students had done to complete their courses despite 'the many obstacles and difficulties'. He didn't use the words 'war' or 'anarchy'. He made no comment on how their country had fallen apart in the past four months, or on how these young students had managed to focus on finishing their courses in the most difficult of circumstances, or on what kind of future they could expect. I sensed that everyone simply wanted to cling to this brief moment of normality without being reminded of the terrifying world that preoccupied their daily lives and thoughts.

The two top students stepped up to the lectern where they were given their special citations and then they rejoined their colleagues to swear the Hippocratic oath. Applause rippled around the courtyard and, as the sun disappeared for another day, the falling darkness was broken by the bright bursts of light from camera flashes while mothers, aunts and older female relatives ululated in celebration. Ali went over to congratulate his wife. As pious and observant Muslims they didn't embrace and kiss in public, instead they shook hands, Maysa gently placing her hand on top of Ali's while he touched her on the shoulder. We arranged to meet for breakfast the next morning and I left them to their privacy.

Their house is situated in one of Basra's prosperous middle-class residential areas in the centre of the city, not far from the commercial district. There is nothing ostentatious about the rows of bungalows and small villas. The gate to the Sharif household opens on to a narrow front garden with the driveway leading to a single garage. A small date tree stands in the corner of the garden providing shade for a swinging bench. Just inside the house, at the end of a short corridor, is an alcove where you take your shoes off before entering the front living room. Ali beckoned me in. The inevitable power failure meant that the family were sitting in the dark, the ceiling fans resolutely still in the broiling temperature. Sweat lined the temples of Ali's father, Maysa and her young sister. At Maysa's feet was Hassan, their son, born four days before the outbreak of war, gurgling as he sat in his baby bouncing chair, reaching for the brightly coloured little animals which hovered from a mobile above his head. It is hard to imagine how difficult it must have been for Ali and Maysa to look after their new child just as the war began; trying to keep a newborn baby healthy amid constant gunfire and explosions was not easy. Clean water was hard to come by, medical assistance would have been impossible to find if Hassan had fallen ill.

The family had prepared an overwhelmingly generous breakfast: bread, eggs, tea, orange juice, cake and chilled bottles of water.

They took it in turns with the reed hand fan, trying to keep Hassan cool while we talked. Ali's family has strong links with Britain. His father used to work for British Petroleum and one of his brothers emigrated to Britain and lives in London. Ali showed me photographs from the mid-1980s when his father and late mother visited his brother. One picture was of Ali's mother sitting in a small, sparsely furnished flat holding one of her grandchildren. Another one captured Ali's father wearing a thick wool coat, smiling broadly as he posed for the camera on a Victorian London street. Ali described himself as an optimist. His observations flitted uneasily between outlining the failures of the occupation and explaining what he saw as the achievements of the war and Iraq's ability to remake itself. It was a difficult circle to square.

'People do not feel safe now after the war. You have seen the disorder and the anger amongst the people here,' he said. Ali explained how he had joined a discussion group of young intellectuals and professionals who met once a week to consider what role they could play in building from scratch the administration of basic services such as schools, hospitals and law offices. He outlined briefly a plan to form a human rights group in the city. 'We all spent the entire war living in this house. Hassan had just been born and we were very scared. The building across the road, an old school, was being used by members of Saddam's Fedayeen as a base. They would leave each day in civilian vehicles to attack the British forces and sometimes only a few would return.' So how had the war changed their lives? What legacy had it left? He thought carefully about the reply. 'The only good thing is that Saddam Hussein has gone. He was a dictator and a lot of people suffered from his regime.' And now? 'Now? Well, now we have so many problems. After the war there is a lack of electricity, fuel and no stability.'

'Having said that, Ali, are you optimistic about the future?' He paused to look down before replying, 'I am optimistic about the future. Iraq is a rich country, with a long history, and we have a rich culture. But we need help to solve these problems so we can rule ourselves in our own way.'

I'd begun to feel uneasy about asking so many questions and I could sense Ali felt awkward. It was as if I was doubting his optimism. Now he looked at his son who despite the distraction of adult conversation continued to play with the toys dangling in front of him. A smile came over Ali's face. Focusing on Hassan's bright eyes and playful grin provided us with a welcome opportunity to change the subject. 'I'd like to prepare him for being President,' Ali said. I joked that Ali should also teach him to give frank interviews to journalists, like his father.

Ali's journey to work was an eloquent illustration of how the occupation was affecting Iraqis. I'd said my goodbyes to Maysa and prepared to accompany Ali on the one-hour trip he makes to his clinic every day. As we walked out on to the veranda, he quietly asked if it would be okay if the crew and I didn't travel with him on the public bus to the village. 'It is better if you follow behind in your cars.' I questioned the change of plan. 'As you know, kidnappings are a problem, and one of Maysa's colleagues, a medical student, was recently kidnapped. So if you please . . .' He didn't need to finish the sentence.

At the gates of the house he kissed Hassan who lay in Maysa's arms, and we followed him to a central avenue in Basra, where drivers hire out their old mini-vans as buses. We filmed him from a distance as he got into an old grey van which crammed in about twenty passengers. Ali was one of the last and, after a brief wait for more customers, the driver slammed the door shut and pulled out of the garage compound. We followed the van as it passed through the city limits and on to the flat, scorching plains around Basra, dotted with small farming homesteads and villages. Ali's clinic was about forty minutes' drive from the city in the village of Adair, just off the dusty main road.

This was just another trip to the office for Ali. And yet his identity as a doctor ministering to a poor community had to remain hidden because nobody could protect people like him in a country now controlled by the most powerful armies in the world. The clinic was lined with low mud and concrete shacks selling produce from the surrounding farms, utensils and small supplies of cooking oil and diesel kept by the front doors of the shops in reclaimed tins and oil drums. The car park to the side of the two-storey brown-stone block was empty and behind the main gate stood one ambulance. Its driver sat in the shade by the glass doors at the entrance of the clinic, smoking a cigarette and staring listlessly out at the midday heat. He'd run out of petrol, and besides, without electricity and with patchy phone lines at the best of times, he was hardly being inundated with emergency calls.

From the outside, the clinic looked like a disused building. By the time we caught up with him, Ali had already gone into his office to check how many staff had turned up that day. The threat of kidnap was not the only thing persuading many of the staff to stay at home. Even as the chief doctor and administrative head of the clinic, Ali is paid just over £100 a month. However, with Iraq's transitional government still struggling to establish a working bureaucracy, doctors and medical staff throughout the country were receiving their pay only irregularly.

The pharmacist and several nurses had already opened up the clinic for the day and we walked behind Ali as he went to examine a young girl who'd been brought into the emergency room that morning. We could hear her screams far down the corridor, rising in pitch as we got closer. When we turned into the room we could see her writhing and twisting furiously on the bed while her parents tried gently to restrain her. Ali bent over her and smiled trying to offer her reassurance. Her name was Leila, and her mother sat by her on the side of the bed, her face expressionless and still with dread. Leila's father explained that their child had been looking unwell for about two days until that morning they had found her crying in agony. Ali began examining her, constantly talking to the little girl whose pain was now exacerbated by the fear of the nurses gathering around her.

'Because of unproper water supplies, we suspect enteric fever, because of infection with typhoid bacteria,' said Ali. Leila was presenting the delirium and chronic abdominal pain associated with the fever. One of the nurses went to the small room at the other end of the corridor that was the clinic's pharmacy and medical store. It can't have been more than six foot by six foot and was modestly stocked with only basic medication. The ideal pills for Leila weren't available and her parents would have to travel to Basra to try to buy them there.

In spite of its derelict appearance, it is in this kind of rural clinic that we should look in order to judge how the war and occupation have changed the lives of Iraqis. It is in these ordinary places where citizens live their daily lives, rather than in the televised ceremonies for new government ministers, military press conferences and visiting dignitaries of Baghdad, that we can judge the outcome of liberation. The clinic should have borne witness to how people were being freed from years of privation, sickness and lack of facilities, and yet it only reaffirmed those experiences – a doctor who travels in fear to his clinic, to manage a staff who see little benefit in attending the facility and parents who come searching for help for their child only to learn that they must go elsewhere. The strength of disillusionment in this quiet rural hospital was almost unbearable.

The father's story

The motorway from Basra meanders through the empty desert of southern Iraq, leading inexorably to Baghdad. The horizon shimmers in the heat and the stirring desert air distorts the landscape as the relentless sun cooks the land and everything on it. In the opposite lanes, heading towards Basra, was a seemingly endless line of fuel trucks. Several American Humvee vehicles led the procession. The soldiers manning large machine guns on top of the vehicles peered out of the roofs wearing ski goggles to protect them from the blasts of hot dust and air. It was impossible to tell whether the lorries were transporting fuel for the people of Basra – an irony if ever there was one given that the city is surrounded by some of the richest oil fields in the Middle East – or whether they were taking the precious cargo to the coalition forces.

Gradually the flat desert land gives way to Iraq's central plains

with those familiar and still beautiful vistas of date palm trees. Past
Nassiriyah and about fifty miles beyond the Shia holy city of Najaf,
you cross the Euphrates river, not far from the city of Babylon. It
was in the verdant Mesopotamian fields that man evolved from
being a hunter-gatherer to sedentary farming, where he first learned
to build a permanent place to live. It was here men transformed
what had been the curse of yearly flooding from the Tigris and
Euphrates rivers into a blessing by developing systems of irrigation
that utterly changed future civilizations. The Sumerians of Mesopo-
tamia grew wheat and barley. Trade and commerce followed their
ability to grow more than they could eat, and they soon bequeathed
to us the first system of writing – cuneiform, developed as a means
of bartering and keeping trading records. This, in the land which
was also the birthplace of Abraham, forefather of all the prophets
in Islam, Christianity and Judaism.

Soon after you cross the Euphrates you come to Hilla. A small
town on the route to the Iraqi capital, Hilla has the air and feel of
a place that has always been overlooked. And yet it was the setting
for one of the most horrific and puzzling acts of the coalition's
military campaign – an act which truly strains the notion of a 'battle
for hearts and minds'. It was here, in the last days of the war, as
what remained of Saddam Hussein's forces in central Iraq crumbled
and fled, that coalition troops dropped cluster bombs on what they
thought were Iraqi soldiers but were in fact the settlements around
Hilla town centre, leaving a trail of civilian dead and injured.
Hilla reminds us of the painful truth that, however accurate and
sophisticated a weapons system is, and however committed an army
is to sparing innocent lives, there is no such thing as a war without
civilian casualties.

It was hardly surprising that our arrival sparked curiosity and
suspicion among the people of the town. Children playing in streets
brushed with sand quickly gathered around. Within only a few
minutes more than twenty young boys and girls were pressing and
jostling against us shouting, 'Hello, mister! Picture, picture!' Some
of the older boys, who were proud of the number of English words
they knew, having had the chance to watch more pirated western

films than the younger children, seemed disappointed when I
replied to them in Arabic. About a hundred yards further up the
lane two men stepped out of their bakery to see what all the fuss
was about. White flour dusted their forearms. One of them was
wearing a Juventus football shirt, and he put his hands on his hips
as he squinted at us through the haze of heat. The other man had a
look of disinterest, which bordered on hostility when he realized
we were a western television team.

We started to walk down the narrow alleyways of the suburb
towards the area where a number of the bomblets had left their trail
of grief. They were no more than passages really, with low-rise
cement and stone houses and uneven walls constructed by hand.
Some of the lanes had small tributaries of open sewerage. I tried to
imagine what the scenes must have been like in these densely
packed, claustrophobic alleys in the minutes after the first attack;
the noise, the smoke and blood, the frantic and useless attempts to
patch up eviscerated bodies. But the ever increasing and raucous
crowd of children distracted me, making me feel and probably look
like a demented pied piper. Salah and Abu Salah tried to reason
with the kids, even offering them the chance to have a look at their
new four-wheel-drive vehicles. But the children couldn't have
cared less. For them, the lure of DC's camera was much more
powerful.

The flimsy tin doors of the dwellings were peppered with tiny
little holes ringed in brown where the rust had begun to set in. I
could see the signs of what had happened even before I stepped
into the house of the al Jubouri family. The living and sleeping
quarters were in a small brick block. There were just three intercon-
necting rooms, all without furniture, where the whole family slept
and ate on mattresses and reed mats. Immediately to the right of
the front gate was another small and dingy brick room that was the
kitchen; in front of it was a water tap where the family's washing
was done in the middle of the large open courtyard. At the back
was a tiny grass patch from where I could hear a cock crowing,
while a small group of chickens scratched about looking for seeds
of grain.

Virtually every wall was pockmarked with shrapnel holes that looked particularly menacing against the whitewashed walls of the main living and sleeping rooms of this family home. This is where Hussein, a young man just out of his teens, lived with his father and four siblings. As the war entered its final week, and with American forces at the very gates of Baghdad, the proximity of the main road to the capital meant that everyone in the area knew that many of Saddam's forces were in retreat. Most people in the village had presumed that the fighting, if there was to be any more, would pass them by, and so few saw any reason to take cover.

On 1 April coalition forces showered parts of Hilla and surrounding hamlets with anti-personnel devices. 'There had been no fighting inside the town or anywhere near our village,' Hussein said, 'so everyone was outside as normal. I just heard a series of explosions, and blinding light and heat. I didn't know what the weapons were at the time. I saw my brothers and sisters covered in blood.' I pressed him, asking if he was sure that there were no Iraqi forces or militiamen in the area. He wagged his finger sternly. 'No! They were not in the area. They were outside the area, on a road far from our village.' I heard the same account from everyone I spoke to that day. Nobody reported hearing or seeing any Iraqi regular or irregular forces in or near the village.

Immediately next door to Hussein's house lives another family, also called al Jubouri, but not related to Hussein. They took a direct hit from two of the bomblets. As soon as I crossed the threshold into their front yard I could see the two small holes left by the explosions. They were no bigger than a tennis ball and around their edges the blast had left grooves and stripes in the concrete, as a child might draw rays around a picture of the sun. The windows of the main living quarters were fractured with shrapnel holes. Ali, the young man of the house, guided me around the damage and explained how his grandfather, Hassan, was killed in the attack. 'When the bombs fell, he was sitting by the wall and I was standing near the front gate. There were aeroplanes overhead, but that had become familiar during the war,' he said, as he walked through the courtyard pointing out the different locations where everything had happened. As he began to talk about the coalition planes overhead, he pointed to the sky, waving his hand in a circular motion to imitate the movement of the aircraft which killed so many that day. 'But then they dropped the cluster bombs. My grandfather was killed immediately. There was panic outside as ambulances and civil defence forces rushed to the area to take the dead and wounded to hospital. There was screaming and crying everywhere.'

While I talked to Ali the children remained inside one of the bedrooms. When I peered through the glass broken by shrapnel I saw his younger brother sitting on the floor, holding a piece of paper in his hand. I went inside to see what had so captured his attention. His small fingers were clasping an identity card from the Saddam Hussein era. In the top left-hand corner was a passport-size photo of an old man, wearing the black-and-white keffiyeh worn by Iraqi men from rural areas. It was the only picture of his grandfather that remained.

By the time I had spoken to these two families, most of the village had come out to meet us. Everyone, it seemed, wanted to talk. Some wanted us to hear their stories, but many more, especially the elders, wanted us to explain why this had happened to them. Press credentials or not, in their eyes we were representatives of the West. One man waved his burnt hand in front of my face in reply to my inane question of how the war had affected his family.

'Nothing has been done for us as a result of this war,' he said, his eyes wide with resentment as he jabbed his index finger in the air with each point of grievance he articulated. 'We have only experienced loss. There are no jobs, there is no electricity, there is not even safety and security in our land. Is this the democracy we were promised? Is this the freedom we were told we would have? I tell you, our lives have been destroyed.' The atmosphere was beginning to change; I sensed that some of the men wanted us to leave.

However, two old men insisted that we should see one more family before we left. I walked with them down the alleyways towards the edge of the village, near to an open field. This was the poorest part, where the houses were much smaller and mostly made of mud rather than from bricks. This was where Abdel Jawad Tamimi lived, a man whose story stood out even among all the other testimonies of suffering I had already heard. As we approached his rickety metal door the older men turned to the swarm of young children and told them to be quiet and go home, for this was a household which everyone wanted to treat with dignity. The kids were kept away from the front gate and I stepped inside. Abdel Jawad was sitting on a stool at the entrance to the living quarters. He got up and limped towards me, holding out his hand as he looked at me blankly. Two of the elders explained who I was and why I had come to the village, and asked if he would mind spending some time with the journalists and being interviewed.

'You are welcome,' he said, almost muttering, and then gestured for us to come inside. He carried his left leg with some discomfort as we sat down on a large stone step inside the house. I hardly knew where to start, but began by asking him what he recalled of the day of the attack. It came flooding out, as though it had only just happened, with all the agonizing details of those dreadful moments still fresh in his memory. He'd heard the initial explosions at the end of the village and, presuming that fighting had broken out, he and his wife, Aliya, gathered their six children together. Deciding that staying inside was more dangerous, they opted to make a run for it. He described how he tried to lead his family out of the village, on to open ground. He kept looking behind him and up at the sky, not knowing whether the explosions were a result of ground fighting or whether the planes he could hear overhead were dropping bombs.

'At first I did not think it could be from the planes, for why would British and Americans be bombing civilian areas?' Then suddenly he felt a devastating blast close to them. 'It was ten o'clock in the morning when it happened. It was horrible. I was thrown to the ground and fell down an embankment into a small river. I could feel a pain spreading across my leg, my arms and chest, like hot knives being jabbed into my body.' He unfurled his dishdasha and showed me where the shards of hot metal had torn into his calves and thighs, ripping off the middle toes of his left foot. Wounded and bleeding, he looked round to see what had happened to his six children. 'My life ended that day,' he said. 'I crawled back up the embankment where I saw the children lying face down, blood everywhere, shrapnel all over their bodies. They are children! They are children! The bombs were very powerful. Adults couldn't have taken it let alone children.' A few yards behind where we sat was a pile of large pictures in gold frames stacked neatly against the bedroom wall. As Abdel Jawad told his story he leaned over to grab them and laid them in his lap. He went through the pictures one by one. 'This is Ali, two years old; Anwar, eleven years old; Noor, twelve years old,' and on and on. Every single one of Abdel Jawad and Aliya's children was killed that day. What do you say in such circumstances? What words can you offer as comfort? No parent should have to bury a child. What then of parents who bury six children not yet teenagers, on the same day?

One thing I found particularly hard to accept was that nobody had come to the village to find out exactly what had happened. After all, it was not as if the coalition forces or the media were not aware of it. I remembered sitting in our room at the Palestine Hotel, looking through the footage from Hilla's main hospital the day after the attack, filmed by an Iraqi cameraman from Reuters Television. It was an obscene sight. I fast-forwarded through the pictures depicting severed limbs and the survivors wandering aimlessly through the hospital sobbing in shock and grief. Some of those images, those we were able to broadcast, were shown on television and were described on the front pages of newspapers around the world. Why then had no coalition investigators or human rights group visited Hilla to hear these testimonies?

I asked Abdel Jawad whether he wanted people to come to hear his account so that something could be done about what had taken place. He looked at me, his eyes heavy with disdain. 'What's the use? If they come, what will they see? Am I something to look at? Would they feel proud of themselves, of how they killed my family? How would I feel if they came to look at me? I would not let any of them come into my house.' He paused to think of the plight that faced him and his wife. Without children to provide for them in old age or help in the house, in a country where there were no economic opportunities for poor Iraqis, they now relied on hand-outs of food from other families in the village. 'I want compensation that will allow me to live because I can't do anything. What's done is done. May God make me patient. My children have died. What should I do? Starve until I die too? That would be another crime against God.'

It is an obvious truth that wars never really end, and the war in Iraq will never end for fathers like Abdel Jawad, and mothers like Aliya. We draw comfort from being told that 'all major combat operations in Iraq have ended', and while news that the guns have fallen silent gladdens some of us, there is a silence of a different sort in the houses of these families.

Return to Baghdad

The blue-and-white sign above the motorway simply said Baghdad, with an arrow indicating the next exit to the right. I could not shake an overwhelming sense of apprehension. It was impossible at that moment to appreciate how much the experience of a war can change one's relationship with a city. Memories of my first journey into Baghdad, nearly seven years before, came flooding back. The mixture of thrill and trepidation returned, the hunger to notice every feature on the approach to the city. Everything, it seemed, had come full circle, as I embarked on this new journey to Baghdad.

We drove through the southern suburbs and along the arterial road that heads to the west of the capital. The elevated expressway runs beside the Tigris river, enabling us to see that familiar flat, low-rise cityscape. The cars, taxis and buses still clogged the roads around Liqa Azahour roundabout. Families wandered through the busy market stalls and shops of the Mansour district, transformed since the last time I had seen them when I drove out of Baghdad at the end of the war. Back then these streets had been lifeless and fearful places. The traffic ground to a halt on the main avenue alongside the old Muthana military airfield close to the Al Rasheed Hotel. The hotel was now an American military post, ringed with barbed wire and sandbags. The traffic had stopped to allow a military patrol to cross the road and return to base. Several cars had been pulled over to be searched by the young soldiers.

As we came into the heart of Baghdad, the city revealed its damaged and scarred face: the Foreign Ministry remained gutted, its façade still bearing the black scorch marks of the flames that had consumed the offices inside; the Ministry of Information also bore the same scars and its windows were still broken from the orgy of looting in the weeks after the city fell. On the right, just before the Joumhouriya Bridge, stood the gates of the forbidding Republican Palace on the western bank of the Tigris. Ironically, and perhaps ill-advisedly, it was now the main headquarters of the American occupation in Baghdad. The enormous, classical columns at the main entrance were guarded by a line of concrete blocks, razor wire and armoured vehicles. In front of this barricade I saw a crowd of about a hundred men. They stared at the five armed US soldiers on the other side, who in turn stared back at them. Some in the crowd were carrying banners written in Arabic and a small number of them chanted, 'We want jobs! We want jobs!'

According to reports emanating from the city, Baghdad had become synonymous with upheaval. Outwardly it projected a deceptive sense of normality – busy traffic, families shopping in the markets – but it felt like a completely different city from the one I remembered. I drove back down Saadoun Street, where I had walked on the last night of peace. Here, too, the busy pavements disguised the reality of life in a city under occupation and racked by insecurity. It led us back to Firdoos Square outside the Palestine Hotel, where the breathtaking image of the toppling of Saddam's statue had fleetingly given us a glimpse of the desire of Baghdad's people to believe that the years of torment were over. The plinth still sits in the centre of the square, daubed with graffiti and posters advertising various political parties.

As I turned round the corner to drive up to the entrance of the Palestine I came across what was by now a common feature of the capital. Two US soldiers stood behind a sandbagged position, overseeing a checkpoint manned by Iraqi guards. We were told to step out of the car to be bodysearched, after which the contents of the vehicle were examined. Then we swerved through a chicane, past four battle tanks, hundreds of yards of razor wire and several gun positions. As though the Palestine Hotel's dubious celebrity during the war as a base for foreign journalists were not enough, it now had the questionable honour of being probably the most heavily guarded hotel in the world. Occasionally the thudding sound of rotor blades in the sky could be heard and, reminiscent of a Hollywood movie about the Vietnam War, the black specks of American helicopters could be seen arcing across the sky.

Baghdad remains a city whose true identity lies buried beneath the image of those who rule it. As in Basra, the statues, murals and posters of the dictator who once muzzled his people have been torn down and defaced. Yet now this ancient Arab capital and its citizens find themselves under the control of the US military, and instead of the image of Saddam Hussein, it is tanks, Apache helicopters and military patrols that dominate the city and the lives of its inhabitants.

I returned the following day to the Ministry of Information. As I drew up in front of the Press Centre, I noticed a small crowd of smartly dressed men and women. Some of the men carried briefcases and folders. One of them approached and identified himself as a telecommunications engineer who, along with other colleagues, now came to the front of the ministry once a week in the hope that western news organizations might hire him for some work. Here were a group of highly qualified young men and women, forced to assemble and ask for work like casual labourers seeking temporary jobs on building sites.

As I walked through the metal gate towards the press hall I heard someone calling out my name. One of the former chief minders from the ministry was walking towards me. Now freed from all the pretence and fear that had inhibited relations between us in the past, for the first time in six years we could be genuine towards each other. He greeted me with a warm hug and asked how my family was. He offered to show me what remained of Baghdad's Press Centre.

In the middle of the hall I could just make out where the offices of the BBC Arabic Service and Reuters News Agency had been. A foot-deep carpet of fine ash covered the floor. The metal supports on the ceiling were twisted and mangled. Anything which had not been damaged by the fire had been stolen. 'We don't understand why this was allowed to happen,' my friend said. 'Even after the Ali Babbas [the colloquial name given to thieves and looters] took everything and burnt the building, more of them come to the ministry to see if there is anything left to steal. But the coalition does nothing about this.' While we were talking a young man with a machine gun – employed by the former officials of the ministry and clearly still keen to do his job despite the rather obvious change in circumstances – walked up to us, demanding to know who I was. My friend quickly explained that I was with him and he should not worry, and the young man walked away.

My friend was more fortunate than his former colleagues who were waiting outside. He now worked as a fixer for an Egyptian television company, while they were still trying to find work. This was the real face of 'regime change' and its impact on Iraqis. A policy which was represented so dramatically and unforgettably by that deck of cards issued by the US Defense Department and depicting the fifty-five most wanted men of the regime, starting with Saddam Hussein as the ace of spades, was a policy with unforeseen consequences. It was based around the notion of excluding any member of the Ba'ath Party who had served in the former regime. 'Regime change' was in actual fact much more like 'state change'. For, in order to have been a lecturer in a college, or a middle-ranking bureaucrat in the Ministry of Agriculture or Health or Irrigation during Saddam Hussein's rule you almost certainly had to be a member of the Ba'ath Party. Excluding all members of the party effectively meant barring thousands of engineers and administrators from working towards the reconstruction of the state and meant they could look for jobs only with western news organizations. The very people who were desperately needed in order to create a new Iraq from the desolate rubble of the old regime were being prevented from doing so.

In this chaos it was unclear how the state – in the form of its institutions and administration never mind in terms of its actual resources – could return to Iraqi control. As ever, I turned to Mohammed to illuminate a way through the confusing uncertainty in which the country found itself.

Mohammed's story

The BBC's new Baghdad office lies in a large villa not far from the Palestine Hotel. The situation in the capital is so precarious that the narrow street in which it sits and which is also home to a number of other major western news organizations had been barricaded at either end. As soon as I walked through the heavy door I saw Mohammed, his desk piled high with newspapers and books, a scene that would have been unimaginable during the tightly censored regime of the Ba'ath Party. We held each other for a long time, barely knowing what to say. He called me by my Arabic honorific title as the father of my son, 'Welcome back, Abu Sami.' I asked him about his wife, Samira, and their three children. We looked each other up and down as if to make sure we were really there and laughed in relief. Quickly we left the office and headed to my favourite place, Hassan Ajmi teashop. The old copper and brass Ottoman urn and kettles had been removed from view. Rashid Street had become as lawless and dangerous as the rest of Baghdad, and the teashop's old owner was not going to risk the precious collection that he had inherited. However, the rattle of domino pieces on the wooden tables still echoed reassuringly around the old building. For the first time it felt good to be back, and the sense of familiarity and affection for the city started to return. We settled into the frayed wicker chairs with our glasses of hot, fresh tea and then, without prompting, Mohammed began to describe his life in this new city.

'The worst time of each day is taking the journey home. I just can't wait to get back and find out that my daughter has returned safely from school. This new trend of kidnappings is really terrifying.' In a city where the US military authorities no longer report the number of Iraqi civilians killed by American soldiers, let alone by criminals, this grim new industry of extortion has gone on almost completely unreported. Young girls are often kidnapped to be traded into prostitution. Other children and adults are kidnapped purely for ransom, often for no more than £200. Mohammed said it had led him to restrict his family to their house as much as possible while he was at work. He told the story of one day earlier that summer when his wife and children had finally had enough of being closeted indoors, and demanded that he take them out for the day.

'I said to them, "Okay, you want me to take you out. Fine, put on your smart clothes and we will go to Baghdad Jadida."' This is a public park with a children's playground where middle-class families used to go at weekends to promenade and picnic. 'We got a taxi to take us from our house in Jama'iya in the Al Dora district. The car headed on to the expressway in the direction for Baghdad Jadida. But when we came to one of the main traffic lights, we heard the sound of gunfire everywhere. I quickly got the family out of the car and we ran into one of the shops by the roadside, where the owner had seen us and shouted at us to get inside for protection. The gunfire continued for at least another twenty minutes. When we got back home, I waited until they had had a chance to get over their shock, and then I said to them, "Now do you see why I have been telling you that the city is not safe?"'

Mohammed told me how Baghdad had had a taste of what it means to be liberated, but he described the new freedoms that Iraqis now enjoyed as decorative ornaments rather than things of real value and substance. 'Of course we can do, say and be things that we could only dream of under Saddam. If my son Marwan wants to attend a top college in Baghdad, he knows that he will not be denied a place because his father is not a member of the party or a military officer. I have no more fears about what I can read or what views I hold. For example, I have lost count of the

number of newspapers in the city. The last time I counted there
were more than a hundred. Everything from newspapers supporting
the Communist Party to those supporting a return to a monarchy.
But yet I am afraid to let my family out on to the streets. Without
a sense of security how can one enjoy these freedoms?'

Look out across the skyline of Baghdad today and you will see
little forests of satellite dishes on the roofs of apartment blocks, a
vision that would have been unimaginable under the previous
regime. The main streets of the Karada shopping district in the
south of the capital are packed with stores that are new to the city
– rows upon rows of shops selling satellite dishes and decoders.
Many are packed with middle-class Iraqis eager to part with precious
foreign currency to buy the satellite equipment, such is the hunger
for international news and entertainment channels. I visited a shop
owned by an Iraqi businessman who did not want to be named.
He told me that he sold 150 dishes a day at £100 a unit, which
makes him over £100,000 a week. As I interviewed him in his
shop, about 100 Iraqis were jostling each other on the other side of
the till, thrusting slips of white paper towards us, proving that they
had paid for their dishes and now wanted to collect them. Three
accountants on the other side of the room counted the bundles of
dollar notes from the day's takings. The shopkeeper said this was
just about the only business that was booming in Baghdad. But he
didn't look particularly happy. Standing in the middle of his heaving
shop, he said wistfully, 'I'd easily give up much of my profits in
return for greater security. Every night I have to have six armed
guards for my shop, and recently I've hired someone to escort my
children to school. I'm just too afraid. Many people leave my shop
very happy that they can now go home and watch things they were
not allowed to see by Saddam. But when they watch this western
lifestyle, the nice things, the pretty things, this is like a kind of
torture. This is not the reality in Iraq. We can just look at this life,
but here, there is too much fear, too much danger. I feel very bad
about this, I want all Iraqis to live this life, like in America, like in
England. But we can't see how we will have this life in Iraq.'

The satellite dishes beam images of our world, the world of

opulence and plenty, of safety, comfort and choice, into the living rooms of people who hear gunfire in their city every day. People in Baghdad are now free to watch international stations showing everything from American wrestling to home shopping. Yet they must live their lives amid the disorder, violence and deep uncertainty of an occupation to which they see no end. If there is one thing that the war has not changed it is the fact that ordinary Iraqis aspire to the things we enjoy: security for their families, a livelihood, essential services. They share with us the fundamental aspiration that binds all humanity: a desire to ensure that their children have a better life than they had. It is on this basic human right that Iraqis will judge whether the war and occupation have transformed their lives, or whether all they did was overthrow Saddam Hussein.

The tearing down of Saddam Hussein's statue was an image that had much deeper significance for the coalition than for most Iraqis: for the United States and Britain it was a tangible symbol of success in their policy of regime change; for Iraqis however, the extent of the psychological damage of almost a quarter of a century of dictatorship is almost unimaginable and Saddam's tyranny could not be erased merely by the destruction of his statues. It would take much more than that to convince the people that their lives had changed. In the weeks after the fall of Saddam Hussein's statue in Firdoos Square the glaring failures of the occupation reinforced most people's belief that the war was unable to deliver the liberation they had been promised, and this belief will continue as long as their country remains in the grip of insecurity and conflict.

However, the dramatic capture of Saddam Hussein on 13 December 2003, eight months after the fall of Baghdad, and the images of the broken leader shown in the press conference that followed *did* convince Iraqis that that part of their lives, at least, was finally over.

The news of his capture was greeted by both British and American leaders in language loaded with rhetorical gravitas; they used words such as 'for ever', 'the end', 'finally' and 'never again', eager as they were to present this as an historic moment for the Iraqi people, something which they could see and feel had been done for them and for their future.

But the scenes in Baghdad told a different story. They were eerily reminiscent of the day the city fell – the crowds that did emerge for a brief time in the streets numbered no more than a few hundred. In Firdoos Square – the place where television cameras had shown Saddam Hussein's statue being torn down on 9 April – an hour after his capture the international media filmed a crowd of about 200 Iraqis, led by Shia clerics, celebrating the news by parading a large portrait of the slain Shia leader, Ayatollah al Hakim. There was no mass outpouring of joy, no seething crowds of thousands of people thronging the streets, no scenes like those that occurred in the cities of Eastern Europe as Communism collapsed. It was as if the people were still cowed, still fearful, still damaged by the tyrant's memory. Instead there was mostly sober contemplation of all the years of cruelty, and a private sense of profound relief. This was the moment when Iraqis finally believed – for the first time in a generation and without any remaining doubts – that Saddam Hussein would never rule them again. But it did not assuage their anxiety and uncertainty about who or what would rule their country now.

As ever, though, Iraqis had a much more sophisticated and realistic analysis of the future than that expressed in the finite and absolute language used by British and American leaders. Most Iraqis knew that it was indeed 'the end' for Saddam Hussein and that any future violence on the streets would not be orchestrated by him, but they were still unsure as to what would follow. Britain and the United States had for so long perceived Iraq and its society through this one barbaric man that it was hard for them to picture the country and its people – with all their complexities, different voices and aspirations – beyond him.

Capturing Saddam Hussein without a doubt boosted the morale of the coalition forces and administrators, but it also inadvertently provided the large number of insurgency and terrorist groups attacking and killing US soldiers in Iraq with a political opportunity. The capture of Saddam Hussein rid them of the millstone around their neck. The many anti-western Islamic militant groups now in the country fighting coalition forces, as well as the many home-grown Iraqi groups motivated by the desire to expel what they see as foreign occupiers, were never driven by a wish to return Saddam Hussein to power. Instead their intentions are varied and manifold: the Islamification of Iraq; the revival of the Ba'ath Party without Saddam Hussein as leader; to kill representatives of the American government, who are supporters of the state of Israel.

The idea that Saddam Hussein had been playing a major role in this insurgency war was dispelled as soon as the pathetic and solitary former dictator was pulled out from his hole in the ground. This was not a man running anything, but running away. As long as he remained free, occasionally issuing audio recordings, people could believe that the groups and organizations fighting coalition forces were doing so in order to bring back the dictator – something the coalition accused the terrorists of and which no ordinary Iraqi would ever support. Now that he has gone, however, these groups can present themselves as freedom fighters against foreign occupiers who have failed to bring about the promises of a new Iraq, whose military tactics have left many Iraqis dead, and who are benefiting economically and strategically by their presence in Iraq. It is an aim that could certainly find support among the country's young and disillusioned population.

The capture of Saddam Hussein is, of course, a watershed in the traumatized lives of the Iraqi people. It could also lead the way to regime change in a way that will benefit them, providing a frame-work for the emergence of an independent, sovereign and stable Iraq – something the occupation has so far failed to deliver. The construction of this framework could be long and complex, yet it is the way the coalition reconstructs Iraq that will prove the impor-tance of Saddam Hussein's capture – the capture of Saddam Hussein cannot, by itself, prove the success of the coalition's strategy. Anything less than a thoughtful and determined course of action for a new Iraq will mean that the legacy of Saddam Hussein's brutal dictatorship will linger for many years to come.

Index

43,